OF PANDAS AND WANDERING GEESE

A Journey Through Shadow and Light in Vietnam, China and Tibet

Thanh and Benjamin Cherry

MINERVA PRESS
ATLANTA LONDON SYDNEY

OF PANDAS AND WANDERING GEESE: *A Journey Through Shadow and Light in Vietnam, China and Tibet*
Copyright © Thanh and Benjamin Cherry 1999

All Rights Reserved

No part of this book may be reproduced in any form,
by photocopying or by any electronic or mechanical means,
including information storage or retrieval systems,
without permission in writing from both the copyright
owner and the publisher of this book.

ISBN 0 75410 709 4

First Published 1999 by
MINERVA PRESS
315–317 Regent Street
London W1R 7YB

Printed in Great Britain for Minerva Press

OF PANDAS AND WANDERING GEESE
A Journey Through Shadow and Light in Vietnam, China and Tibet

*For those who know what it is
to stand on the edge*

About the Authors

Benjamin and Thanh Cherry met in 1972 in Vietnam, he as a journalist from the West, she born and brought up in a country torn apart by war. In 1994, after twenty-two years away, they went back with their eighteen year old son, and from there travelled further through China and Tibet and many other parts of Asia on their way overland towards Europe. This book covers the first part of their long and often arduous journey. From Tibet it continued on through Nepal, India, Pakistan, Central Asia, Iran, The Caucasus, Russia, Eastern and Middle Europe to England. It took nineteen months.

They are back now in the Southern Highlands of New South Wales, Australia, teaching in the school they founded in 1983. They are also increasingly involved in teacher training in various Asian countries, something for which their journey was both a preparation and an inspiration. Their son lives in Sydney, fulfilling his dreams in the world of music, television and film.

The authors describe their home town as a meeting place of many influences. In the Australian Dreamtime it was a boundary between different groups of people, where they would trade and sometimes fight – and where they are thought also to have carried out initiations. It is an area of geological diversity, where the native vegetation blends readily with plant life from Europe and Asia.

In their writing is a similar signature, for it embraces a wide spectrum of cultural experience, but looks always beyond outer differences to what is essentially human in all people. If, after journeying with them in the pages that lie ahead, you would like to get in touch, you may do so via benthanh@hinet.net au.

Authors' Note

This book is not the story of one journey only but several, taking place on different levels. Writing it has been a further journey in itself, as we have tried to weave together the many strands in a form that is both readable and true. In doing so we have been faithful to what Life, the greatest of storytellers, has brought us, but, partly out of respect for people's privacy, have taken the licence to recast certain details.

One of these has been the names of the various people involved – even of those who tell the story and reveal their inner secrets. It has allowed us all more freedom, we who write and they who act and feel and think. The characters have developed on in subtle ways and the book has moved from a travel journal to being a story, touched by imagination, with its own unfolding drama.

A second challenge has been that of writing together. If the journey itself was not already a sufficient test of marriage, then trying to write about it in this way certainly has been, as the cherished words and images of each of us have been progressively questioned and rearranged by the other, not once but over and again. Despite this, the perspectives of the narrators, which alternate chapter by chapter throughout the book, remain faithful to our personal experiences – even those of Luke, whose words were also written by us.

Bowral, Australia
1st September, 1999

Contents

Part One

Sydney	13
Vietnam – South	23
Vietnam – Centre	80
Vietnam – North	111

Part Two

China – South	149
Hong Kong	192
China – East	206
China – North	231
China – West	255

Part Three

Tibet	311
Postscript	397

'These days happy time,' she said quietly. 'Now you all go. You wandering geese, fly with stars. I panda, home in bamboo forest.'

> (Spoken by a Chinese friend as we left Xi'an, China in September '94)

*

Geese travel vast distances across our planet.
They fly at dizzying heights, close to that of Mt Everest.
They are said to navigate by the stars.

Pandas barely move from the place where they are born.
They depend mainly on particular kinds of bamboo,
which they eat voraciously each summer.
They can spend days and weeks,
sitting placidly in caves or hollow trees,
in apparent contentment.

Part One

The human heart can go to the lengths of God.
Dark and cold we may be, but this
Is no winter now. The frozen misery
Of centuries breaks, cracks, begins to move;
The thunder is the thunder of the floes,
The thaw, the flood, the upstart Spring.
Thank God our time is now when wrong
Comes up to face us everywhere,
Never to leave us till we take
The longest stride of soul men ever took.
Affairs are now soul size.
The enterprise
Is exploration into God.
Where are you making for? It takes
So many thousand years to wake,
But will you wake, for pity's sake?

Christopher Fry
A Sleep of Prisoners[1]

---

[1] Christopher Fry, *A Sleep of Prisoners*, Oxford University Press, Oxford, 1971, p.55. By kind permission of Oxford University Press.

Sydney

The seventh night after the operation I had a dream.

Something was weighing on me, constricting my breathing. It became a black snake. I lay still, stifling fear, as it started to move. I could feel it sliding across my chest and under my back, and realised it was heading for Thu who – in the dream, as in reality – was sleeping next to me. I dared not call in case she stirred. In agonising slowness I willed my body to stand, supporting my right arm with my left hand to raise it upwards. I flicked the light switch – and was suddenly awake, still lying in bed. The room was dark. Thu slept on undisturbed.

It was not the thought of surgery that had scared me. I had a high level of trust in the doctors and the facilities at their disposal. Why then had my body been trembling beyond control, as it was wheeled into the operating theatre, my mind still active? One of the team must have noticed, for he came over to offer comfort – a young man from the sound of his voice, but all I could see were spectacles and a forehead, between cotton mask and cap. 'We know our job,' he said kindly. 'All *you* have to do is sleep.'

The surgeon had been more brusque. He lifted the dressing beneath my left eye and looked at where the cancerous tissue had already been cut out under a local. 'Ah,' was his comment. 'A big one!' Then he reached down to my shoulders and on each marked an area for the transplant. Why two?

As I lay in bed now, the feel of the snake still palpable, it became clear that my fear had been of death – or, more precisely, of not being yet ready for it. This, despite all my years of working with thoughts of the spirit's immortality. It was the fear both of surrendering my body so utterly into the control of others – and of losing myself in the blackness.

Something else, perhaps, had played into the dream. It was what our friend Greg – a surgeon too, though not of skin grafts – had said when I asked later what an anaesthetist does during an operation. 'The injection only puts you out for a short time,' he replied. 'Then a tube is put down your throat.'

'You mean I was gassed?'

It was three thirty in the morning. Sleep was out of reach. I dressed and went outside, needing to move, to take in air. Sydney street lights, orange in the darkness. My feet sought the high ground, my soul the ocean. I followed the path leading up to the Heads. It was unknown ground.

Fear was with me again. It grew as I climbed the steps, drawing away from the bay and the protection of the headland. I entered the wind, massive, solid. Far beneath, the surge and swell of the Pacific, boom and thunder against rock. Fear of what? Of people in the night, the night itself, this world of elemental power. Of the unknown path and being drawn off that high place by the ocean's sucking and the battering of the wind.

On the cliff top I lay down, sheltered by bushes. Above me, past shredded clouds, the stars of the southern hemisphere. In those moments I knew for sure, it was not there I had wandered during anaesthesia. I had gone, not up, but *under*. Hence the vivid turmoil of my dreams since. Compared with sleep and the ordinary darkness of night, anaesthesia is a sun eclipse, a gap in the daylight, a chunk of time somehow cut out.

The wind blew. Was I breathing it – this wind that brought the touch of the world into which Thu and I would shortly be entering – or it me? The terror had gone. In its place, simple gratitude for being there, now, on the brink.

The following day, I saw the damage on my face for the first time. Getting to that moment was a mini-journey in itself, a testing of qualities that would be indispensable in what lay ahead – learning to wait, for example, and accepting one's self-unimportance. With a bandage round my head, I went to the hospital by bus and train. It gave me a feeling for how it is to be old and at the mercy of what is around, of how much energy we expend in coping with noise and pollution and being jolted about. We only realise this when the energy is not there.

What I did have, though, was time. That was the secret. We speak today of conserving resources. It was a new thought for me that one of the most precious is time.

There was a long queue at the hospital, and most people in it – beneath wall posters warning of skin cancer and unsafe sex – were in a worse condition than I was. One elderly lady had hugely swollen legs and a dressing extending over half her face. Next to her was a man with livid burn marks on arms and neck. With my newly acquired ugliness I found it easier to look into theirs.

'It looks good,' says the nurse, when my time comes at last. She removes the stitches and guides me to a mirror. Half the nose and cheek are a deep-purple pulp. It is a far more atrocious colour than the burn marks on the man's face.

'It's going to change, is it?' I manage.

'Of course it is.'

On the bus back, a girl of about five kept peering at the thick dressing when she thought I was not looking. 'What has that man got under the bandage?' I heard her whisper to the elderly lady with her. 'Is it a hole or a big lump?' Her attention was sombre but intelligent – a foretaste, perhaps, of how it was going to be for us in the coming months as objects of curiosity in foreign places.

It was also different for me, looking out. The bandage and the residue of shock created a distance between myself and the reality around. I could look at people's features – the beautiful and the sexy as well as the gnarled and pitted – without seeking to attract their gaze. I was closer in those days to the Buddhist experience of non-attachment. In its small way it was a preparation for being with people in poorer parts of the world who have disfigurements that will never heal.

Neither Thu nor I were strangers to the process of preparing for a long journey. The difference now was that we were at an age where it is normal to dig roots rather than cut them. In Western cultures, at least.

In the weeks that followed, until my skin graft got the okay from the surgeon, our evolving plan to travel overland through Asia to Europe would be in our conversations almost daily. Along with the excitement were the doubts and questions. Were we up to it physically? Psychologically? We knew, from an African journey thirteen years before, the despair of not knowing where one is going – in life, as well as space. A long journey requires a long will, something quickly devoured by impatience and anxiety. It is a test of trust, not towards others only, but oneself.

During the intensity of our lives as teachers, we had had the security at least of being able to say, 'I know what I am, because I know what I do and where I live. What's more, others appreciate my work.' Now? The essence lay in this –

that we were on our own, with no commitments to go to or come back for. Nobodies, again.

'Are we trying to relive our youth, then?' It was me. 'Blown by the wind, flowing with the clouds. Like hippies?'

'Why not as people of the Tao? Or Zen? Not drifting, but being open.' Thu searched for words. 'It's going to put us on the spot, you know. Bring us up against the question: what do I really know? Not just because I've read or been told it.'

Outer aspects are perhaps the easiest to deal with, though they involve hard decisions – such as whether to spend money on travel insurance. We did. We applied for visas and bought new backpacks, each small accomplishment a milestone and a new source of anticipation. Then we got our one-way tickets to Bali, the start of the journey. Beyond that, the only fixture was to meet up with our son, Luke, in Vietnam a month later. It was there Thu and I had met twenty-two years before when I was a journalist during the war – and we had not been back since. For Luke it would be the first time and he was keen to get there under his own steam. He was in no hurry. Having just emerged from school, he wanted time to 'hang out' with friends, before 'hitting' the unknown. He had a year's deferment for his course at university.

We began sorting out what was going to travel with us, knowing well the drudge of lugging along possessions one never uses. One of the problems was that we were heading for extreme variations of temperature – torrid heat in the tropics, snow and ice in the Himalayas. Not to mention monsoons and deserts. Another was that, leaving a wealthy country for places of comparative poverty, one easily panics and buys too much, forgetting that most of our belongings originate in the so-called 'Third World' anyway.

We had sleeping bags and mosquito nets but no tents. Much of the weight came from books and notebooks, too many medicines and too many clothes. Then there were such things as a torch (later to be stolen), batteries, toilet items, sunglasses (hardly used), a pocket knife (confiscated in Iran) – and a neat automatic camera.

In the Africa journey, we had opted for not taking one. We figured there was enough already separating us from the local people. We sought to be there in pure experience, uncluttered by thoughts of how things would look on a piece of paper in the future. That had been during our early thirties. Perhaps it was a symptom of older age now, that we valued the recording of events as well as living them. Whereas then we had kept no journals, only a bare logbook of money spent and miles covered by our Kombi, this time we planned to write each day. We knew we would need to honour our encounters by remembering them in detail.

Next came the question of vaccinations. Our wish was to cultivate openness, which means not only standing aside from prejudice but travelling without armour. Vaccinations are a kind of inner armour – as well as bringing something alien into the blood. I was impressed when the doctor suggested that Thu, having been born and brought up in Vietnam, was probably immune to Third World nasties. My situation was more problematic, but the fact of having survived in Africa and South-east Asia before obviously counted for something.

We ended up with malaria pills and a tetanus boost, plus polio for me and – for reasons I have puzzled over since – hepatitis B, though this potentially lethal strain is only passed through blood and sexual fluids. A clear mind is a still lake, as Thu often used to remind me. Fear sends tremors that ruffle the surface. 'I shouldn't have taken it,' I said later.

'Why?' Her voice had a whisper of an edge to it. Regretting is not her way and she gets uncomfortable when I do it.

'I guess I lost trust. I had decided I wouldn't have an injection and then I did.'

'Why did you decide not to?'

'Well, why didn't you have one?'

'I didn't need it.'

'Exactly. Nor did I.'

Pause. 'Then why did you have it?'

Luke, who was with us at the time, opted for everything the doctor recommended. 'I don't see why you make such a big thing of it,' was his comment. 'It's stupid to take risks that aren't necessary.'

Risks! If there was an angel looking over me when I plunged into Vietnam the first time, back in 1971, I was unaware of it. I had had no sense of being guided or led, though it is true I did feel pushed. The furthest my faith could reach then was to the naive belief that somehow nothing too terrible could happen to *me*.

I had been working in Hong Kong, in a well-paid job with the prospects of an excellent career. There was every reason to stay, but for the chaos of emotions within. I turned to drink, to the pleasures of the senses, even to hard work. Then I became ill, with that strange, non-specific exhaustion that goes under the name of glandular fever (or now, perhaps, ME). And all of it because I could not rid myself of the thought that just across the South China Sea, a war was raging.

Of its politics I knew almost nothing; it was the war itself that haunted me, and the image of those shadowy figures in black called the Vietcong, who were defying the world's most powerful nation. What was it they believed in so strongly they were willing to die for it?

And how was it for the draftees who were being forced to fight there? I had seen a documentary about a group of them in California, on the eve of their departure. Some were gung-ho about 'fighting the commies'; others, close to panic. They were my age, speaking my language, as naive and terrified as I would have been in their place. By what right did I live my own pampered life? I had no wish to fight; but I felt compelled to be there.

It was different this time, of course. The war was over and we were going there freely. Yet there was a similar sense of something beyond consciousness urging me on. I knew it as a kind of haunting wish to encompass what is foreign, to learn to find it not just 'over there' in some other part of the world, but 'right here' inside me.

'So, are the hippies ready for the long trail?'

It was Easter Saturday and we were picnicking with Greg and his wife, Liz, near the Opera House during a two-hour interval in Bach's *St Matthew Passion* – based on the events leading to the crucifixion of Christ. We had known each other since their participation as parents in the school we had founded eleven years before. In the course of time their involvement had become yet closer, Greg as a member of the board and Liz as a teacher herself.

We had finished our picnic and had a further half-hour to get back to our seats. The others were talking quietly. I turned to Greg. 'I have another question about anaesthesia. Can you bear it?'

'Ah, Justin, for you…'

'Okay. I need to say first that I now see it as a spiritual experience, a kind of initiation. Something that takes you – how can I put it – into another… realm.'

He listened silently. We had had enough conversations over the years to have respect for our different vocabularies.

'So I want to ask you how it is on the outside during an operation. Is there an atmosphere you don't experience anywhere else?'

There was another question pushing around inside me, but I could not yet focus on it with words. To my surprise, he answered seriously. 'Of course. It has to do with the fact that a person's life is involved. Every action must be clear and precise. Time is of the essence.'

'Do you feel the presence of death? A guardian angel?'

'Ah!' He had a way of drawing out this single sound to include a variety of unspoken moods – affection, playfulness, delight, seriousness. 'I have a sense of being more fully present than at any other time. Does that satisfy you?'

We got up to go, the shell domes of the Opera House drenched in sunset as the huge Australian day slowly merged with the night. 'It's true,' he said after a while. 'There is something extra.' We were walking strongly now, realising we might have misjudged the timing. 'At such moments, I somehow seem taller than I normally am.'

We mistimed by about thirty seconds, and had to wait until the first pause, receiving the music second-hand through the video system. It was when we were back in our seats at last that I realised what the question was inside me. It had to do with this event of which Bach's music – and Matthew's Gospel – is a celebration. And with the sense I had had on the cliffs that night, of having gone into a place of utter blackness. The feeling of it had been with me ever since the operation. It was 'just there', beneath the surface of everything I looked at or felt. Entering such a 'space' in ordinary consciousness would have shattered me to pieces.

Now the thought came that it was into that very nothingness that the Christ had descended at the first Easter, and so came the question: the fact that one doesn't come back demented after anaesthesia, does it not indicate that there is something there, in the blackness, protecting one?

Vietnam – South

1

Justin shouts in his sleep. Pale light is filtering in through the shutters, the noise of traffic building into spasms of frenzy. I turn and doze, to wake up in bright daylight. 'Can you open a window, Thu?' he mutters, as I get out of bed. I push the stiff frame, and shut it immediately. 'Come on, we need air,' he says, joining me. Then he laughs. 'You're right. We'd better keep it closed.' The fans give an illusion of freshness as we stand and stare through the glass.

Below is a roundabout at which five roads converge, packed with motorcycles, *cyclos* (tricycles with a sofa-like seat and a driver pedalling behind), push bikes, *xe lams* (three-wheel mini-vans into which as many as twelve bodies can be crammed), carts, pedestrians and trucks, like whales among fish. On scooters built for two are families with up to five kids. There seem to be no rules, apart from the one of keeping vaguely to the right. Currents flow like a river in spate, complete with back eddies. From above, it has the grace of a dance – except when there is a collision. Then the bits become flotsam, flung out of the flow and angrily shouting.

Here and there are women with an *ao dai* – the long-sleeved, tightly fitting garment with two flaps reaching below the knees, which is our traditional dress. It is worn with black or white loose pants. More common are tailored trousers and short-sleeved blouses, gloves up to the elbows to protect the skin, wide straw or cloth hats. The men wear Western clothes.

Along the street is a hill of garbage, at which shabby-looking figures are picking with long sticks. A woman arrives and puts up a red and white parasol. She lays out a trestle table, six folding chairs and lo! a food stall, pots, bowls and all.

A truck appears, and its mechanical arm shovels the ooze into its dark entrails. It cannot hold it all, but enough at least to give hope. I feel clammy and unrefreshed. I have slept little in the heat and humidity of our first night in Ho Chi Minh City.

I was a bundle of nerves on the plane from Jakarta. We had been travelling for three weeks already in Indonesia, and were getting used again to the world of cheap hotels and madly packed buses, the noise, the smells, the food, the spices, the vibrancy and poverty of Asia. Yet it was as if our journey was only now beginning; from here to Europe it would be overland all the way. As we swung low over the snaking coils of the Mekong River, burnt gold in the twilight, paranoia flooded through me. Would the officials treat me with contempt for having married a Westerner? Might I be arrested?

We joined a queue in the same hall I remembered from twenty-two years earlier – faded tiles, fans overhead, hostesses in *ao dais*; but cleaner and more orderly. Most of the officials wore uniforms. They looked normal enough, even kind. And none of them had guns. How different from before – and my whole time of growing up in Vietnam!

When I was born, my family lived in Hanoi in the North, during the time of the war with France. My first contact with the West, when I was six, took the form of two French soldiers carrying long rifles. They were huge with hair all over their faces and up their nostrils – as gruesome as the images my wet nurse had fed me of 'foreign devils'.

In '54, when the French were defeated and Vietnam divided, we fled as refugees to Saigon – now called Ho Chi Minh City – to escape communist recrimination against my father who had been in the French colonial service. For the rest of my childhood, we lived under the shadow of another war, in dread equally of the army and the anti-government Vietcong and in crippling inferiority towards the West, represented by America. Police had a free rein to search and interrogate. They could detain people, confiscate their possessions, extort bribes or simply taunt them with terror. The sight of armed police and soldiers still provokes fear in me.

'Taxi? Taxi?' Voices in the sultry, spice-laden darkness, as we left the building.

'We've made it!' I exclaimed. 'I can't believe it. It was so... normal!'

All the more so for being with an American traveller called Carol, whom we had met on the plane, and who was as excited as I was anxious. She had been studying Vietnamese in college and was jubilant when the taxi man responded to what she said. His car, he told us, was owned by the government. It was air-conditioned and comfortable – with a meter he did not use.

We drove along boulevards and well-lit roads, past clean pavements and villas with high metal gates, barbed wire mingling with dusky bougainvillaea. What a relief! It was like showing guests around one's house and finding the beds have been made after all. I knew it so well, yet I recognised none of it. I had no idea where we were. The driver dropped us at the *Dong Khoi* – an old colonial building with suites as large as small houses, dilapidated walls and ceiling fans that creaked alarmingly. All this for eighteen dollars, but none of us wanted it.

We headed on to the backpacker area in a medley of cyclos, their drivers calmly chatting across the din of traffic. Ignoring our instructions, they stopped at a private doorway and rang the bell. A woman in bright red and yellow emerged from the grille gate and greeted us. She was small and robust, and looked about our age. A crowd gathered, chatting, inquisitive. 'There's been a mistake,' I said, exulting still in the language I know well but now rarely speak. 'We want the *Hoan Vu*. Do you know it?'

'It's round the corner, sister. But have a look here first. I charge less and it's safer.'

So it was we came to Mien's house – up concrete stairs and surprisingly spacious considering the narrow entrance on the street. She had converted it into four guest rooms, keeping for herself a single area which served as family room, kitchen, large cupboard and bathroom. In the kitchen was a low tap where the family would squat to prepare food and wash. Into the main part, less than twelve square metres, were crammed a bed, a table, shelves and a stereo. On one wall was a clock and a poster of Buddha above a small altar; on another, framed photos of two young women and a man.

'My husband,' she said, following my eyes as I looked at a youngish face, with high forehead and glasses. 'He was a lawyer; then an officer in the army. He died in the war.'

'And your daughters?'

She nodded. They were in their twenties, the one on the left strangely dark-skinned, both wearing the mortar boards used at graduation ceremonies in the West.

Here, and in the large cupboard, slept Mien, her son, daughter-in-law, five year old granddaughter and nephew. During the time we stayed there, various relatives would show up and pile in somehow. Later we discovered a family with four children living in a small room on the roof –

more cousins from the country.

I had gone out that first evening in euphoria. It was late but the streets were still a buzz of activity and the small shops open, with their meagre array of electrical wares, clothes, shoes, groceries. Cyclos swooped mercilessly, until we agreed to squeeze into two of them and purred our way to a brightly lit street with tables on the sidewalk. Beyond was a shabby soup place, serving all sorts of noodles and soyabean 'meat'. It was excellent and cost thirty cents each. We began to relax.

Carol was here to further her studies at Hanoi University. She spoke Vietnamese well already – with a Northern accent like mine. Justin mentioned he had been a journalist during the war. She had been a child when it ended in '75, but remembered its effects on her parents. 'Hey, you guys,' she said suddenly. 'Was this where you met?'

It had been in a café in the centre of Saigon, a place where artists and journalists used to hang out. 'I was with some friends,' I began. 'I had recently returned after five years in Australia. Justin came in with a Vietnamese man who knew me and he introduced us. We spoke for a while, then they went to another table.'

'As you can see,' said Justin, 'an event of no importance to Thu; while for me, the world had been turned upside down. I daily harassed another friend who was an artist to draw her face as I remembered it. He did drawing after drawing, but couldn't get it right. Then one day she showed up at the café again and I asked if we could have a meal together. She thought for a while and said, "Okay. What about now?"'

'Wow!' Carol laughed loudly and turned to me. 'So you fancied him?'

'My main feeling was, "Let's get it over with!" I wasn't looking for a boyfriend, certainly not a Western one. I was impressed that he spoke Vietnamese, but it was only when he asked to borrow money to pay for the meal that I started to take any real interest in him.'

Carol was quiet for a while. 'What are the chances of two people meeting like that?' she said at last. 'I mean, from such different backgrounds. Both of you just happening to be in a café at the same moment.'

'It may have been even more unlikely than that,' said Justin. 'It seems that Thu and I were in Hong Kong at the same time at one stage, though we didn't meet. Then we overlapped in Japan where I was on a business trip before going to Vietnam.'

'Like a meeting that was waiting for a place to happen,' said Carol.

We wandered back through streets, dark now and deserted – except for a few lone figures in white singlets half-lying on deck chairs, and women in uniform sweeping up garbage with long straw brooms. Gutters still flowed with the afternoon's rain and we walked with ankles bare, our sandalled feet splattered with mud.

Our priority the next morning was the post office, near the centre of the city, where Justin and I went to check for mail – a sacred ritual for any traveller on a long journey. There was nothing waiting for us, except the girls selling postcards outside. One ran up barefoot, in a tattered skirt and shirt, and thrust a cedarwood fan into my hand. 'Auntie, buy my fan,' she says in Vietnamese. 'One dollar. Please.' She looks about six years old. Her face is ingrained with dirt.

'I don't need it.' I put it back into her hand. 'Where are your parents?'

'No mother, no father. Auntie, buy my fan.' She starts crying.

'She's lying, she's lying. Buy postcards from me.' A chorus of voices. I hold up the ones I have already bought as we head for the red-brick Catholic cathedral.

A guard of beggars is on the doorstep, but inside it is serene. Women lighting candles, bowing low. Statues of Mary and various saints – Francis, Theresa, Michael; above the main altar, Christ on the Cross. In Mary's chapel, the walls are covered with shining plaques: 'We thank you, Holy Mother, for having protected our dear husband and father...'

I was a stranger to this world of churches as a child. Most Vietnamese were Buddhists, only ten per cent Christians, and I gave it no thought until a friend at school whispered some Gospel stories to me during a literature lesson. It impressed me that Christ had not tried to avoid suffering. Until then I had thought that the purpose of human striving was to escape from it. At sixteen I met an unusually gentle boy who was a Catholic. I felt terribly naughty, sneaking away with him twice to the park in front of this cathedral. The first time, we sat on a concrete bench at twilight, discussing Antoine de Saint Exupéry's *Little Prince*. The second, he talked about Jesus Christ and why he is nailed to the Cross. I wanted to ask more; but before I had another chance he left for a priests' seminary in France...

Justin wants to give money to two men on crutches at the door, but only has one small note. He gives it to one of them and we walk on.

'Why didn't you give to both? That's not right.' It is the girl with the fan. I tell her the only other note we have is too big. 'Give it to me,' she says, holding out her hand. 'I'll sort it out.' Whereupon she gives it to the beggars, instructing them to divide half of it between themselves and give us back not only the change, but our original note!

They told us they had been soldiers in the army that lost, but appeared to be without bitterness. There had been recriminations at first, security checks, barely enough food to survive and they had not been able to get work. There was also paranoia about subversion from overseas and people needed permits to go anywhere; but, though many disappeared into the infamous 're-education camps', their own period of internment was brief since they had not been officers. (So it was with two of my brothers, who were released after six months. A brother-in-law, who had been high up in the air force, however, was kept for thirteen years.)

The other girls are running across the road to join us. Immediately the one with the fan starts sniffing. 'Auntie… uncle… please buy my fan.'

'Postcards, one dollar.' They jostle to get near. I squat down to their level and ask why they are not at school.

'I have to sell cards.'

'Only my brother goes.'

'Mother's had a baby. There's no one to help.'

'What about you?' I touch the first girl, whose hand is in Justin's.

'Buy my fan,' she moans, tears flooding.

The only friend from the past I still had in Ho Chi Minh City was Lan. We had been out of touch for many years and it took us a whole day to track her down, as she had moved several times since. We even found the cyclo driver who had transported her belongings to her present address, and it was with him that we covered the last part of the trail.

Halfway, it started to deluge. The driver put up the roof for us and draped a cover over the front, but the rain still came through. He himself was totally soaked and we joined the people huddled under awnings and balconies, while the heavens opened, blazing arcs of lightning followed by thundering drums. Only cars continued, splashing up fountains. Water swelled over the sidewalk, stalls on wheels thriving on sudden business – sweets, cigarettes, Coca Cola. A boy put out his hand to catch a trickle from the canvas, and his well-dressed mother smacked him, then wiped his arm with a handkerchief. The rain lessened... and stopped. People hurried out in the hush, engines backfiring. We were wet and cold.

The house was in a flooded alley. Lan was at work, but her two teenage children were at home. Also her sister. 'Lan got divorced two years ago,' she said. 'Her life's been hard.' The previous month, she had fallen off her Honda and broken a shoulder. After a week in hospital, she had had to go back to her job, as an interpreter in a foreign company.

'What about you?' I ask.

'My marriage has broken up, too. Men aren't for me. I've got my shop.' Her laughter rings like a bell, but cold.

When I was young, girls were not encouraged to think or ask questions. The brain is a man's domain, we were told, so we should concentrate on looking pretty, being virtuous and getting a good job, until someone might want to marry us. In Australia, where I went to university as a scholarship student after leaving school, I swung to the opposite extreme and learnt to appreciate my independence from family and tradition.

To begin with, it had been paradise. I remember biting into my first crisp apple on Bondi Beach, the sea breeze and ice creams. No money worries, no bombs. The glitter of shops was like a fairy tale, and I felt sorry for people in Vietnam. I used to send half my allowance home. Then, strangely, the excitement waned and I became more and more isolated. In this land of plenty I felt starved, but did not know why. I read avidly, as I always have, and through this came to existentialism. I saw life as arbitrary and godless; and conceived of an exhilarating but terrifying freedom, without responsibility to anyone except myself.

When I came back to Saigon after five years, I rejoiced in the subtleties of the East and my native language. I saw how pictorial it is – precise, yet with a wealth of innuendoes. My own name, which is really Le Thu, means 'Autumn Teardrop'; and what I am now as a wanderer is a *nguoi phieu luu*, or 'person cloud flow'. I delighted too in the musicality of its tones, which are such tripwires for foreigners. There are six altogether, each bringing a different meaning to a given sound. Justin was to tell me later of an occasion when he was addressing an elderly lady and got the wrong tone for the word '*cu*' which has meanings as diverse as owl, tickle, the, used, elderly person – and penis!

Nuances of mood and relationship are expressed even in pronouns. Talking to my mother, 'Can I help you?' would be, 'Can daughter help mother?' To a boyfriend, 'Sister gives brother a present.' After an argument, perhaps, 'I want it back.' I address my father's younger sister as *co*, my mother's as *di*, while their older sisters are *bac*; my father's younger brother is *chu*, my mother's, *cau*. Thus to an older woman I express something minutely different if I say, 'Can niece help *co*?' Or *di*, or *bac*? Or *cu*! The varieties are infinite, you and I changing like a chameleon with the environment.

Combining this new awareness with the free spirit of a Western education, I delighted in my new life. I became a manager in a pro-government public relations office with Lan as my assistant. We had uproarious fun, welcoming foreign journalists, businessmen, high-ranking officers and other important guests to the conferences we organised, and distributing our newsletters worldwide. I had a flat in the city centre, an unheard of thing among good family girls, and enjoyed all the modern facilities imported from the West. The cost of my dinner each night in nightclubs and restaurants would have supported a poor family for several weeks.

But little by little, doubts began to lodge. Was it true, what we were broadcasting? Where did all the money come from for our expenses? My employers were evasive – while Lan carried on unconcerned.

That was when I met Justin and discovered the other side of the war.

'It's you,' she cries, tears in her eyes. 'It's you. I thought I'd never see you again.'

'I'm sorry I didn't let you know we were coming. But here I am. And Justin.'

'Hello, Justin. You look happy together. Unlike me.' She laughs and as she does so, the sensual carefree face I used to know reappears. Then it vanishes. 'Have you eaten?' She looks exhausted.

We said we had, but a plastic sheet was spread on the tiled floor, and food brought in – sweets, green rice cakes, sesame buns, lotus tea.

In soft but urgent tones, Lan told of the nightmare she had gone through in '75, during the last days of the war. She was in a Catholic hospital awaiting the birth of her first child, while rumours ran wild of the advance of the communist forces. The American authorities were already evacuating their citizens and those who had worked closely with them; and as the hours ticked by, the exodus became a stampede. Friends brought messages that there were still places on aircraft bound for the US, but that she must come instantly. The nuns checked her womb and shook their heads, while her husband raced around demanding a decision.

Panic grew, people rushing in the corridors, words of terror exploding in her mind… violence, massacre! They're here! They're heading for the hospital! Her labour began and in the delirium of pain she heard that tanks had broken down the gates of the presidential palace and the war was at an end. The baby girl arrived as the liberation flag was being raised on the palace roof and the battered city awaited its new fate in terror and excitement.

'We must get away,' she says suddenly. 'Can't you help? America. Australia. Anywhere.' In the years following, they had had a son; and she had involved them in five attempts to escape, failing each time and exhausting their funds. Her husband finally got fed up and left her to fend for her children on her own. After her accident, he had suddenly reappeared and now visited often. She thought he had a new family somewhere.

'Isn't life better now?' I reply. 'There's so much to do here.'

'You think I'm doing nothing? I'm flat out each day, with no prospect of getting anywhere.' She pauses. 'I'm a realist, Thu, not a dreamer. I work to make money, to look after myself and my children. Is it so different with you?'

It churned me up, the contrast between our lives. Northern Vietnam is closer to China, not only geographically but culturally, while the South was once, through the Chams (its earlier inhabitants), connected with Cambodia and the Hindu tradition of India. The climate ranges from icy winters to tropical heat. The differences are even in the accents – the Northern, earthy and clear; the Southern loose and airy. Through Lan, I had opened to the warm-blooded South; while she had been affected by my Northern thoroughness. We had become like sisters. Now we were strangers.

I told her of how, years before, Justin and I had run a reception centre for Vietnamese boat people in England; and of the unexpected feeling of fulfilment we had had through such work. Was I being patronising? My words seemed to echo back, unreceived. 'Many of the refugees were disillusioned,' I add. 'They had expected a land where money grows on trees and instead were met with the dankness of English winter and streets empty of people and filled with cars.' I remember one group that was bussed in from London airport in January asking piteously, 'Are all the trees dead in this country?'

'But they're free,' Lan exclaims. 'Look at you, you can travel.'

Thoughts came to my mind, which I did not know how to express. The only time she had had an offer of a way out, she was physically unable to take it; she was giving birth. Then came the failed attempts with the boats. 'I know your despair, Lan; but if only we can accept what destiny brings – even be grateful for it – doesn't that make us freer?'

She was silent. 'Why didn't *you* stay, then?' Her voice was sharp; and then she smiled. 'Why don't you stay now? Maybe we can work together.' For a moment something opened, a warmth we both knew. Then the clouds rolled over and she had to go off to work again.

That night the demons of the mind taunted me mercilessly with what I had said to her for I had heard it before, addressed to me. Justin, distraught, trying to bring reason into the maelstrom between us. Though his words had sunk in, all I heard at the time was arrogance and hypocrisy.

For nearly twelve years, the school in Australia had been our life. We had lived its joys and pains with the intimacy that comes from having witnessed its birth and experienced every aspect of its growth. We put everything we had into it, fired by the ideal of educating children holistically, in head, heart and hand. It was a call to learn the language of childhood, but to speak it without losing our centredness as adults. It meant re-evaluating what we ourselves had learnt at school, so that we could teach it in a fresh and alive way. It called forth the artist in each person.

In my secluded world of kindergarten I could witness daily the accomplishments of children, which are often not seen in the rush towards intellectual excellence – the moment when a withdrawn five year old first opened her arms and hugged me; or when a mother came to say her little boy had managed through the night without wetting his bed; Fiona, with new colour in her cheeks, starting to sing; Daniel doing a painting without muddying the yellow. Signs of inner nourishment – from fairy tales, imaginative play, artistic and practical activities.

I too was nourished by the children, the daily rhythm, the stories, and the friendships with colleagues and parents. There were great and memorable moments; but there were dangers too. The school grew; but it took its toll on us as a family. I became ill during the last few years, though I continued to work. And Justin, for reasons connected with his own life, came into crisis.

I saw his suffering but had no energy to help. And when at last he turned to another woman for support, our partnership deteriorated into a bitter and hateful duel. It opened up in me all the scars of a childhood deprived of love. We could have separated; we were tearing each other to pieces and each saw in the other a terrifying well of darkness. But we did not. Instead, a year and a half later, we left the school and decided to go on a journey – only realising, now we had begun it, that it was a further step on a modern path of initiation. The path called 'marriage'.

We spent the next morning in our room, shut off from the world. Each day was so rich in outer happenings, it was hard to fit in inner work; yet the longer our travels continued, the more we realised its importance. Experiences, like food, need to be assimilated. Our way of doing this was through meditation, writing and conversation. And of course sleep.

We would write whenever the opportunity arose but aimed to meditate at roughly the same time each morning. When travel schedules intervened, we would fit it in somehow – easier in the East where people take less notice of one's strange behaviour. Amidst the noise and crowds, we would try to school our consciousness into focused clarity – a word spoken silently, an image recreated, an idea entered into and held in stillness.

In the evening, we would go back through the day, lighting up significant moments. How often does one carry into sleep problems to which the next morning mysteriously brings solutions? And how much better one seems to know a person whom one meets again after a night's sleep. During waking hours I am immersed in all that comes to me through this world of space and time; during sleep I am in a different dimension, of which at present I have no awareness. It is here all the time but on another level. And the more consciously I prepare myself for it, however briefly, the more I begin to sense sleep as an activity which has an influence even on the small details of the day.

Yet the encounter with Lan was still like something undigested within me; and there was another meeting coming that I knew would shake me – with the only member of my close family who still remains in Vietnam. My family I say, but in truth she is not related to me. Like several others, Nhuong came into our lives when I was young and lived as one of us, though my mother already had thirteen children to care for.

She used to have a juice stall near our house and in the evening would wheel it into the living room and squeeze in beside one of my sisters to sleep. Her parents had died earlier and she adopted my mother as her own, nursing her through illness to the end. She continued living with the family, even after my father died, until most of them fled to the States in '75. Now she was the custodian of my parents' ashes – two porcelain jars in a Buddhist temple.

'I don't know if it's wise,' I say to Justin, nervous as always about meeting anyone connected with the family. Why is it like that?

Ever since I can remember I felt a stranger in my own home, most of all with my mother. For reasons I still do not understand, she disliked me as a child. I have no memory of her ever touching me with affection, let alone hugging or cuddling me. At special times when gifts were given, I would somehow miss out and be laughed at when I tried to participate.

The grown-ups called me *vung ve* (a kind of Humpty Dumpty) because I was clumsy and dropped things. I have a vivid memory of coming down the stairs one day, carrying a pile of clothes. My mother was in the room with some of my aunts and older sisters, when someone said, 'Look, here comes Humpty! I bet she drops it.' And sure enough, I did. Laughter everywhere – and Mother sternly telling me to take the soiled clothes to the wash room.

Then there were times when my sisters were taken on holidays and fed rare foods while I did not seem to exist. Or so it appeared to my six-year-old heart.

'It's a matter of recognising one's roots,' Justin replied. 'Isn't that what we're here for?'

So in the evening we took a cyclo to the outskirts of the city, passing a shanty town district with shacks of tin, tyres, plastic and old timber. I could understand why Nhuong had chosen to stay with us each night rather than go back through such places in the dark.

She greeted us with excitement, a small woman in her fifties with curly hair and sad full eyes – and ushered us into a surprisingly spacious house which she shared with a sister, a brother, his wife and children. We took off our shoes and sat on new carved chairs beneath whirring fans. At the back was a generous verandah with a hammock and a sleeping dog. Chickens wandered freely among banana trees.

The only person with a job was Vinh, the brother, who managed a furniture factory. He earned forty dollars a month and they lived mainly on money sent by relations in America. Nhuong was not well and this perhaps played into her despondency. 'The government is no good,' she declared. 'All corruption and greed. The country is in a mess.'

'Wasn't it worse before?' said Justin. 'At least there's no war and it's one country again.'

'There have been other problems,' Vinh continued quietly. He said that in '75 communist cadres had been put in senior positions everywhere, regardless of their lack of expertise, and they preached a spartan lifestyle. Then some changed their tune and became the most corrupt. Feelings had run high and many people were arrested. He reckoned that if things had not opened up, there would have been a revolution. The change began about the time of the collapse of the Berlin Wall, though politically it remained tight. 'Until a few years ago, one could be arrested simply for speaking English or having dollars,' he went on. 'Now, much of the business is done in dollars and people are paid extra if they know English.'

We asked him whether he was a member of the Communist Party. 'Even if I wanted to, it wouldn't be open to me,' he replied. 'One's invited on the basis of pedigree, going back to one's grandparents. But now it's only in politics and government that it matters.'

'Do you regret not having gone to America?'

'Never,' said Nhuong, looking at me tenderly. 'This is our home. Besides, who would visit father-mother's shrine if I left?'

And then I ask about my mother's death so many years before. It had been while I was in Australia, and when I came back eventually to Saigon I never felt able to talk about it. 'She died at home,' says Nhuong. 'Cancer of the uterus. She never complained.'

'Did she say anything?'

'She gave instructions – how she should be dressed, what type of coffin, what each of us should do in life. She was a saint.'

'I mean… about me?'

'You were not to know. You should finish your studies first.' She lowers her voice to a whisper. 'For a long time she would not shut her eyes. I got your photo and held it in front of her. She looked, then left this world.'

2

The flight from Hong Kong to Saigon on the first day of '71, eighteen months before I was to meet Thu, remains with me as one of the low points of my life. The plane was filled with men in army and civilian clothes, enormous, loud and showing no signs of anxiety. I could share neither their jokes nor their heartiness.

I knew no one in Vietnam. I had a month's tourist visa, savings from my job and a knowledge of French – and I travelled as widely as I could by bus, from the lush Mekong Delta to the old imperial capital of Hue. A few days before the visa was due to expire, I found myself in the scenic and peaceful town of Dalat in the highlands north of Saigon.

How I met Sandy I do not remember, but knowing his outgoing nature he probably approached me in the street. He said the Catholic university, where he was working, needed an English teacher – and there and then, scruffy as I was, took me to meet the Vice-Dean, a priest in immaculate clothes, speaking immaculate French. He expressed the university's gratitude for my being willing to work there and said they would take care of my permit.

It was a beautiful setting in which to begin and I stayed for six months, sleeping in the attic of the old villa in which Sandy lived with his Vietnamese wife and baby. Altogether there were three Americans at the university, all fluent in Vietnamese. I set myself to emulate them. It took me several months even to hear some of the sounds and tones, let alone reproduce them, but at least I did not have to learn a new script, as the written language was changed from Chinese characters to the Roman alphabet several centuries ago – foreshadowing the tragic but strong connection Vietnam seems to have with the West.

I also plunged into its history – the kinship and struggle with the Chinese, colonisation by France and the conflicts of this century. Much of what I read came from the library of the Military Academy where there were books from all shades of political persuasion. Most valuable to me were those of the French correspondent Bernard Fall, who was there during the war with France and was later killed by a mine as the American escalation was beginning. His work was thorough and dispassionate and I sensed a man of courage, who cared.

There was even a book by Wilfred Burchett, an Australian communist who had visited the North and been taken into Vietcong areas in the South. Photographs of this large man in black pyjamas haunted me.

From their writings I learnt that when the French were defeated at Dien Bien Phu in '54, the United Nations Security Council decided on a temporary partition between a communist North under Ho Chi Minh and a non-communist South, with the proviso that nationwide elections take place within two years. While around a million people fled from the North to escape communist reprisals, a much greater number elected to stay behind in the South, though their allegiance was to Ho. They became the seed of the National Liberation Front, or Vietcong – a derogatory term meaning Vietnamese communist, though it is acceptable today.

Often people said that if the elections had taken place Ho would have won. He had been active in the independence movement since the twenties and was, for most Vietnamese, the last in the line of heroic leaders against foreign invasion.

This was later confirmed in the leaked *Pentagon Papers* which revealed the CIA's forecast of an overwhelming vote for Ho. I began to realise that the democracy I had taken for granted in the West could appear in a very different light to people in other parts of the world, in whose lives it was interfering. It was an open secret that the CIA had prevented the elections from taking place.

If ever one needs evidence of the effect thoughts have on reality, it is to be found in what led to the US involvement in Vietnam as its foreign policy swung from one extreme to another.

During the Japanese occupation in the Second World War, the only real resistance came from Ho Chi Minh's 'Vietminh' guerrillas (as they were then called), who received drops of arms and supplies from American planes in the Northern jungles. When the British army took the Japanese surrender in '45, it was met with Ho's proclamation of independence (modelled largely on that of the USA). The British response was to use Japanese troops to police the country until the French arrived to claim it back. Ho approached the French – and was put off by one delaying tactic after another. So, in November '46, the war against France began. The US government (outwardly at least) put pressure on France to withdraw.

Three years later, Mao Zedong came to power in China and the world's largest nation became communist. American attitudes swung a hundred and eighty degrees, the 'domino theory' was spawned (of one nation in Southeast Asia after another being toppled by its neighbour if communism was not 'contained') and battle lines drawn in Korea. Almost overnight the colonial war in Vietnam became a war to save democracy from communism. American money, weapons and advisers poured in to shore up the French.

And when the French at last withdrew in defeat, American experts were already there in their place, building the dykes of the free world against the threatening tide. It was as irrelevant to them as it was to the Russians in Berlin that the Vietnamese dyke (like the Korean one) went right through the middle of an existing culture.

So began the deadly battle for the 'hearts and minds' of the people of Vietnam. What had begun as a struggle for independence became systematically distorted into a civil war of mutually hateful ideologies, in which all three superpowers were involved. Many Vietnamese saw their country as the arena for a world war that had finally found a place to happen.

Often in Saigon, after I had left my apprenticeship time in Dalat, I would play the Japanese game of *Go*. The board, a scroll of paper or cloth, was filled with squares and each player had a bag of counters, one white, the other black. At each turn, one put a counter on a square, the idea being gradually to surround the opponent's pieces and capture them.

The mystery of the game lay in this – that in the process of surrounding, one was being surrounded. It taught me much about Eastern thought. I learnt that reality is never simply black or white; there are always other perspectives and what may appear in one light as solid and reliable can seem in another to be illusion. It taught me also about the war and gave me the feeling that the American army would never be able to win.

Like the French, they relied on a network of outposts bristling with technology and supported by air power. During the day, one could have the illusion of these gaunt outcrops as a kind of encircling wall of armour. But during the night, it was the spaces in between – the rice paddies, jungles and mountains – that were the reality and the fortresses but islands in an ocean that could rise up and engulf them at any moment.

I stayed on in Saigon for three months teaching English at a Buddhist university. The students were as polite as in Dalat, but there was far more tension in their lives and a keener awareness of politics. I enjoyed the contact, but felt the lure of travelling on further through Cambodia, Laos and beyond.

I decided to leave. Three days before doing so, I was introduced to Du. In that first encounter I only caught a glimpse of the culture in his soul, but the fire of his eyes was enough to pull me back after three months of wandering, and he invited me to share his room in downtown Saigon since his wife was overseas on a study scholarship.

Through Du – pronounced *Zoo* by Northerners, *Dju* in central Vietnam, and *Yiu* in the South – the experience and book learning of my first year matured into understanding. He had been a student leader in the sixties and was arrested for his opposition to the American presence. Torture was everyday practice in the political prisons and he emerged after three years considerably weakened. Though his mind was as clear as a bell when I knew him, his body grew quickly tired and he had no work. What he did have was time – and patience. And during the months of our friendship he would speak to me each day about the East.

He spoke slowly in Vietnamese, often pausing for a deep drag on a cigarette, his language rich in imagery. His silences became part of the conversation and helped me to realise how much passes between people supersensibly, our words simply pointers for the sharing of thought and the meeting of souls. Although not in the Vietcong, he knew people who were and held them in high respect. Where he differed was in the matter of personal freedom. Their ways were often brutal, partly because of the extreme danger in which they lived. He was one of many who sought a middle path, and he introduced me to people who cared deeply for the culture that was being eroded equally by capitalism and communism.

As the weeks passed and I plunged more deeply into the cultural landscapes through which Du was leading me, there grew inside, like a child in a womb, an urge to express. The Vietnam I was experiencing had little in common with the daily news, most of which, I realised later, was a rehash of government briefings to journalists. I started to write and sent articles to various newspapers around the world. Nothing came back – until one day I saw one of them in a magazine from Hong Kong! The day after came confirmation in the post that they liked what they had received and would appreciate more.

Something else was growing too. In that shadow society where a person's real identity was always a question, I longed to meet someone whom I knew to be in the Vietcong. It was a selfish desire, for the risks for such a person would be enormous and it is perhaps fortunate that Du's attempts to put me in touch with a friend in the tunnels came to nothing – the wife of a doctor, due to come into Saigon to have a baby which she would then leave with relatives.

The image of the tunnels haunted me. There was obviously a network stretching for miles underground; Vietcong and North Vietnamese units could appear and disappear at will. The American response was to turn suspicious areas into free-fire zones in which anything that moved would trigger off an air raid.

One of the most bombed, mined, booby-trapped and poisoned pieces of ground in Vietnam was the 'iron triangle' near Cu Chi village, west of Saigon. It was not only devastated with rockets and B52 bombs; it was systematically gridded with walls of bullets from helicopter gunships. But the small people in black continued to appear and disappear.

I passed through Cu Chi in my days as a journalist, but never stopped. For that I would have to wait twenty-two years. It was now on my return to the country that I finally had my meeting with the Vietcong...

It was in the room known as the kitchen. Today the upper level of tunnels and entrances has been enlarged for Western tourists. There is electric lighting and one can forget that there are no windows. We were there with Carol who was still staying in our guest house in Ho Chi Minh City, and were offered a sample of the food the guerrillas used to eat.

The lady serving us was dressed in black pyjamas with bush hat, black and white check scarf and 'Ho Chi Minh sandals' cut out of tyres. The skin on her face was tight, her body thin and fragile. Her manner was gentle but somehow aloof. I wondered. Then I asked. As a girl of seventeen, around '64, she had become a cook in this very 'room', emerging in the evening to work the fields. This was before the area was devastated and the village destroyed.

She served us tea, cassava and some 'rice bread' with sesame salt. Normally there would only have been cassava and sesame. The bread was reserved for those on the move.

It was made by moulding cooked rice into the shape of a loaf, grilling it until burnt on the outside, then wrapping it in banana leaves. The crust would keep the rice fresh for four days.

Haltingly, in Vietnamese, I told her of the longing I had had to meet people in the Vietcong and she replied with sudden emphasis, 'It could not have been.' I wished to say more, for I felt the touch of destiny which years before had sown a wish and now had brought fulfilment; but I lacked the subtlety of expression. She agreed at least to be photographed with us, formal and in silence. She was the height of my shoulder.

We explored the tunnels further, bowed horizontal from the waist upwards and at times fighting claustrophobia. Our guide was a young man. He knew the information but not the war; and the depth of what was unspoken, so eloquent in the cooking lady, was lacking.

We experienced the top two levels and saw trapdoors leading farther down. We were shown a hospital area, places for sleeping, a conference room and the small space used by the commander. There was a photograph of him – young then, eyes shining, a shock of black hair, thin and black-pyjamaed like the others.

At the museum I had my second encounter – an elderly man in army green, who offered to be our guide. A calm dignity held his meagre frame together; but for his uniform, I would have taken him for a monk. Here again was a photograph of Burchett in black pyjamas, this time with a man called Nguyen Van Linh who had been commander of Vietcong forces in the Saigon area. It was the same man whose picture we had seen earlier. Our guide took us on past an assortment of booby traps, mortars and mines, ingenious and gruesome. He spoke quietly and with the simplicity of someone who knew well how to make and use them.

On one wall was a photograph of a GI waist-deep in a tunnel opening, a pistol in his right hand. His face was in profile, young and with all the poignancy of that moment, as his eyes linked with those of a mate leaning over him. Teams of men were trained specially for going into the tunnels. Most of them died. Later dogs were used. It is said they never penetrated lower than the top level. 'Who took this picture?' I asked.

'We did.'

'But how? It's so close.'

He laughed. 'We always kept close to the Americans. It was the safest place to be. We trusted them not to call in bombing raids on themselves.' He saw my bewilderment as I struggled to keep up with what he was saying. 'We knew when they had found an opening. We could see them. We would go in another way. Unless there was no need...' And he touched one of the booby traps. 'We even had tunnels into their bases.'

Again we stood together for a photograph. His hand touched mine and held it in the way that is natural in Asia. As we said our thanks and farewells I asked how it was for him now meeting Western people, especially Americans. 'They're friends,' he replied. 'The war was not between individuals but systems. People fought because they had to. Now it's over.'

We made our third encounter during lunch at a simple restaurant a few kilometres away. She was an old lady, almost toothless, with a face of a thousand wrinkles, laughter raying through her sun-hardened skin. We asked if she came from Cu Chi and she told us, in her rough rural accent, that she was one of the people who had built the tunnels.

She looked with tenderness at Carol who was wearing the black clothes with hat and scarf she had bought at the souvenir shop. 'You remind me of my daughter,' she said, wiping away a tear – and touched her. Then, unstoppably, laughter alternating with grief, she told her tale, her face transparent to the thoughts and memories that stirred in her.

There was something, I saw now, which all three people had in common. As well as gentleness, they each had in their eyes a deep-etched sadness which somehow heightened their individuality. They had the faces of people who have seen and suffered, perhaps I can say who have looked into evil; but the darkness in them was also beauty. I believe this is because, having seen and having done, they have also somehow been able to accept.

She had worked in a group of four, from '62 to '65, always at night. They would be given tools, guns, a kilo of cassava and a kilo of candles. While her group dug, a second one would scoop up the soil and a third carry it above ground. A fourth group would take it away and scatter it over the fields, she never knew where. The village was divided into hamlets and they shared the work, usually in one-week shifts. There was no pay. If one unit excelled, it would be rewarded with a pot of *che*, a sweet bean porridge.

Now she lived alone as a caretaker in the tin shack outside the restaurant. She had a curly-tailed piglet which Carol picked up and cuddled, while the old lady almost burst with laughter and tears. 'When you go,' she said, 'you'll forget me. I'm old and you live far away.' She looked again at Carol and went on, 'That's how I used to wear my scarf. Just as you have it. To keep my hair out of my eyes while digging.'

Back in Ho Chi Minh City, we made enquiries about the man whose name we now knew as Nguyen Van Linh. Our friend at the museum had spoken of him with deep respect. We learnt that he had later become general secretary of the Communist Party. It was through him that Vietnam changed course in the late eighties, opening its doors again after the years of isolation. We also discovered that he had retired. Though originally from the North he lived in Ho Chi Minh City. What is more, Mien, our landlady, knew him.

'I call him Uncle,' she said in fluent English. 'My husband's brother is married to his wife's niece!' I asked what she thought about my writing him a letter and she offered to take it to his wife.

'How can this be? Wasn't your husband in the South Vietnamese army?'

'I told you he was in the army. I didn't say which one.' In the silence realisation dawned. I looked at her smart clothes and permed hair and thought of the elegant silk elbow-gloves she would wear on her Honda. Could it be? 'Both my parents were in the Vietcong,' she went on. 'I joined at the age of seven.'

She came from a village in the Mekong Delta. In her teens she had become a soldier in a unit within which she only ever met two other people face to face, never the leader. 'He only knew me by a number and a false name. We went to meetings blindfold. If any of us were arrested we had no names to give away under torture.'

'How did you receive instructions?' Thu and I were still reeling.

'By word of mouth from the leader to someone else who passed it down the line. Always in casual encounters – with a beggar, for example, or a stallholder in the market.'

'Could you turn down a mission?'

'Yes, but I felt privileged to be given one and always found a way to carry it out.' She said a friend of hers was instructed to contact an officer in the government army and enlighten him about the Vietcong. She became a bar girl and did her task so well she married him.

Later in the war Mien worked as a secretary in the sprawling US base at Saigon airport, her real task being to mix with certain of the officers.

I look up to the photographs of her daughters on the wall. I notice now the brown hair of the fairer one peeping out beneath the mortar board. 'She's studying physics in Germany,' says Mien softly. 'This one, medicine in the States.'

My main problem in asking to meet Mr Linh was that we had nothing to offer in return. All we had was who we are, with our interest and our wish to connect.

It kept echoing in me that this man had affected history, for while America was changing Vietnam, Vietnam was changing America. And through the latter there spread into the world a growing awareness about the dangers of materialism. Prior to the sixties, warnings about nature's decline and the consequences of denying the spirit had been largely ignored. What happened then was a revolution in consciousness and the most potent outer influence in it was the Vietnam War. It became for many the epitome of destruction and deception.

Things reached exploding point in early '68 following the so-called Tet offensive. Having been told over and again that the war was nearly won, the American public woke up on the first day of *Tet* (Vietnamese New Year) to the news that during the night virtually every city, town and hamlet of South Vietnam had been occupied by the Vietcong. Though most of them were later driven out, the deed had been done. The peace movement became unstoppable.

I wrote of this in my letter, adding that I was glad Ho Chi Minh had experienced the war's turning point, if not its conclusion; he died in '69. By the time we had written about ourselves it was embarrassingly long. But Mien said, positive as always, 'Never mind. I'm sure he'll see you next week when you come back from the Mekong Delta.'

3

'It must have been on old tubs like this that the boat people escaped in the seventies,' remarked Justin as we stepped on board. Theirs, though, had been not only more heavily loaded but bound for seas and oceans, not just the Mekong River, wide and deep as it is.

It was a low wooden boat with two levels. Below, people squeezed on benches or squatted in the narrow aisle; above, it was crowded with old deck chairs. On both were rows of hammocks, hanging from the ceiling over planks thick with stretched out bodies. We were crammed in near the back, by a wood fire for cooking and two large vats holding water. A breeze was blowing in through an opening in the side.

The wharf was still a bustle of people in black or white pyjamas bargaining and chatting, the women wearing conical hats of dried pineapple leaves, their lips stained with the red juice of betel nuts. Children were playing among the sacks, bundles, baskets and animals yet to be sorted. No one seemed to know when we would leave. I went out to buy some food; it would apparently take six hours to reach My Tho.

I came back to a commotion around an old woman moaning on the floor. 'She was trying to get on to her hammock,' said Justin. 'But she didn't spread it out properly. She fell with a real thud.' She was helped to a chair and women fanned and stroked, smoothing her hair, drying tears. A green bottle of Tiger Balm appeared and they rubbed the liquid on her temples, pressing salt poultices onto swollen shoulders and a twisted thumb.

There was a sound of wings fluttering under Justin's chair from a sack with bulbous forms clucking inside. The engine started, the boat inched out into the brown voluminous Saigon River and we went to perch near the bows. On both sides were shacks on straggly poles, river craft of all sizes weaving among them, weighed down with produce, and with a palm-leaf cover or cabin housing a family. Naked bodies of children glistened in the murk.

As we emerged from the slums the water changed to topaz, rippling, life-reflecting, the breeze a whisper. Palms and thatched huts glided by. How different from a bus! Twilight fell, mosquito-free, and the first stars appeared – Venus in the west; in the east, Jupiter. Voices droning, muffled laughter and the chug-chugging of the engine. Such a journey would have been impossible during the war.

'Police.' Someone touched my arm and one of the men signalled us down. 'They'll fine us if they see you there,' he shouted. The boat stopped to take more people; then we were allowed back on deck. The wind was blowing harder. Rain spattered. Two boys and a woman joined us, bubbling with curiosity. 'Is he your husband? Where do you live?'

Most of the people, they said, were from a village beyond My Tho. They were on their way back from selling produce in the big city – especially durians, the large spiky fruit with succulent flesh which smells like body odour to the uninitiated and divine to those who have succumbed to its temptations. There are stories of people selling house and wife to attain one. 'You're sitting on their stones,' said the woman with a laugh, as she prodded the lumpy sack beneath me. 'They'll make your bum itch.'

It was dark now, the stars large and close. Speeding on our right, Scorpio; on our left, even this far north, the Southern Cross. Justin was chatting with the boys. They were twenty and had never known war. Its memories pass, like the flowing river, and life carries on anew. They said they did not like the city and were happy in their village.

I wove my way back in paraffin light through the creaking cabin, past swaying hammocks and gleaming bodies, the engine a harsh clanking din. A woman was cooking at the stove. At a low table people were eating rice and chicken, talking and laughing. A boy rushed about fetching bottles, cracking ice and shouting, 'Anyone for a drink?'

'How are you enjoying it?' A grey-haired man with kind features sits down next to me, saying he is the captain. He is dressed in long white pants and a singlet.

'Very much. Is this your boat?'

'It's been in the family for thirty years. We always run this route. That's my wife cooking, my grandson serving drinks. My son's at the wheel. Not a bad business. It's up to oneself how things go, you know.' He excuses himself and climbs onto a hammock over the vats. I realise that, except for our time as refugees in the South, I have never been as close as this with country people in Vietnam.

When I was a child, society was still feudal and my parents, coming from a line of aristocrats, or mandarins, had never mixed with the 'lower' classes. The only exception for us children were our wet nurses, or *vu em* (literally, 'breast child'), village women who would leave their own infants with relatives and breastfeed the children of wealthier families. Mine was with me from the day I was born until the age of six. She then went home, had another baby and, again leaving it, came back to take care of my newborn brother. Though I grew up not knowing my mother's touch, for some reason I was not close to my nurse either.

In the North, communism did away with all this, but in the South it stayed the same and even as refugees we kept the stamp of our breeding. Yet I enjoyed the camp with its rows of wood and iron shacks in a government barracks. We were a family of fourteen at first – my parents, my father's second wife and her daughter, nine of us siblings and a maid. I was the fourth, turning eight. Soon after, the second wife left with my half-sister to set up house on their own in town, and my father divided his time between the two places.

In that mass of homeless humanity I discovered warmth for the first time. Our life in the North had been of servants, chauffeurs and governesses, our parents out of reach. Now we were all cooped up together with two large boards as communal beds. I still felt distant from my mother, and my father was hardly there; but I became closer to some of my siblings. We attended makeshift classes and spent hours playing in the streets of the camp, mainly with children of poor and uneducated families. Mother was unhappy about it but had to accept.

One of my best friends was Marie, a girl of twelve, as huge as she was black, with frizzy hair and flat nose, but speaking only Vietnamese. Her father was Moroccan and had been in the French Foreign Legion, a giant married to a tiny peasant woman with a squint. They shared a bed-space with their two daughters, Marie being the older. She took me for a walk one evening to the zoo and we sat by the lotus pond, while she read from a book of poetry. She had the most beautiful voice I had known. Then they left for France.

I got to know our maid too – a woman of forty from our ancestral village who had been a captain in the Vietminh army against the French. She told me how she had been wounded and operated on under a paraffin lamp in a tunnel without anaesthetic. The surgeon had extracted the bullet but punctured her bladder, which resulted in urine trickling out all the time. She got discharged and came to work for us. Mother had agreed to take her south as a helper – or rather to be helped for she was not well. I remember her for her kindness. She would get upset when Mother seemed to favour my siblings over me and said she thought I was not my mother's child. Discord developed and she left, saying she did not like being a servant.

Only in the last few years have I learnt that she was a Communist Party member all that time and had gone south to gather information. She must have done her job well, for she was sent to Moscow after, to have a proper operation. It did not work. She died there.

We reach My Tho at ten. Somewhere in the dark we must have joined the Mekong. Our boat pauses mid-river and a sampan takes us to the rambling Grand Hotel – a relic from French days and seemingly without maintenance since. Mould-spotted blue paint is peeling off the walls, the taps trickle and the drain is almost blocked; but we are provided with towels and soap and cracked plastic slippers for the lady!

We woke to the deep throb of an engine, going on and on. Below us, in the humid heat, was a canal crowded with boats and barges, one so heavily loaded as to be almost sinking. Men in loincloths were carting baskets up rickety planks into warehouses, each one stacked high with a single kind of produce – onions, cassava, pumpkins, sweet potatoes, durians, jackfruit, pineapples. Women cleared out the holds and cooked, home life expanding as the cargo disappeared. Sampans skimmed lightly, ferrying people and merchandise to shops and shacks on stilts. Tufts of green floated in the water, children's heads bobbing, bodies glinting. Voices from the street, the gentle sounds of water.

I finished reading John Cornish's *The Raising of Lazarus*. One detail he related became a theme for my meditation. When Jesus came to the house where Lazarus had died, Martha went out to greet him while Mary stayed inside wrapped in sadness about the loss of her brother. Jesus called, for she was needed too, alongside her worldly sister, in what was about to take place. At the moment of seeing him, her self-absorbed grief was transformed into a love that overflowed to others. Only then was Lazarus raised from the dead.

It gave me the strength to realise that the awful feeling of being a victim of circumstance to which I am prone – going back to childhood – *can* be changed into something worthwhile. For a few special moments I had the conviction that what took place historically in the Gospel scene can happen in one's own inner space, if only one works at it hard enough.

The sudden rain was startling but life went on as normal. Cyclo men pedalled without raincoats or hats, boatpeople plied their trade. A bicycle passed with three teenage boys on it, one at the handles, another on the rack behind and in between, the third, barefoot on the frame. They honked and shouted deliriously, water streaming over them. I could not make out whose feet were doing the pedalling.

The deluge was over in minutes. In the coolness that followed, we walked to the park by the Mekong River where locals gather at dusk, the expanse of amber water reaching almost to the horizon. A man with a forearm missing perched next to us on the wall. He told us bitterly he had got drunk and shot it with a gun to get out of the army during the war.

A younger man approached, bare-chested and dishevelled. 'Aunt-uncle, the police are persecuting me,' he said, ignoring our neighbour. 'I'm a woodcutter. My village is far away.' His words poured out. He said he had fled here with his wife and baby who were asleep on the grass. 'They say it's forbidden to cut trees. How are we going to live? They are *devils*.' And he threw himself on his knees, begging powerfully amidst the flame trees and the soft hum of laughter and lovers' whispers.

Strangely, in this place of peace, I do not sleep well. My reading in the afternoon, coupled with the wildness in the young man's eyes, has touched something in me; and now there well up, from beyond the borders of the mind, past scenes of war between Justin and myself as we reached breaking point. Waves of resentment flood through me – while Justin lies asleep, oblivious. How can I put this to rest once and for all? Is this what it means to forgive?

It cannot be a question of having to say the hurtful actions are good. But there's a choice there, somewhere: to blame, or no longer to blame but look on objectively and accept. What an outcry the thought brings up! 'Forgive? How naive! Do you not know that there are things so bad they are not meant to be forgiven?' Then comes the familiar pain, the pain I long to hurl at the person who provoked it. Do I have the strength to carry *that*? Why should I? Or transform it, like an alchemist?

Without a higher source of power, how can one do such a thing? It is too great for the ordinary self.

I remember a story I have read about a man who used to visit an Allied hospital in the aftermath of World War II. His presence brought light and hope to the patients, regardless of which side they had been on. His capacity to love achieved healing where medical treatment alone had failed.

A few years before, he had witnessed the murder of his entire family – parents, wife, children – in a Nazi camp. By what incomprehensible power had he chosen the path of forgiveness?

'Now *this* is a river!' Justin exclaims with delight the next morning as we rock dangerously in a sampan with a shrieking outboard engine. It is the fourth longest in the world. Rising in Tibet it journeys through China and Laos before splitting into two branches in Cambodia, both of which flow through Vietnam. The Vietnamese know it as *Song Cuu Long*, the River of Nine Dragons, dancing and multiplying on its exuberant way to the ocean.

We were on a branch of a branch of one of the earth's arteries, yet how wide and full! It felt as if we were going out to sea. In the middle the current was more gentle, and the owner cut the engine and let us drift. A boat floated by, its cargo of straw so tall it was almost toppling over. At the back was a figure in black with a conical hat, steadying it with a pole. Palm fronds, bobbing coconuts, clumps of lilies, colours fragmented on the ripples; no sound but the lap of water against wood, and in the distance, a radio, a child's voice. 'Do you realise we'll be at the place where this river begins in a few months?' said Justin dreamily.

'And in three days we'll be seeing Luke.' I felt joy and anxiety in the same instant. What if he does not like Vietnam? After all, it is a part of him even though he has never been here. I imagine him in Bali or Java, suddenly no longer a child but a young man. Is he finding his way? And is it important for him, as it now is for me, to come to terms with his roots? What if he denies that part of his nature?

The engine spluttered into life again and we skirted a number of islands, thatched huts amidst rain forest green, some with TV aerials. 'Shall we stop here?' said the boatman. He seemed strangely reluctant to go on.

'No, we're going to Coconut Island.'

I closed my eyes; and all at once we were in a narrow rivulet between dense foliage and reeds. The engine fell silent and the man took out a paddle. 'We'll wait until it's passed,' was all he said, as he started tinkering with a spanner. We heard the noise coming closer on the main river. Small waves rocked us as it went by, out of sight. 'Government tourist ship,' he explained at last. 'Small boats not allowed. Unsafe. There's a twenty dollar fine if they catch us.'

Now it was gone, he relaxed and took us to our destination – a long island with a pretty village of shady trees and whitewashed walls joined by a red dirt lane, and a temple made famous by the man known as the Coconut Monk. The ticket lady let me in free as Justin's guide.

As a young man, Nguyen Thanh Nam had studied chemistry at university in France. Back in Vietnam he married and had a family which he left to live here as a monk. He founded a sect combining elements of Buddhism and Christianity, and immersed himself in meditation to find a solution to the war, allegedly living only on coconuts for three years. For his opposition to the violence of the Southern government he was repeatedly put in prison. When the communists took over, he was victimised again.

The temple this eccentric but courageous man built is in sad disarray – faded columns entwined with dragons; derelict world globes; a map of Vietnam painted on a slab, festooned with broken shells; a rocket-like tower; two bare thrones, an inside one for meditation, outside for teaching. An old photograph shows him dressed as a Catholic priest; in more recent ones he is wearing the robes of a Buddhist monk. 'A few years ago they pushed him off a cliff,' said an elderly man who looked as bedraggled as the temple. 'That's what happens to people who are different.'

*

The day had come. Early in the morning, we headed back by bus to the city (along with the ducks, chickens, bicycles, dried fish, rice, durians, pineapples and soya sauce that were bound for its market). Luke's plane was due at noon.

People squeezed in. All the double seats were occupied by three, the air toxic with smoke and blaring music. Into the mêlée came an old man carrying a net with a sharp rod, which he wedged against a seat. What if it falls over as the bus hits a pothole and the spike goes into someone's eye? I wondered. How Western I had become! In Australia, there would be insurance claims and maybe lawsuits running into millions of dollars. Here, it would be taken as karma. The focus would be on the victim rather than the wrongdoer, on accepting what had happened rather than seeking compensation.

Back 'home', Mien – no longer just a landlady but a friend – told us she had delivered Justin's letter to Mr Linh's wife and that she was optimistic about our being able to see him in a few days. She had also organised a minibus to take us to the airport.

Her son Tuoc appointed himself as our guide. He was the eldest of her children, in his thirties, small, thin and with a scar across one eyelid. 'He fell off a chair at five months and damaged his brain,' she told us blandly. 'That's why he's not so bright.'

'Bright enough to have a wife and child, eh?' he chipped in.

'Where is she, by the way?' I asked.

'I've sent her to her mother. She kept singing this silly song about a baby falling out of its cradle. She didn't stop when I told her to.'

The flight was delayed and we had a long wait, during which Tuoc several times approached staff saying he had important clients and that the plane must land without further delay. It came at last. Passengers pour out; then the flow diminishes, and stops. No Luke. Has he got lost – or had an accident? Is he sick?

It is his brightly patterned shirt I see first, then the strong eyebrows from his father's side and brown eyes from mine. His hair is short; he looks happy. 'Sorry I kept you waiting,' he says. 'The guys in there wanted to know about Australia. There was also a woman in the queue who asked me to marry her. Is that the normal way over here?'

He was overflowing with stories about his experiences of travelling as we headed back through the afternoon flood. He told us of a volcano he had climbed in Bali, and of how he had strayed from the path and got lost in the dark. He had caught his leg in a crevice and, by the time he got it out, realised he was going to be spending the night there. 'Man, it was dark,' he said. 'And I kind of felt things.'

'You mean insects?'

'No. There were ants; all over me, biting. But this was something else. Eerie, scary.' He paused. 'I did something I never thought I'd be capable of. The sort of thing you'd do, I guess. I talked to them. Aloud. I asked them to leave me alone.' He laughed. 'I even spoke to the ant spirit, asking it to stop the ants.'

'Didn't you have a torch?'

'Yeah, but I dropped it somewhere. And my matches were wet. By then I couldn't do anything for shaking. I wondered if I'd make it. I even prayed.'

Later we went out into the steaming streets, Luke's astonishment enabling us to look at everything we saw with fresh eyes. We wandered on foot in the rain-fresh smells, tasting the fruit, pastries and drinks, then took cyclos going nowhere in particular – Luke pointing his camera in all directions. 'This place is a paradise for photographers,' he shouted. 'I love it. I love travelling.' My worries had been groundless.

It rained again and we came back soaked. In the night he developed a fever and stomach pains, which continued into the next day. Mien prescribed *chao* – rice porridge – with salt and pepper, and a bed rest. 'You know what helped me that night on the volcano?' he said, still sorting through his memories. 'It was the stars! They were so bright, so alive. And I realised, yeah, they're there all the time, while we're so wrapped in our problems. It's hard to remember how it felt, though.'

4

It was to be one of those days, so full one's soul almost bursts.

It started with a meeting at seven with Minh, a man who was famous when I was in Vietnam as a journalist for having written a letter from prison to the American president in his own blood. My friend Du had known of him and held him in high respect, as did Thu. Now he was a doctor, working with a growing number of Aids victims. We met him in his clinic – his face, like Du's, vivid with life experience and big for such a thin body. It was gentle, with deep lines and dark eyes.

He told us of his time as a student leader in the sixties. He had not worked directly for the Vietcong, but had links with them and could count on their support – for example, in organising demonstrations. 'They were everywhere, sister,' he said to Thu. 'Anyone who genuinely wanted to make contact could do so.'

He was in prison for many years. His name must have been well known, because a US senator visiting Vietnam on a fact-finding mission insisted on seeing him. 'I knew something was up,' he went on. 'My food improved. Then people came and cleaned my cell. They even dabbed on some paint!' The prison toilet was over a river in which were bits of paper used by villagers upstream to wipe themselves. He got hold of a fragment, washed it and took it back to dry. With a pin he pricked a finger, using a twig as a pen.

I spoke to him about Du who had shown similar courage, yet who in the years following the communist takeover had been arrested again and put in solitary confinement. 'Yes, I know such things happened,' he replied. 'For those who had known the tunnels, all city people were bourgeois. Many of the new officials had little education and were suspicious of "intellectuals". Where is he now?'

'In England. That's the irony. He says he left to preserve his Vietnamese culture.'

Our second appointment was with Mr Nguyen Van Linh who had responded warmly to our letter. We were ushered into a ground-floor room, accompanied by an interpreter and an ambassador from the Foreign Office. Luke was carrying his bulky camera case, Thu our day bag. No one asked for our identity papers or searched our belongings. In how many countries can one meet an ex-head of state without a security screening?

Inside was Mr Linh, small with age and wearing a high-collar suit and sandals. He had glasses, but they did not hide the life in his eyes and the extraordinary growth of his grey eyebrows. He beckoned us to a sofa and ladies in traditional dress brought fresh orange drinks and small cups of tea. The room was unadorned, the furniture comfortable but far from new. He sat upright with an impassive face which would suddenly light up in response to something said. It made me think of how it might have been conversing with a mandarin in earlier times.

I asked him what had kept people going during the war. His reply was a narration of Vietnam's history of struggle, leading up to the initiative taken by Ho Chi Minh against the French. He spoke of the tradition of loving one's country and that it was natural for it to hold its own against America. He said nothing personal. It was as if a mask had descended. His voice was flat with the reeling off of facts so often stated before.

'What about faith?' I persisted. 'There must have been something more than tradition to give people the courage they showed.'

'Faith?' he replied. 'If you mean religion, as a Marxist I have none. We allowed people to hold on to superstition so long as it did not interfere with their duties.'

He then began a second narration, this time about Christianity. Jesus lived at the time of Jewish suppression by Rome. Born of a working-class father, he fought for his people's independence, his closest followers peasants and workers. He was crucified between thieves, however, and this did not lie well with his supporters. So the stories were glamorised about his supernatural powers and about paradise in a world beyond. Catholic colonisers later used these to distract oppressed people from their misery. I was reminded of the Marxist statement that religion is the 'opiate of the masses'.

He paused. 'Was there ever a time when you yourself felt tempted to give up?' I asked.

He smiled and looked at me directly for the first time, his eyes clear and bright. 'Never!'

The event lived on through the rest of the day and for several days to come. Two hours later as we were having lunch at the home of Du's ninety year old father on the outskirts of the city, the rain a torrent outside, flu descended like a wall separating me from the world. I knew it was not only a physical matter; I felt shaken inside.

I had the sense of having encountered the spirit of communism and it weighed on me. I wished I had asked Mr Linh, having been surrounded by so much bloodshed, what he thought happens after death. Was he truly a man without religion? I realised that behind my initiative to meet him was the same question which had drawn me to Vietnam in the first place: what *was* it that enabled the Vietcong and North Vietnamese to endure the suffering they went through and prevail?

Maybe after all, it really was no more than indoctrination, as their enemies had said. But no. The image came back of the people we had met in Cu Chi; of our landlady, Mien, too. And the way in which Mr Linh had spoken that single word, 'never'. In that moment the spirit had been there – not of communism but the human spirit. He had believed in what he did. Was this not, in truth, his religion and his faith?

I wondered again why the meeting had affected me so strongly. Maybe, in eternity, our simple encounter with Du's father was of more importance, for we met as equals. Was it a symptom of my own ambition – despite years of working to overcome it – which fawns on the power in others because it seeks power for itself? I thought of the Zen master who sweated in nervousness before welcoming a visiting dignitary. In self-disgust he renounced being a teacher and left the monastery.

'I guess he's a hero of yours,' said Luke, on our way to the Ho Chi Minh museum.

He used to be, but now I needed to delve deeper. People argue about whether Ho was primarily a nationalist who wanted independence for his country, or a communist who wanted to bring about a social revolution. Of course he was both, but what interested me now was his inner life as a leader and an individual. 'Since you're here to find your roots,' I replied, 'sooner or later you'll have to form a relationship to him. Of all Vietnamese he's had the greatest influence on Vietnam this century. On the world too.'

I told him of Du's description of the demonstrations in Saigon, following his death in '69 – streets filled with the white robes and headbands of mourning, among them a procession of veterans and war widows. They walked in silence, in defiance of the curfew and uninterrupted by the armed police. Men on crutches or being pushed on wheels, bandaged, deformed; and behind them, the women, young and old, many needing support. Would a 'mere communist' have inspired such courage in a people supposed to be fighting against him? The museum helped me towards an answer.

It brought home how much of the world Ho visited between leaving Vietnam in 1911 as cook boy on a French ship and returning in '41 as leader of the resistance. Ironically it was in France that he encountered communism – among workers who were suffering, as Vietnam was, from a system that rewarded the rich at the expense of the poor. He attended several congresses in Moscow in the twenties.

The thought nagged: how different might history have been if, instead of Lenin, he had encountered Gandhi in Europe – or Rudolf Steiner who, as the First World War was grinding to an end, presented his ideas of a threefold society in which culture, politics and economics could work alongside each other rather than in competition. In contrast, what came about was the divide between capitalism and communism, each increasingly dominated by economics.

As with Gandhi, British law had its part to play in Ho's life. As a Comintern agent wanted by the French, he was arrested in Hong Kong in the thirties. The judge before whom his appeal was heard, a man called Prit, was impressed by his integrity and persuaded the British government to withdraw its case. Here were two men from polar opposite backgrounds who met at a critical moment in Ho's life. Had he lost his case, he would have been handed over to the French and almost certainly put to death.

Ironically again, it was not in the West but neighbouring China where Ho's mission was almost extinguished. He was arrested in the chaos of a country torn apart by rival fiefdoms. Amongst the poems he wrote as he languished for over a year in a succession of overcrowded jails, was this one:

> Thy body is in jail,
> But thy spirit, never!
> For the great cause to prevail,
> Let thy spirit soar... higher.

In the old Zen stories a breakthrough can come at the most unlikely times, such as while walking in front of a butcher's shop. So it was that what spoke most to me in the museum was a tiny detail in a photograph. Taken around 1960, it showed Ho wiping an eye with a handkerchief. In the caption we read that he had been brought to tears by news of yet more suffering in the South. It could easily have been staged; such things are common worldwide. What affected me however was not his face or the caption, but his wrist – its thinness and fragility, the gentleness of its gesture sculpted by years of hardship.

Inwardly I placed Ngo Dinh Diem, Nguyen Van Thieu and others who had held power in the South, next to him. It was like putting a wax model next to a human being. In the one there is just appearance; in the other, spirit. They had seized what was not theirs. Ho's stature outshines them because through him there spoke the spirit of a people.

In saying this, I am not defending his methods. From communist Russia he imported the brutal ways of cadres and secret cells. His land reforms in the North after '54 were extreme and he could be ruthless with opponents. Nevertheless, like Churchill with the British and Gandhi in India, he had the destiny of leadership.

5

Tuoc knocked at six thirty in the morning to announce a visitor.

'They're half an hour early,' Justin muttered grumpily.

'Come on, Dad. It'll be great at the beach,' said Luke, for once up earlier than his father.

'I'm not leaving until it's time.' And he made a point of fussing about, tidying the room, while Luke and I went on down without him.

In front of the house was a flashy black saloon. A man came towards us. 'Sister Thu, I'm Dong,' he said excitedly. He was tall and thin, casually but neatly dressed. 'I was out yesterday. I'm so sorry.' I had been given his name by one of my brothers in America, but only his wife Thuy had been in when we looked them up. Their home was a luxurious penthouse in an otherwise shabby street and its contrast with the poverty all around had put Justin on edge ever since.

We waited awkwardly until he emerged, at one minute to seven. Dong shook his hand with gusto and we piled on to the spacious back seat, while the driver took his place in front. 'Nice car,' I ventured. Its luxury was bewildering.

'I bought it last month. It would normally have cost seventy thousand dollars. I got it for fifty.' He flicked a button and a husky female voice flooded the interior. The stereo and air-conditioning made the street scene distant, as if in a film.

We met up with Thuy and her children at an open-air restaurant outside the city, famous for the *pho* that originated in Hanoi – rice noodle soup with beef or chicken slices and a mountain of herbs. 'Good stuff,' said Luke, finishing off two bowls, as beggars watched closely. Justin remained silent whilst Dong effervesced with goodwill. Thuy sat down next to me. I liked her – a friendly and unassuming person despite their new wealth. I felt Dong was too.

It had come to them since the new economic policy. They had started with a demolition business, then expanded to recycling the scrap metal into parts for the booming construction industry. They made phenomenal sums, enough to buy two houses and a car, and talk of sending their children to Australia for tertiary education.

Vung Tau has been the seaside resort of the Saigonese since French days. Sparsely populated, it has facilities for thousands of holidaymakers pouring in at weekends and school breaks. Most of the villas now seemed empty and dilapidated amidst the fiery flame trees and mauve jacarandas; but the beach was packed with tightly spaced deck chairs and parasols, and the water a mass of heads and bodies and bright plastic balls. We settled into our seats, surrounded by the peel and plastic on the soft white sand, and ate lychees.

Luke merged with a group of men throwing beach balls. Now and then someone would talk to him and be bamboozled when he could not reply. Beggars hovered. Dong spoke of plans for the future. He was excited by the new opportunities opening up, also by the power money brings. 'If you have initiative, you can do anything here, sister.' One of his ideas was to make surfboards. 'There was an international surfing competition on China Beach up north recently. The next thing is to advertise and create a need for it among the young. That's how they do things in the West.'

A man appeared, carrying a baby with a grossly inflated scrotum. He thrust it towards me, mumbling, 'Ladies, be merciful.' I asked why he did not take the child to hospital and he said he could not afford it. I gave money on his promise to see a doctor. It soothed my conscience and no doubt resulted in him telling a lie.

'It's strange,' said Thuy. 'I used to wish I could have lots of money. Now I wonder. We have everything we need but our lives are frenetic. We seldom have time to talk, like now.'

'It's true.' It was Dong. 'Everyone was dirt poor before, but we looked after each other; and whatever we had we valued. I like this too, though. I get energy from it.'

'And if the government were to take it all away?' Justin asked. It was almost the first time he had spoken.

Dong smiled in his carefree way. 'We'd cope. Money comes, money goes. The important thing is to enjoy it while you have it.'

Justin got up and we wandered along the beach together. 'I'm sorry I've been irritable,' he said. 'They're generous people and I like them. Sometimes the conflict of feelings becomes too much, that's all.'

He paused, then spoke of how he had come here once with Du during the war. The beach was deserted and they spent the night sleeping under trees. He woke up in the moonlight to find Du talking with a man who spoke Vietnamese fluently, but looked different. He had been born German and joined the Foreign Legion in North Africa. He fought in the French war in Vietnam and after it was over, married a local woman. When she died he became a wandering monk. 'That's the image I had retained of Vung Tau.'

Our time in Ho Chi Minh City was drawing to a close. Three things remained that I needed to do, all connected with my past. The first was to see my friend Lan again to try and bridge the distance between us; the second, to glimpse the house where my family used to live; and the third, to visit my parents' shrine.

We arranged to meet Lan in the afternoon but she was not at home. Her daughter let us in and we waited in the confined space – Justin in front of a Singer sewing machine with bits of cloth and tangled threads; Luke on the tiles, against a wobbly table that was the family's work surface; I on my feet, gazing at two ancient Chinese heroines in pink ribbons and robes on a pile of magazines. No one seemed to know what was happening.

She came an hour later, loaded with bags specially for us, from a famous vegetarian restaurant. Her daughter changed into a bright orange dress in honour of the occasion and we laid the exquisite food on the floor. Then, while the young people played on a guitar and sang, Lan spoke again of her desire to leave Vietnam. I felt a growing sense of impotence.

'Look, I can't help you in that way,' I blurted out at last. 'I don't have the influence. But isn't it what we make of life that matters?' And I shared something of my own lifelong struggle to accept. 'When I was a child I used to wish I had never been born. I felt cursed, as if my whole existence was a mistake. At least you had the love of your parents.'

I used to delight in visiting Lan's family. There seemed to be such natural intimacy and I was welcomed into it. I thought of her parents as liberal-minded people and of Lan as much more Western and adventurous than I was. Why then this jinx on her life which had prevented her from travelling to the West, while I, who as a teenager had had no desire ever to leave Vietnam, had seen so much of the world?

'What made you apply for the scholarship to Australia all those years ago?' she said suddenly.

'A friend suggested it. We went and enrolled at the same time.'

How often have I had anxiety dreams about sitting for exams! Yet for this one which changed the course of my life – and for which I made no preparation – I had not the faintest nervousness; because I did not care about the result. 'Why didn't you go for one too?' I asked.

'I did. Several times. But I didn't succeed.'

'Then maybe there's a purpose in it,' I burst out. 'Maybe, for some reason, it's been important for your children to be brought up in this country. Who knows? How must it be for your daughter, knowing that it is through her that you've been forced to stay here?'

She was quiet for several minutes; then spoke more lightly of a retreat she had made recently, to learn to accept karma and change one's habits. 'I was refreshed at the time but it's worn off. I realise now one doesn't just change once and that's it for ever. It's a continuing thing like eating! We have to keep doing it again and again.'

I mentioned a sequence of exercises that Justin and I had been working with since our journey began. The first involves mastering one's thoughts, even if only for five minutes each day at the same time, for a month. One pictures an ordinary object, the less interesting the better, because then it is entirely one's own will power that carries one. One allows in only those thoughts that are connected with it.

In the second month comes an exercise for strengthening the will, again for about five minutes each day. It is a question of deciding beforehand to do something quite trivial one would not normally do – like moving an object from one place to another. The less utilitarian or interesting it is the better. One does it purely because one has decided to.

The third month is devoted to equanimity in any situation; the fourth, positivity; the fifth, open-mindedness. In the sixth and final month, the aim is to repeat all five exercises in a regular rhythmical alternation. 'It may sound very simple,' I went on, 'but, believe me, if one can focus on a paper clip for five minutes each day, it becomes a lot easier to deal with more important matters. The concentration is the same.'

'I know,' said Lan; and she smiled. 'Isn't that also the Buddhist way?'

Our time had gone. She had to rush off to her evening job and we said goodbye in the darkened alley. How much easier it would have been to hug! But it is not done in Vietnam. She pushed the kick-start on her Honda and I touched her arm.

'It looks like a doll's house,' says Luke as we stand in the lane with its rows of terraced dwellings, outside the house where I once lived. The door is open; I peep inside into a single long room with partitions, the ceiling so low I wonder if Justin and Luke would be able to stand. How had we all fitted in, sixteen of us at one stage including the maid and Nhuong?

The street is now sealed with concrete and strikingly clean. In those days it flooded at each monsoon. Water would overflow into the main room and I remember walking on planks to get through to a small courtyard at the back, which would be filled with sunlight when the rain stopped. Here, in the heady days after my return from Australia, I spent magical hours with my sisters when tired of my other life. We would sit on stools on the scrubbed tiles while they sewed, separated stones from rice or combed each other's hair...

The light comes on. There is someone sitting near the window under a fan. She glances up and we move away.

In the same lane live the in-laws of my brother, Hao, where we were invited for dinner. The shock of seeing where I had lived was with me still as a dozen people surrounded us warmly welcoming, among them Dong and Thuy from our day in Vung Tau. As in the other houses, the front window and door were open and voices, smells and the din of the street merged with the blast of the fan.

'Your brother Hao is a dear boy,' said the mother, a gentle person with noble features and grey hair in a bun. 'We miss him and our daughter Lien very much.' She held both my hands, eyes misty, the archetype of a Vietnamese mother – like my own, but less stern.

She told me how Hao and Lien had fallen in love but kept it a secret. On the eve of Saigon's fall, amid the panic of thousands trying to escape, he had come to say goodbye. In the morning he would be leaving on one of the US planes. Early next day, the fate of the country still unknown, he reappeared saying he had decided to stay. He was twenty-one. Soon after, he was taken away for re-education but was released after a few months. He lived on alone in our house until the cadres appropriated it for a family of ten. Lien's mother took him in and got him work in a factory with her husband. 'One day,' she reminisced, cackling, 'he came to me and said, "I love Lien. Can we get married?" Can you imagine? I hadn't suspected a thing. Now they're in America and their children are in their teens.'

The flowery plastic covering on the long table was almost hidden by all the dishes. Delicacies were loaded onto our bowls and plates, followed by fruit and sweets. Laughter and chatting. Someone sang. We were urged to make toasts with the hundred year old 'medicinal' rice wine and my head began to swim and ache. 'Brother Justin, sister Thu!' Dong was raucous after a few beers. 'You should come back here and make a fortune teaching English.'

'Don't,' said the charming elder son of our hosts. 'Life's much more interesting abroad. But come and visit us each year.' He was an engineer and said he wanted to stay and work for his country although he knew he would be better off elsewhere.

There was a partition wall at the end of the table and one of the daughters beckoned me towards it. The space behind was cut in half to create a corridor and a tiny room, no more than two metres by four. In front of shelves stacked high with paper and books was a dental couch surrounded by modern equipment. There was a chair for the dentist but no space for an assistant. 'My surgery,' she said proudly. 'Do you need anything done?'

A staircase led to the low sleeping loft with beds for parents and four grown-up children – two daughters (the dentist and a doctor) and two engineer sons. The youngest son, a student, slept downstairs on a camp bed. 'You must stay with us next time,' said the old lady. 'There's no point in wasting money on hotels.'

Beggars swoop relentlessly as we wait for Nhuong and her brother Vinh outside the *Vinh Nghiem* Pagoda. It is a large sanctuary, built in traditional Chinese style with red roofs curling up at the corners. Justin and Luke give money to some old men and it rouses the others into heightened activity. There is only one to whom we decisively do not give, a boy with a cage. 'Buy my birds and you can set them free,' he shouts.

'And tomorrow your cage will be full again,' Luke throws back. 'No, thanks.'

Chanting from loudspeakers fills the air, people everywhere with flowers, food, candles and incense. Women in *ao dai* and conical hats bustle up the steps to the prayer hall. 'It's always busy,' says Nhuong, suddenly here, 'each weekend when I visit father-mother.'

She leads us into a dark area on the first floor, its altar ablaze with small flames around a golden cross-legged Buddha. She puts down fruit and flowers and gives us three joss sticks each. Justin and Luke light theirs and hold them between pressed hands. I join them, then turn to the urns – ceramic pots, many with blue dragons and phoenixes, on shelving throughout the room. Two little windows stare at me, in one a picture of my mother, age of death, fifty-seven; in the other, my father, sixty-seven. I feel my mother's presence, less so my father's.

My mother was an only child of a mandarin; her mother died when she was still small. She was brought up in loneliness, surrounded by servants and tutors and the love of a father often preoccupied with state affairs. I had heard stories of him, regaled in the silk robes of office, holding her on his lap as he presided over official ceremonies.

She married my father at fourteen and had her first baby a year later. It was an arranged marriage as custom dictated, he five years older, the son of a mandarin too. To begin with they were happy and abundantly provided for. She gave birth fourteen times in her life. Four of her children died in early childhood and one as an adolescent. I was the fourth of those who survived, my elder siblings all female. After the ninth birth, my father took up with another woman and they had a baby girl. We were still in Hanoi, but I was conscious enough by then to notice my mother's red eyes and hear their arguments.

One morning at the time of the new year, we were summoned in our best clothes to the large room upstairs filled with incense. My mother and father were sitting on dark ornate chairs, she solemn and dignified, he rather agitated. A strange woman, young and full-bodied, stood on one side holding a small girl's hand. 'This is your father's 'little' wife,' said mother. 'From now on she'll live with us. I want you to call her *di* – Auntie – and her daughter, sister.

We will live in harmony.' That is all I can remember of her speech. My father said nothing.

We each lit a joss stick and paid our respects at the altar before leaving.

Harmony did not last long. Mother behaved with outward impeccability; but she hardly spoke, only vaguely smiled. We ate together as a family, Auntie addressing her respectfully as 'older sister', while Mother called her 'younger sister' in a neutral voice. We children did not know how to deal with it, so kept quiet and separate. After a few months Father and Auntie argued. Eventually she moved out and went to work as a teacher. He continued to spend time with her, which caused strife between him and Mother.

During all this time I knew my mother's pain but was absorbed in my own. At times I wanted to reach out to her. I didn't know how. The distance between us was too forbidding. Why could she not love me like her other children? Why?

The incense curls over, touching my hand; behind me are people whispering. The image of my mother lights up with dark eyes, questioning. Something dissolves – a hardness in the chest. I feel my breath released, and tears prick my cheeks.

Since her death I have often felt her support, sometimes through dreams. One of the most important of such 'experiences of the night' occurred after Luke's conception, before I knew that I was pregnant. Justin and I were living on a Greek island at the time, a place wrought by volcanic action where the ash-soil is white and the lava-sand black, and which we felt to be a midpoint culturally between East and West; even physically each of us could pass as a local. She appeared showing me a rainbow-coloured fish. She opened it and inside, like matriochka dolls, was a smaller one, then another. Within the last, the seventh, was a baby.

The thought fills me now. There is a meaning in my having been born into such a relationship; and it is up to me to find it. I recognise the impetus it has given me to find my own life and venture outside my culture. I can see now too, how it has prepared me to work with children. Having known how it is to crave love, I recognise the same pain in some of those who have come to me and can see beyond the ugly behaviour with which they express it. I have learnt the value of love that one has to build from scratch, regardless of whether one is related to – or even likes – the other person.

I have always known that despite everything, my mother was an upright and compassionate person, in some ways my best teacher. Only now, standing before these small pots, do I understand it in my heart. In that moment I know what it is to forgive. Within it is the need to be forgiven too. And I ask her then for what I have never dreamt of asking before: forgiveness for the grudge I have carried so long.

Vietnam – Centre

6

Dalat again after twenty-three years, first stop on our way north. Clear sky and sunshine, but with a breath of coolness from the altitude. I stand at the gate of the university, not alone this time but with a wife and a son. Was I so unconscious before that now I recognise nothing except the calm order of the place and the conifers on the slope beneath, soughing in the wind? Such students as we see are tidily dressed and polite; they are here to study, not to get involved in politics. Dalat has long had that hill station aloofness. We walk down to the lake. Surely here memories will stir?

'You marry me?' Her question seems to be directed at me. Then I realise – her gestures more eloquent than her English – that she means, Will I marry her to my son?

'You'll have to ask him,' I reply, enjoying Luke's embarrassment. She was the fifth person who had proposed since his arrival less than a week before, but far the most forward. Usually such words were enveloped in giggles and coyness. There were to be many more such half-playful propositions, often from mothers. They had a fascination for this comparatively large person who looked Vietnamese and had the sproutings of an Uncle Ho beard, but could not speak the language.

'Why you ask father not me?' he says, already versed in pidgin.

'In my country father-mother decide. Your father like, we marry.'

'In my country I decide.'

'Why not I decide too? Like United Nations, right?'

We were staying in a hobble-de-hoy wooden house in a field of lilies, bright white against dark green. At the entrance was a glassed area festooned with tropical growth; nearby, a sty with three large pigs. Hens scuttled. There was even a dog. It was the home of a young couple, friends of Thu's friend Lan, but with a very different attitude towards life.

Huong and Van worked for the town council, she as an architect, he for the electricity board. They were unambitious and, that rare quality, happy. What is more, they accepted the government's ways and chose to work with them. As a result their children were nine years apart – a daughter of fifteen studying in the city, a four year old son at home. The general rule was for civil servants to stop at one child. If they wanted two, they were encouraged to space them out so the mother could remain employable.

Their salaries were small but their needs were met. They owned the house and because of long service would be eligible for a grant to upgrade it. Huong was confident the authorities would accept her current project for a more efficient garbage disposal in the town and the cleaning up of a creek drain near the house. They were overjoyed at having us to stay and insisted we take their bedroom (up a ladder, beneath the ridged roof) for which they had even bought a new pink mosquito net in our honour.

The next day we rented a taxi to take us into the surrounding countryside, to waterfalls and a new Buddhist monastery above the reservoir built by the French – places spoken of as though in legend before, for the wilderness belonged to the Vietcong and the bombs and bullets of war planes. There had also been teams of US Special Forces operating in the mountain areas, who often developed more of a kinship with the indigenous tribal peoples than with the Vietnamese themselves.

The falls were powerful and the scenery spectacular, but already they were being tamed by tourism. What stood out for us was our encounter with the monks at the monastery – co-designed, we later heard, by Huong. It was a fine setting with a vista of pine-clad hills sweeping down to the water below, the architecture clear and clean.

'It is good to see you again. Where do you come from?' Each syllable enunciated in clear English, goodwill flowing from his gestures and face. He wore the russet-brown robes common among monks and was tall for a local person.

'Australia,' said Luke. 'Mum's from here.'

'Ah, your mother. I wondered. And this is your father? Come, I invite you to have tea with us.'

'What did you mean by "again"?' I asked, walking next to him.

He laughed. 'When I saw you, I wanted to meet you. Perhaps that is because we have known each other in another life.' He took us into the spacious reception room with its heavy dark wood furniture. A second monk was at the table and he too greeted us with warmth while the first went to prepare drinks. He came back not only with fearsomely strong tea, but cups containing a potent liquid tasting like medicine.

'It is fortuitous you have come,' said the other monk, with the same clear enunciation. 'Here we have a text by our master who is a saintly man, nearly eighty. He has been meditating for many years and discovered a new method. We are translating his work into English for the foreign visitors who come to learn.'

He showed us a piece of paper, handwritten. 'Meditation is the path to our Buddha nature,' I read.

'Through meditation we achieve mastery over thoughts, feelings and actions.'

It was invigorating to go through the remaining sentences and search for words in English that could convey their meaning. I realised that to do this, we had at least to glimpse the experience out of which the monk had written. The translation had to come, not word for word, but out of inner perception. Using the concepts with which I am more familiar, I would have translated 'Buddha nature' as 'higher self'.

Unlike some Buddhist practices, their meditation was without chanting or the reciting of mantras. From what they described, it was a strengthening and clarifying of thinking as a foundation for understanding and 'seeing' – something one could call 'spiritual research'.

We were there for several hours, and as we left the first monk read out a haiku by the Japanese Zen master, Basho:

> Friends part
> for ever – wild geese
> lost in cloud.[2]

We stayed up late talking with Huong and Van. Though no strangers to hardship, they were too young to remember the war. So it is now with the majority of people in Vietnam. There was an innocence about them and a delight in nature; but they could also be objective about the society within which they had been brought up. 'It works for us,' said Huong simply. 'Maybe we're lucky. The government treats us well.'

'And do you feel free?'

'Provided we don't get involved in politics, yes,' said Van. Then to our surprise he said that many of their

---

[2] Reproduced by kind permission of Penguin UK.

relations lived in the States. 'We could go there too, but we're happier here. Besides, my parents are still in Vietnam.'

I asked what they saw as the main differences between the two parts of the world. 'Here we can still love our nation,' he said after a pause. 'And our family. Over there many people seem only to love themselves.'

We compared perspectives on the two main social philosophies of this century – the capitalist one in which the economy is dominated by competition and the desire for profit; and the socialist one in which it is controlled by the state. In the first, freedom runs rampant, in the second, equality; and nature seems to fall foul of both. I suggested that there is a third way, based on altruism. 'That's the ideal of the socialist system too,' said Huong excitedly.

'I know. But how has it been put into practice? Aren't people forced to be altruistic?'

'Is there any other way?'

Our drive to the coast early the next morning was awful. The girl next to Thu threw up repeatedly and the smell mingled with that of dried fish. My window was stuck shut; the slide door near me had to be man-handled violently each time anyone got in or out. The saving grace was a large monk in dark glasses, his fingers on rosary beads, lips moving soundlessly. I drew comfort from his stillness. When he reached his destination, a neighbour helped him out and I saw he was blind.

The final descent to the sea was truly frightening as we overtook on the hairpin bends; and though we had been assured our bus would go the whole way to Nhatrang, farther north, no one protested when the driver told us to get out halfway in Phan Rang, site of an immense ex-US naval base. We shunted across into an ancient Renault which reminded me of the armoured personnel carrier in which I had hitched a lift to the battle zone in '72.

It was phenomenally slow. At first this was a relief; we assumed we had a cautious driver. Then we realised that thirty kilometres an hour on a flat straight road was the fastest the vehicle could go. This would have been no problem had it not been for what was inside. If it is possible, the pressure of bodies and things was even greater than in the minibus; also the seats were of bare wood and the legroom an impossibility for Western limbs.

One solution was to pile things on my seat so that I was half standing, bent forward to avoid the ceiling. Another was for Luke and me to sit sideways, legs on each other's laps, as he stretched forwards to take photos out of the window.

The bus stopped repeatedly, including three times to fill the water canister on the roof from which a pipe led down to the engine. I presume this extra cooling device, common in large vehicles, is not only because of the heat but the absurd weights they carry. It took a further three and a half hours to reach Nhatrang. But how good to be at the ocean!

Perhaps it is time to explain why we chose to go by bus; many tourists travel in reasonable comfort by other means. We could have flown or hired a car; but our wish, so far as possible, was to share the experiences of local people. It was also a matter of money. With such a long journey ahead we had to economise all the way – though not to the extent of chronic masochism. Trains were a possibility on the coast, but getting tickets at intermediate stations was problematic and there were higher prices for foreigners. We could have opted for the lowest class, but with jam-packed hard seats this was little better than being on a bus. In Hue, farther north, we did try to get sleepers. They were booked out.

Besides, though the bus rides took their toll, they had their own charm. Simply to survive, we had to learn patience (and humour) and sharpen our sense for beauty. Some writers speak of the 'morbid pleasure' of such discomfort. Can one not say the same of the pain one endures training for sport or overworking at the office? We had chosen this way and it gave us strength. For most of the world's people, it is the only option available.

It was nearly the time of the full moon. There was a swell in the ocean and it was too dangerous to swim. I was tired and my spirits were sinking. Right to the water's edge I was on the brink of toppling into gloom.

And then it happened.

It was about twenty minutes before sundown and the light reaching up from the west was all at once a gold-pink glow through the entirety of air and sea and sky. Froth-white foam, darkened by sand, glistened with flames of saffron and rose. We seemed to have entered a world adjacent to our own where all is beauty and each thing for ever new and unrepeatable.

Then, from the east, the glowing whiteness of the moon weaving into the halo of gold its melodies of silver, lilac and mauve. All this upon that heaving mass of ocean water crashing upon itself, wave after wave, rushing upwards, sucking back, with a power that became a torrent as it swept past our legs.

We played like children, splashing up fountains of coloured jewels, tempting the waves (watchful as leopards) then tearing back to safe ground at the last moment, or trying to hold for eternity that leaf-thin film of reflection and form, when the wave has spent its force at the extremity of its stretching and for the smallest of seconds… stands still.

'I can't handle it,' said Luke, angry and distressed. 'Why do people suffer like this?'

It was evening again and we were at the old Cham temple in Nhatrang, on a high rock by an estuary, a beautiful place. The bay was crowded with the blues and reds of fishing boats; up river, to the west, valley and hills green with tropical growth. Once a vibrant Hindu shrine, it is pretty much unused now except by tourists and beggars – the Cham culture, out of which it was created, long vanquished in Vietnam.

Many of the beggars were wearing army fatigues and were without one or more limbs. Thu and I had given a few notes and walked on to look at the architecture but Luke had stayed on to talk. Partly he did not know how to disengage himself; partly he wanted to encounter them, maybe even take photos. 'They asked me about Australia and how much you earn,' he went on. 'It makes me feel so guilty.'

We sat among the boulders. From a neighbouring hill gleamed the whiteness of a gigantic sitting Buddha. I told him of something I had read in Valentin Tomberg's *New Testament Studies*. We see so much wrong in the world and are pierced by guilt and shame. Such emotions paralyse but if we can listen to them in calmness, their thorns become a 'crown' – the inward taking of responsibility for what is around.

'That's fine, but what about these people? They say the government does nothing, nor does anyone else. They have no choice but to beg.'

'I'm afraid we're going to see a lot more of it,' said Thu. 'Most of the world is poor.'

'I know, dammit, and that's the point. It doesn't have to be.'

The sun was just above the hills, the evening casting its

spell of stillness and orange as we sat and spoke of suffering. It has been at the root of many, if not all, religions. In Hinduism it is accepted that we suffer what we deserve, as karmic consequence of past lives. From Buddhism comes the method of mastering it – and oneself – through detachment. The message of Christianity is the bearing of suffering and its transformation into love.

'All that's fine,' said Luke again, still angry. 'No doubt suffering has its place; but that doesn't mean we have the right to create it – or allow it to go on when it isn't necessary.'

'What can we do, then?' It was Thu.

'I don't know. But whatever it is, it has to be real. People like Doctors without Frontiers, they have my respect, going into remote places and saving lives. That's the problem with all these religions. They don't face what's real.'

'So is communism the answer?' I said. 'Capitalism? They're pretty down to earth, aren't they? Are they coping with reality?'

The sun had set, Venus high above it, Jupiter to our left over the sea. There were no beggars on the steps as we started back towards the street.

'I know how it *could* be,' said Luke more gently. 'People caring for each other, working together rather than in competition. That's how Huong and Van seem to think it is already. But it isn't – and I don't understand why.' A few shapes were curled up under the trees in the growing moonlight. 'Somehow we all have to work it out for ourselves, don't we,' he went on. 'But how?'

Although his stomach was not well, Luke joined an outing the next day to some of the islands. In the late afternoon Thu and I visited the temple of the white Buddha. As an active place of worship it was a more lucrative haunt for beggars and we were swooped on from all directions as we walked to the steps with our young cyclo driver.

First was a man who scuttled on hands and knees, legs bent into a curve and far too thin to support his weight – the legacy of imprisonment in a cage. He signalled with genial movements of face and arms, muttering incoherently. We put a note in his hands and he grinned like a child.

Beyond was a mother carrying a naked infant. She pushed it towards us, eyes practised in pleading. We gave, but reluctantly – prejudiced by the stories we had heard of parents making their children sick to elicit sympathy. We had met a number of travellers who refused as a matter of principle to give anything to such people.

At the top of the steps three more women descended on us like harpies. 'No, no money,' I said in Vietnamese. 'First we talk. Why do you beg?'

They patted their stomachs and mimicked pain. They said the government had forced them into the mountains where the land was infertile and they could not support their families. 'Now we sweep the ground around Buddha and he looks after us.'

In their wrinkled faces was a richness of expression that comes from having made the most of life. They were a bit batty, but there was calmness too. It was easy to laugh with them and I asked to take their photos. They acted coy and held out their hands with new vigour, chanting, 'Dollar, dollar.' We gave, not dollars but Vietnamese dong; and as we parted I said, 'I think you no longer fear death. Am I right?'

'Buddha looks after us. Him we trust.'

We walked round the statue and our cyclo companion told us about his life. He was just a few months older than Luke, but had lost his mother as a child and left school early, because his father did not earn enough money as a barber. He used the cyclo to help support his three younger brothers. 'I wish I could study more and learn English,' he said sadly.

Behind us the three old ladies were hen-pecking a new cluster of visitors.

Back down the steps was a blind man, waiting in quietness. He held a cup, but made no gesture of pleading, although he must have heard us. I put a note in his hand and told him what I was doing. His face became illumined by a smile I have to call radiant. While he spoke the radiance was with him; when he stopped he withdrew again.

In simple sentences he told how at the age of nine, during the Tet offensive, he had been in an explosion. He had little recollection of the event. It had simply happened; and ever since, he had had to fend for himself. He said the government ran a hostel for cripples but it was like a prison. 'They give you food but there's nothing to do. They lock you in.' He had escaped several times and sought refuge in the temple, away from the dangers of the street.

'How do you know how much money people give you?'

'I trust what they tell me. It's the same when I spend it.'

We moved on, then stopped and looked back. He was standing as before. Waiting.

As we passed the lower temple, I heard a quiet whimpering and became aware that someone was lying nearby, more imagined than seen in the dim light. It was a young woman of perhaps twenty, skin and bones, and trembling. The cyclo boy asked if she was hungry. She shook her head and gestured for us to leave. We walked on, shamed by our impotence. 'If she wishes to die, this is the best place,' he said. 'In the temple of Buddha.'

All the beggars had gone except the one with useless legs, scuttling around still on knees and wooden blocks, smiling conspiratorially.

What can one do in the face of this misery? Like anyone else, we had the option of hardening ourselves. We could also take refuge in the safe areas created for tourists; and at times we did. But turning away made a nonsense of our journey. The only answer lay in being as 'present' as we could, trying to acknowledge the *person* who was there and taking this into our inner lives. Luke met it head on but could not digest it, and the outrage started to weigh on his shoulders and chest. His cough became a symptom of his overload.

We headed for the ocean and the rising of the full moon. It was a moment to which we had been looking forward; but I felt let down. There was a haze in the air and brown slime on the waves. The world was without the radiance of two evenings before.

Above our heads were what looked like fruit bats on their journey to resting places in the west. They were too high for us to appreciate their full size but the strange bat shape was evident. They flew in huge clusters, wave after wave, away from the moon, silent.

'Isn't that enough?' said Thu.

> Moonrise on ocean...
> Anticipating heaven,
> I almost miss the fruit bats.

At four thirty in the morning two cyclos came to take us to the bus station for the ten-hour marathon to Quang Ngai up the coast – one pedalled by our friend of the day before, the other by his father who had come specially to meet us. When we arrived, still in the dark, he gave us their address, saying, 'Next time you will stay with us.'

We piled into an overcrowded coach to the blare of a martial arts video. The road was narrow, potholed and crumbly at the edges, but the driver used his air horn like an instrument of war as we blasted forward. Pedestrians, *xe lams*, cycles, ox-carts, animals and minibuses were all our inferiors and must make way. As to trucks and other buses, it was better not to look, rather to pray. Our bus rides were becoming a daily training in faith.

I remembered a story about a person injured in a crash. Convalescing in hospital, he realised his injury had been made worse because he tensed. He resolved that if it happened again, he would stay relaxed. It did – and he survived unscathed.

We stopped for lunch at a derelict restaurant with little variety of food and a distinct lack of hygiene, a symptom of the poverty in central Vietnam into which we were now entering. Previously cut in half by the so called demilitarised zone – or DMZ – between North and South, it was a strongly Vietcong area during the war. They paid a high price for it in US retaliations. An example is what took place in the group of hamlets known as My Lai. Here in '68, a US company, unnerved by the shadow-like universality of their enemy, wreaked vengeance, burning and killing everything they came upon.

We expected our time in Quang Ngai to be difficult but we were wrong. Though the signs of hardship were clear, what we found stirring everywhere was a wish to be part of the world. In the small bank where Thu and I changed money, the three young ladies in traditional dress bubbled over with questions and goodwill. 'It's lucky Luke wasn't with us,' Thu said as we left. 'They wouldn't have let us go.'

Where My Lai was is now a museum and a shrine. We went there by motorcycle on dirt roads past paddies and villages of bamboo, mud and thatch. Looking at the men, women and children wading in the flooded fields, trading at the markets, stooping under bundles on poles across their shoulders, sitting by the roadside, I thought not for the first time, So these were the enemies of America!

A paved avenue leads to a towering monument. Along the way are smaller sculptures of women and children in pinioned states of suffering, death and dying. We left the path and were among the graves – not in rows but seemingly at random amidst the shrubs and scattered trees. It dawned on me that they were at the very places where each family had had its home. Most of the names inscribed were female; the only male ones were of children and old men.

Our feet took us naturally, not to the statue, but towards the irrigation ditch on the right where the people had been herded together, hands behind heads, and gunned down. On a plaque were the words: 'This ditch reminds that on March 16th 1968 the GIs killed 170 villagers.' What has been done is not forgotten. How can it be? Memorials in the West carry the words 'Lest we forget'. What matters is what we do with this not-forgetting.

We sat in silence by the muddy water. In this place of murder there was a peace such as we had experienced nowhere else in Vietnam, though we had glimpsed it in certain people, such as the man at the museum in Cu Chi. On the still water a duck wove in and out of the secret places of mud banks and grass, trailed by six ducklings. Above them a ripening pomelo hung from a branch of deep green leaves. There was bird song.

We turned inwards, alone yet united in being there... Here, strange as the thought may sound, through this most terrible of actions, East and West have met. They could not meet sufficiently in peace. Pride and fear made sure of that. But meet they must for it is what our times demand. So they met in war.

What we think and feel and do does not only have effect on the physical level of reality. Through such deeds as these, soul encounters soul in the inevitability of inner consequence. A number of the US soldiers involved have since had breakdowns. Through the torture of not-forgetting, some have made their way back to My Lai.

Yet there was peace. We each felt it. Not sleepiness but a kind of holiness. Such peace as can only come, I believe, because on some level of existence there has been forgiveness. I can make sense of it in no other way.

We walked to the huge statue of stone. The central figure is of a woman, right fist raised in defiance, left arm encompassing a lifeless child. In front, on the ground, is an old man dying, supported by a female figure; to the left, a body shielding a prostrate infant.

Above the museum are words calling for undying hatred towards what the Americans did. Inside, the horror lives on in photographs taken, astonishingly, by the unit's official photographer. They knew what they were about to do and he smuggled in film of his own, as well as what he handed in to his superiors. This was later leaked to the press.

The moments of death and the terror before it are preserved, like the sculptures wrought by nature in the lava at Pompeii in Italy. One sees the faces of uniformed men setting fire to the thatch, firing at screaming women and children, their gestures matter of fact and calm. According to what is written, they were given alcohol and other drugs to dull their sense of responsibility. One of them, a black man, shot himself in the foot to get out of it.

A lady invited us into the reception room to have tea. Her manner was gentle as she asked our background. 'What about you?' said Thu. 'Are you from this area?'

'Yes.' She was silent.

'Are there many foreign visitors?'

'Almost every day. It's a special place and they come with goodwill. Many cry.'

'And the older people nearby? How is it for them?'

'Most have accepted. Some carry hatred. Those ones suffer most.'

She told us then that her sister had been one of the victims. She herself and her mother had been in another village at the time.

It was midday by the time we had checked out of our hotel and were standing on the main street of Quang Ngai, along which buses to Danang and Hue must pass. We bought soup at one of the ubiquitous stalls and were immediately the centre of attention from vendors and passers-by. At one point Luke asked if he could lift an old lady's shoulder pole. He staggered under its weight, the baskets swinging dangerously, while she almost fell into the road with laughing. It was searing hot. An old Renault trundled by, 'Danang' written in several places on it. The boy conductors assured us they were going the whole way to Hue. We did not believe them but needed an escape.

The speciality of this particular can on wheels was that there were no seats in the middle part by the door. We were directed to a bench behind the gap as to a place of honour. The bus clattered on raucously to the edge of town while we exulted in its emptiness. Then it stopped, reversed and turned, and we headed back the way we had come – the boys hanging out of the two doors, banging, cajoling, abusing, persuading all and sundry to jump on board.

We slumped to a halt and the driver turned off the engine, while visions rose before my mind of all the express coaches that were passing by on the main street where we had begun. It took forty minutes; and by the time the machine rumbled again into life, we were fully laden. The merit, I realised now, of not having seats is that one can cram in more bodies standing than sitting. As we moved out of town, we were so full that the person in front of me was sitting on my lap. Had I vacated my section of plank and stood, the ceiling, just okay for locals, would have been an archetypal torture instrument for my back and neck.

And still they piled more on. The boys at the door shoved them in and then hung outside or climbed onto the roof which was loaded with bundles and bicycles and men. Every time we overtook a slower vehicle – an ox-cart or wretched cyclist – they would shout and beat on the sides of the bus to get them out of the way. As if the horn (for once, it is true, not an air horn) was not enough.

Though we started next to each other, Thu had been prised away by the mêlée and I could see she was having a hard time. She was feeling sick, she told us later, but every time she closed her eyes, the full-bodied woman next to her would 'prod and poke and shake' her in an exuberance of friendliness and fire another question. Why wasn't she wearing a wedding ring? What was her husband's job? Why wasn't her son married? Why was he so big? Why couldn't he speak Vietnamese? And then again, as she was just dozing off, and with sudden urgency, what do you eat for breakfast in Australia?

We stopped for water, we stopped for petrol, we stopped to do something to the engine, for water again, for the driver to have a drink and perhaps just for the fun of it. A few people became irritable, most simply endured; while in me there welled up at moments a strange comfort in being almost organically connected to the mass of bodies around me.

We reached Danang in the dark. There was no question of the bus going on to Hue. Jets shrieked overhead, a rare sound in Vietnam today, and the cyclo drivers were hard bargainers. But they got us to a hotel that was good enough for the single night we planned to stay, in this city which had hosted one of the largest of America's bases and on whose beaches the US marines had made their first fateful appearance in Vietnam, back in '65.

This time round, Danang stands in my mind most of all for what we did not do. We missed out on the museum which is said to have the best exhibition anywhere on the civilisation of the indigenous Cham people. Instead, we booked Luke a flight from Hue back to Ho Chi Minh City to meet up with friends from Australia in a few days' time.

As a special treat we hired a car to go on to Hue. It cost twenty dollars for the day and enabled us to take our time on the stunningly beautiful coast road between the two cities. A Russian machine of unrecorded age, the driver coaxed it over the mountain headland north of Danang, seemingly unconcerned about its state. His stops to fill the radiator enabled us to breathe in the sparkle of space, ocean and light far below. It is a vista comparable to that of the mountainscape of olive groves that stretch from sacred Delphi in Greece to the distant sea.

In the midday heat we stopped at Lang Co, described in our guide book as 'paradisiacal' – as indeed it was with the sky vast, the white sand deserted and the still emerald ocean almost transparent. As we swam lazily two at a time (the third on the beach with our money belts) I wondered stupidly what would happen to counterbalance such beauty and peace.

There were no prices on the menu in the restaurant nearby, but the bright and friendly girl assured us they were very reasonable. We ordered three dishes and four appeared. At a neighbouring table a Canadian couple were grumbling loudly about being 'fleeced' in the hotel and maybe this affected how I behaved when we found our bill was over twice what we had anticipated. One of the dishes had been written as large, though we had ordered a small one. 'The cook thought you'd prefer it like this,' the girl said. 'It's more special.'

I was outraged and said so; but paid what she demanded. We drove on, while an all too familiar drama played itself out inside me. It has an impressive cast. First came anger and a wish for vengeance. Why not write and tell the guidebook people so they can warn others against them? At last, disgust at my own pettiness. What were we talking about? An extra three dollars! But it's the principle of course – and the pride. That subtle dignity which in the East is called 'face'. Sometimes it only needs a spark...

It took forty minutes to re-establish order – during which the car was systematically falling to bits. It had begun with the front seat collapsing backwards as I slumped down into it in a huff. Next the chassis started to jar against the rear tyres. Shock absorbers? The driver changed one of the wheels. The noise continued. He exchanged the other with a front one, two separate operations with the jack. He said the rear tyres were wider and therefore more likely to cause obstruction.

The jarring continued. We started to lurch. Was the steering disintegrating as well? Thirteen kilometres from Hue, a violent grating brought us to a halt. Exhaust? Rear axle? A rod was hanging loose at the back. He hooked it up with wire, but the lurching went on. 'I'll have to go on alone,' he said calmly and waved down another vehicle. The new driver claimed he did not have a licence for carrying foreigners and demanded a high price. We waited by the roadside while the haggling ran its course. For once we were not involved.

Hue, capital of Imperial Vietnam, has many connotations. Once it would have represented everything fine, fragrant and dignified. It was the city in which my friend Du had been born and the site of the country's oldest and most prestigious school at which many of the leaders of North and South had been educated.

It was also the scene of the bloodiest fighting of the Tet offensive. It took three and a half weeks and the destruction of much of the old part of the city for the Americans and South Vietnamese to drive the Vietcong out; and among the shattered remains they found shallow graves in which some three thousand people had been massacred. All told, ten thousand are thought to have died, most of them civilians.

I had last been there in '72, shortly after the Northern army had blasted across the DMZ, storming US bases and reaching the Quang Tri River, north of the city. Despite terrible losses they held on to the ground they gained until the end of the war. The only sense I could make of it then was as a bargaining tool in the Paris peace talks with the US. I rode in planes, taxis, a helicopter, jeeps, trucks, buses, a tank, anything that was moving towards the fighting. I slept in hotels, houses, villages, US bases, bunkers, weaving in the way one could then as a foreigner between the simplicity of the Third World and the extravagance of the war machine – even though I was not yet accredited as a journalist.

I was away for three weeks and when I returned to Saigon and walked into Du's apartment he thought at first I was a ghost. He had assumed I had been captured or killed and had already begun a ritual of prayer for my soul. At the office of the news agency whose typewriter I used for my articles there was a telex from the magazine in Hong Kong: 'Why the hell haven't you written? We want you to be our correspondent.' So it had begun...

There is a blackout as we enter the city. The air is warm and balmy. After Ho Chi Minh City, it has the quietness of a village, the purr of cyclo wheels as common as the crashing of combustion engines. Drains are open by the side of the streets; we know of them from the smell and walk with caution in the darkness.

After a simple meal by hurricane lamp in the open, we go off in search of the tourist office. It is a blaze of electric lights and the smartly dressed officials are taking bookings for a tour to the DMZ the next morning – Quang Tri, Camp Carol, Khe Sanh, the Ho Chi Minh Trail, names that are etched into the minds of anyone connected with the events of those days.

Quang Tri was the only one I had been to, initially to visit the home of a student from Dalat. His grandfather was a refined man, a Catholic and lover of French culture, staunchly opposed to communism. During one of our talks – he was praising the French practice of washing out one's bowels – the floor had started to shake as from an earthquake. It continued on, an awesome pulse of drumbeats vibrating through our feet for about thirty seconds while the ceiling lights swayed. It had been my first experience, from a distance, of a B52 bombing raid.

When I went back in '72 the town was deserted and in ruins, the area north of the river completely flattened. At intervals jets appeared, silent then screaming, low above the ground, followed by the empty crashing thud that is a rocket exploding into something out of sight. Bits of bodies lay in the derelict streets, being pecked by crows.

7

From Luke's Diary

I've never really thought of Mum as Vietnamese. She's just Mum – and, like me, Australian. But she's like a new person when she's speaking her own language and people here take me for a local as well, though I feel big and clumsy next to them. Something in me is waking up. I'm glad, but it also makes me nervous. As if I don't know who I am any more. I mean, I'm who I am independently of any nationality. Yet this is me too. Not just Vietnam, but Asia.

I like the energy. There's always something happening in the street. Also the food, though I have to say I couldn't live on rice every day. Then there are the girls. There's a kind of grace about them, especially in their traditional dresses. They seem pretty timid and it's fun to make them giggle. I feel at home. But it's the poverty that gets to me. Sometimes I feel sick with all the emotions it brings up. There's so much food in the world, so much of everything. Why isn't it shared more equally? It just doesn't make sense.

Dad says the root of the problem isn't here. It's in the wealthy countries. Or in ourselves, of course. Is that what he means when he goes on about the connection between inner and outer? He and Mum seem to believe in some kind of moral power that can guide one's life. They speak about spiritual beings.

Maybe they're right, but the proof of the pudding is in its eating. What are the effects in the world? How could higher beings allow all this destruction and suffering to take place?

Today is an important day for them – this tour of places near the DMZ which featured so strongly in the war. I feel a haunting connection myself, partly because of the many films I've seen about it. But it goes deeper. It has to do with war, any war. How can it be, at this time when there's so much knowledge about everything under the sun, that we still fight wars? What would I do, if I was called up to fight?

We lunch at Dong Ha, a town that was virtually erased during the fighting in '72. Among the shattered buildings is the shell of a church, split down the middle by a rocket.

The restaurant's bustling owner comes and strokes my wispy beard, speaking energetically in Vietnamese. It's not like the bushy ones Dad's face seems to sprout. It must be an inheritance from Mum's side. Next she invites me in outlandish English to marry one of her daughters. She calls them in peremptorily and they stand near our table, giggling and looking awkward. 'Her, seventeen,' she tells me, pointing to the younger one. 'This, number one wife,' she goes on, prodding the other. It seems a hard sell. Is she joking?

'Er, thank you,' I reply, and curse myself for blushing. 'Not fit in back pack.'

'Okay. Fit bus!' Whereupon she shoos them away to change and, lavishly made up, they squash in with us as we head on westward along the infamous Route Nine, through country rugged, mountainous and stunning. Dad says it was the supply road for the string of bases south of the DMZ and terrible bloodshed took place on it. The girls' perfume percolates through the minibus.

We pause at Camp Carroll, overrun in '72, nothing left but craters of red earth and a plaque honouring a South Vietnamese officer who stayed behind when the US soldiers pulled out, and later became a colonel in the Northern army. Our guide tells us not to leave the path because of unexploded mines.

Clusters of people, thin and ragged, are shifting dirt with old spades. Children approach us, hawking rusty bits of cigarette lighters, coins and bullets. What a life! According to our guide book Vietnam became the world's leading exporter of scrap metal after the war. The price being paid to those who risk their lives digging it out is around three cents a kilo.

I squat down and take a photo of a little girl of about five with an incredibly sad face. She stares back motionless, her grubby orange dress trailing on the dirt. I beckon for her to come and look through the lens but she makes no response. I hold out a hand and turn it up and down. She looks at it dully. As I stand up, she reaches forward with her own hand and turns it, like I did. So a little game begins: I move and she copies but always in her own time, as though it's nothing to do with what I'm doing. I stand again and suddenly her hand touches mine. She taps it once and I tap back. Then twice and three times, each copying the other. In silence.

The guide calls us back. It's time to move on. 'I you girlfriend,' giggles one of the girls from Dong Ha, as we squeeze back into our seats. 'I you write letter,' says the other, and shows me a photo of them both in Vietnamese dress in front of flowering rhododendrons.

Next stop is one of the many branches of the Ho Chi Minh Trail. There is a bridge there now, high above a mud-red river – made with help from Cuba. In those days, says our guide, it would have been crossed by swimming or with rafts, usually in pitch dark. On the far side is a stretch of road leading upwards past rocks and scrubby hills. From here the trek to Cu Chi and Saigon, along Vietnam's forested mountain spine, used to take about four months.

'Many people died,' says Dad, standing next to me. 'But the flow continued like a force of nature.' In patches on the hills we see the legacy, even now, of 'agent orange', the poison used to kill the tree cover. 'It's the same thinking as with pesticides,' he goes on. 'Eradicate the enemy, whether it's an insect or a human being, regardless of what else is destroyed.'

Near the trail is a village belonging to one of the many tribal people who lived the land before Mum's ancestors came south from China. Their 'long houses', as they're called, are of wood and bamboo on poles above the ground with pigs, ducks, chickens and dogs wandering freely beneath and between, and smoke spiralling through the thatch. They remind me of dwellings we once visited in the rain forests of New Guinea.

A group of people stare at us, women and girls in sarongs with large silver rings in their ears, one with a long pipe in her mouth. There's a sort of 'gap' between the two groups – we tourists, Vietnamese as well as foreign, on one side; the villagers on the other. As if we're caught in a time warp and can't move.

A memory floods in of Africa when I was six years old, standing motionless within a circle of children in a jungle village. Eyes flashing white all around me, total stillness. I know Mum and Dad are nearby watching, but they're not there in the centre. Only I am, alone...

A man steps forward, the only one who can speak Vietnamese, it seems. He has incredible biceps and a face that's as rugged as the land. As he speaks the spell is broken and we are somehow back in life again. Someone asks why their houses are on stilts and he replies that it is to keep away from bad spirits in the earth at night. It also creates a shelter for the animals.

Back by the van the girls ask me to take their photo – not once but twice, three times, *four* times – while they stand on the gravel in their high-heeled shoes and frilly dresses, and smile. They're okay. They just seem oblivious to what's around them. 'You here before?' I suggest.

'No, first time.'

We drive on to Khe Sanh near the border with Laos – a wide plateau, endless shades of green merging into the blues of distant mountains, the soil rich, red and fertile. I feel the exhilaration of being in a high place.

Here was the site of an ill-fated US base intended to block an artery of the Trail, but itself attacked and besieged. In French days there were apparently coffee plantations; now Vietnamese settlers are reclaiming the land with vegetables and grains. There's no sign of tribal people. Strangely peaceful, the air somehow filled with memories. Or am I being fanciful?

Our guide says he recently brought some Americans here. 'They sit on the ground for three hours,' he goes on. 'They are silent. They talk. They sing songs. When we leave they are crying like children.'

Back in Hue, a special day. It includes an intimate family conversation at an open-air café by the Fragrant River which flows languidly through the city. Weeping willows and here and there a sampan gliding by. In three more days I'm due to fly back to Ho Chi Minh City to meet two school mates who are coming in from Australia. Hopefully we'll catch up with Mum and Dad in Hanoi, before they begin their long trek into China.

The subject of our conversation is me and my future. Also my past. It's not surprising perhaps. It's my birthday. I'm nineteen.

I guess I've had an unusual upbringing. At the age of one our home was an old barge on the canals in England. I know it from photos and the stories they have told me: tar-black hull and a bright red cabin made of planks, with a yellow and blue peacock on the front – and strings of nappies drying in the air. Age two and three, we were at a home for handicapped children, where Dad was the gardener and Mum the cook. Years four and five were with Vietnamese refugees – first at a sprawling ex-airforce camp where we shared a Nissan hut with a Buddhist monk; then at an old hotel by the sea, with space for about a hundred people.

Here first memories stir. It seems I was something of a celebrity and would often disappear into one household or another at the invitation of the occupants. One room I remember particularly. It seemed to have bunks everywhere, which I scrambled up and down with the other children. Mum tells me now that a family of sixteen stayed there. For me it was as wide and varied as a village. One man had the top end of his bed raised on bricks at a crazy angle. The children said there was a bad spirit in his stomach, and sometimes his head.

Next came the journey through Africa. I had my sixth birthday in the Sahara desert, though I was only told this later, when we were safely through and could have a small party. Memories of the desert? One at least, of rolling down a great sand slope at sunset. We climbed with gumboots because Dad was worried about nasty things called scorpions. But at the top it was so warm and still, we took off our clothes and 'swam' in the sand-silk.

By the next year we were in Australia, and the year after that at the school Mum and Dad founded. From then on life was more settled, until the past two years when I moved to a school near Adelaide. I guess my education has been unusual too. Instead of the final state exam, we all had to do a major project of our own choice alongside our normal school work.

Mine was to make a film, in partnership with a class mate called Jim. It was great. Incredibly hard work to get it all done, but really exciting. We had a teacher and a specialist as supervisors, but were responsible for every aspect of it – from writing the script, to auditioning, directing, shooting, editing, arranging publicity, funding, and screening. With a third friend, Jake, we also designed and played the music. It's Jim and Jake I'm going to meet in Ho Chi Minh City. Hopefully we'll be able to 'jam' there together.

The film was of a young man, Chris, and his other self, an innocent clown called Curious. As Curious he could talk with animals, trees, bulldozers and tanks, listen to 'racist' conversations between beer bottles of different labels, or see behind the arguments of children and politicians. It was a kind of fairy tale journey beyond outer appearances – a young person's initiation into the modern world...

'Where you come from?' A boy of about ten is standing at our table, looking me straight in the eye. His face is shocking, torn and shredded by burn marks; his English surprisingly clear.

'Australia,' I reply.

'You Vietnam,' he goes on emphatically, and the right half of his face moves into a smile while the left remains chained to the wasted inert flesh. His left ear is completely gone.

We've been talking hard, the memories rich and strong, and I've only been dimly aware of the people drifting by or coming to peer at us. In fact there's quite a cluster – an older boy, perhaps my age, who's wheeled his cyclo over; a well-dressed woman holding a child with a giantly inflated head; and the normal gaggle of children watching, giggling, chasing. Mum talks with the woman and tells me she has four more children, but that this is the one she and her husband love best. He is three years old. From his eyes upwards his head is the shape and size of a soccer ball.

'Husband leave. Go, gone,' the cyclo driver whispers to me. 'She crazy.' And he twists one of his fingers against his temple, gesturing wildly with his eyebrows.

The burnt boy sits down between Dad and me, then goes over to the sugar cane juice stall and orders a drink, nonchalantly indicating that we will pay for it. Dad asks him in Vietnamese what happened to his face and he replies it was from an accident with a petrol stove, when he was eight. He says he's now fourteen and has left school. 'He crazy,' the cyclo boy whispers again, eyebrows in full spate. 'School – no can do. Head – brick!'

Dad buys the woman a cane juice and she sits down and spoons it to her child, cooing now and then to get a response from it. She seems quite self-contained. She makes no attempt to ask for money.

Twilight falls. Where is my life leading now? Mum and Dad are keen, as I guess most parents would be, for me to take up my place at university next year. It seems absurd even to think about it in this environment. My own wish is to 'get into life', to *do* something. Even the coming months are uncertain. Will I join them in China after spending a few more weeks in Vietnam with Jim and Jake – or can I earn some money for a ticket to the US, where I've been offered work on a film shoot?

How unequal life is! Is that the way it has to be? Here I am suffering from a glut of too many possibilities, while the others in this strange circle of misfits (my birthday party!) have so few.

During our remaining days together the three of us do the tourist thing, exploring the city and the surrounding country on rented Hondas. It's a beautiful way to see the sights, weaving in and out of the streams of cyclos, scooters, cycles and pedestrians. I like this city. It doesn't have the buzz of Ho Ville, but you can feel its history and culture.

Mum says the Fragrant River takes its name either from the flowers and herbs once brewed in ritual on its banks and poured into its waters; or else from the perfumed women in lamp-lit boats, now gone, whose skills included music, poetry, preparing opium and pleasing men. She says one of her ancestors wrote a poem in hundreds of verses about one of them. It's apparently a classic in Vietnamese literature… That's to say, one of *my* ancestors.

Following its flowing water one afternoon we come to an old pagoda with a seven-storey tower and temple, and buildings for the few Buddhist monks who still live there. Among its prized possessions is an Austin car in which a monk was driven to a square in Saigon back in 1963, where he set fire to himself in protest against the Southern government. Strangely, Dad, who was still at school in

England at the time, knew more about it then than Mum did. 'All news was censored in Vietnam,' she says. 'I only heard wisps of it through rumour.'

'While outside,' Dad goes on, 'those flames that consumed his body became a symbol that haunted the world's conscience, as the momentum of war grew ever stronger.'

We wander into the garden at the back, past those crazy up-curling roofs, figures of Buddha, bells of prayer, the hum of chanting. What a change from the streets! 'You know, once I saw a soldier try to burn himself in Saigon,' says Dad. 'The police got to him before he'd finished. The flames became black smoke as they drenched him with chemicals and dragged him back to life, charred, twitching and disgraced. Then they carted him away.'

Next morning is a scorcher and we venture farther out into the hills to the temple and tomb of Tu Duc, one of the emperors from the past. It is a huge secluded park enclosed by walls. Walkways and steps lead past pines and frangipani to intricately carved buildings with Chinese roofs and musty rooms. We take refuge by the lotus lake in the blessed coolness of the pavilion. A place of peace and culture; yet it was built with forced labour and such cruelty that it triggered an uprising.

Tu Duc apparently had over one hundred wives and countless concubines. At each meal, so we were told, he had fifty dishes, each prepared by a different cook and served by fifty servants. After he had eaten, all the utensils from cooking pots to plates, chopsticks and spoons would be broken and replaced with new ones.

Stone elephants, horses and mandarins guard the way to the twenty-ton slab on which his life is chiselled in Chinese characters. His official tomb is in an enclosure by a half-moon lake, but the real burial place was kept secret to protect the wealth it contained. And the two hundred servants involved in the ceremony of his death were executed. This was just over a hundred years ago!

What strikes me is the influence of China – in the architecture and paintings, the old costumes and calligraphy. Despite Vietnam's thousand-year struggle against Chinese domination, its cultural legacy lived on; and I feel an unexpected thrill at the thought of perhaps meeting up with Mum and Dad there after all.

Vietnam – North

8

It is ten in the morning, the summer solstice. 'How can so much history accumulate in a simple river?' says Justin, craning out of the bus window. 'And a bare metal bridge?'

Like other Vietnamese, I grew up with songs and poems lamenting the separation of our country into North and South at the Ben Hai. It was compared to the story of the King of Heaven creating the Silver River (or Milky Way) as a barrier between his daughter and her earth-born beloved, of whom he did not approve. They were condemned to gaze at each other from either side and were allowed to meet only once a year in the rainy season when ravens gathered to form a bridge.

The air is sultry, damp; beneath us, water the colour of clouded jade, flowing fast. Do all our wishes come true? I suspect they do; but not in the way – or time – we expect.

Forty years ago exactly my family fled south. How strange! Then, as refugees, we flew straight from Hanoi to Saigon; now, as free people, we are crammed into a dilapidated hulk like refugees. Hanoi, the city of my childhood, is only four hundred kilometres away. My closest relation there is a distant cousin of my father whose wife, 'Aunt' Ngo, used to look after us. Why am I nervous yet again?

Two hours along the rutted road we come to a halt in unassuming and almost empty Dong Hoi. Looking out at the rice fields and villages along the way, I realise suddenly what a different experience the people here would have had of America's presence during the war. Apart from shot down pilots and commando groups, they encountered no human beings from the country they were fighting, only the impersonal, destructive detritus of its science.

The driver unloads crates of soft drink bottles and glasses into a small café crammed with merchandise, then disappears inside. We have been assured it is an express bus, so sit and wait, not daring to eat in case it leaves.

Next door is a juice stall and although fresh ice drinks are unsafe in small places, it is so hot we take the risk. The lady squeezes a green lime into a glass of indeterminate cleanliness, adds ladles of water from a bucket and two large spoonfuls of sugar, stirs vigorously, then pours in a cascade of ice smashed from a steaming block with a hammer. One sees these large blocks being wheeled on carts or dragged with ropes along the streets. I could have gone on drinking for ever.

Midday. I go to the tap in front of the café to wash my hands. It is what I have chosen to do as the second exercise in the six-month process I began on leaving Australia – an exercise for strengthening the will, the idea being to discipline oneself to an action one would not normally take, at the same time each day. With no other motive for it (such as usefulness or pleasure) it is one's own will alone that brings it about – not easy when one is on the move, and sometimes I have had to pour lemonade on my hands through a bus window instead!

The driver reappeared, abrupt and surly. We had been waiting for an hour and a half. 'Another bus will take you,' he said without apology. 'We go no farther.'

'Why didn't you tell us?' someone protested. 'What about our fares?'

'We'll take care of that.' He slammed the door and drove off. A couple of buses went by without stopping, then one pulled up, already full. We scrambled on and squeezed next to a man on a double seat. The atmosphere was different – no prodding with questions, no fussing over Justin. Then I realised: their accents were from Hanoi, their disposition like mine. Women sat upright, silent; men proud and inward. There was no music or blaring radio.

'Have some food,' said Justin, producing some dark-looking duck eggs, greasy fried tofu and pressed rice in yellowing banana leaves he had bought at the last minute; I gave it a miss. Shortly after, his stomach cramps began, but it was to be three hours before the driver pulled over into a bare roadside restaurant for a meal. The biggest nightmare of bus travel, apart from its danger, is that of being caught short between breaks – coupled with the state of the toilets when one finally gets to one. Justin came back white-faced. 'Avoid it,' was all he said.

We spent that night in Vinh, halfway to Hanoi. By the time we got there it was dark and deluging like a waterfall. We clambered out into a vast puddle and were drenched in the instant. Glistening in the headlights, with his bush hat and the lump on his back beneath sodden plastic, Justin looked like a giant frog risen from the water. I knew he was still not well, but the sight was so bizarre I forgot the cold wetness creeping down my own back and burst out laughing.

We went this way and that, following contradictory directions in search of a hotel. A woman beckoned us into her tea shop – rickety low tables and benches under threadbare canvas. We sipped glasses of scalding black liquid, sharing our tale with strangers while large drops of water made music on our covered heads through holes in the awning. 'You walk that way, my pets,' she pointed, refusing our money. 'It's a decent place. Have a good rest.'

It was damp, bare and cold, at four dollars a night but it did not leak. We showered, washed our clothes, hung up mosquito nets, swept the concrete floor and lit our crooked candle. Outside it continued to pour. Our spirits were low. Justin was afraid he had a recurrence of giardia, a kind of amoebic dysentery he had contracted in Vietnam before. He went without eating and I accompanied him.

What were we doing here? I felt myself sliding into a black hole... Justin ferreted in his pack and took out a notebook with quotations gathered from various sources. 'When we look up to the stars,' he read quietly, from a passage by Rudolf Steiner, 'we are actually looking towards spiritual beings. What shines upon us is a kind of symbolic light which they send of their presence, so that here too, even in physical life, we may have an inkling of the living spirit which fills the entire universe.'

Vinh is the capital of the poorest, least fertile province in Vietnam. People from the region have the reputation of being tight-fisted; yet from among them have emerged many artists, intellectuals and leaders, not least Ho Chi Minh. My ancestors came from there too.

Because of its port which fed the supply lines of the Ho Chi Minh Trail, the town was devastated by bombing, and what we saw the following morning was depressing – grey multi-storey blocks, built with aid from Eastern Europe. Many were half completed and the main streets and pavements, though generous in width, were shoddily made and seemed chronically flooded. The cyclos were goods carts, the banks had no foreign exchange. But the people we met were civil and helped us.

Our problem was that the normal Hanoi buses had left by seven. We had taken things easy and it was now nine. Justin at least was feeling better. A man in a suit took us in hand and a small crowd gathered round, each person with an opinion.

'It's too late. They'll have to take a train.'

'The train's gone too.'

'The only way is to stand in the road and ask for a lift.'

A cyclo drew up and the driver offered to take us to a good place for waving down vehicles. He was wearing army fatigues and a pith helmet, his face lined but with clear eyes and strong cheekbones. 'The town's not what it used to be,' he said, as our bodies jarred against wood and metal. 'It was fine when Uncle Ho was alive. The bombs were nothing, nor the poverty. When he visited or spoke on the radio, our spirits would soar.'

He said he had been a soldier from the time he could hold a gun. His company had defended Vinh against the air raids. Friends had died, so had his family except a wife and an old father. Then in '72 he was sent south in the massive assault across the DMZ. 'None of us thought twice about it. If your time comes, that's how it is.' He paused as we negotiated a hole in the bumpy main street. 'Now it's different. People only think of money.'

Another crowd gathered as we got off. Three school girls, graceful in white *ao dai* and Vietnamese hats, practised their English with Justin while some boys listened in admiringly. Two young men watched the road, stopping every bus that went past. As each one slowed down, they would hop onto the step shouting questions, negotiating with the conductor. At last they succeeded – a bus with Hanoi written on the top.

'Three dollars each. Come quick,' they shouted excitedly, grabbing our packs and shoving them inside. They asked for a tip and while Justin was getting out some money, the bus started moving. I hung on to the door, wavering: stay with Justin or go with the packs? The cyclo man pushed us in from outside.

Justin was moved by our encounter with him. 'He would have been there when I went to the front as a journalist,' he said later. 'If we'd met then, he'd have shot me without thinking twice.'

It is dark. Here and there an electric bulb gleaming among trees; then suddenly, a blaze of lights. The beginnings of Hanoi. I am in a daze, panic threatening at what lies ahead. Houses tightly packed, recently built by the look of them. Shopfronts, more lights, a festival of electricity. It must be the glassware district for there are streets of it – chandeliers, mirrors, dinner sets, glasses. 'That's the polytechnic, the university...' the man across the aisle is telling Justin. The streets fan out wider. Multi-storey blocks then rows of offices...

We get down. Leafy trees on large pavements, lamps glowing yellow. Justin and the man haggle for a cyclo, then our packs are on our laps and we're moving again, our friend hitching a lift on the driver's seat. I can no longer take it in.

And then we're there. The house where I once lived. What a let down! I remember it as a palace. An elderly woman slides back the grille. 'Ah, niece Thu, at last.' She is smiling widely. 'Come in, come in... You too.' She speaks no English.

'*Thua bac manh gioi khong a?*' The only words I can find in those first moments. 'Respected Aunt is well, isn't she?' From then on we simply call her *Bac* – or Aunt. She and her family moved here from the country when my parents left for the South. The communists divided the house up and gave them back a sixteenth part. Of course – that's why it's so small!

She led us in past two motorcycles behind cupboards and boxes of electrical goods belonging to a man who used the front portion of the room as a shop during the day – to a wickerware couch against a partition. Beyond were three small rooms, separated by further flimsy walls with a small kitchen, shower and toilet attached. Her husband, the distant cousin of my father, was bed-ridden on a low camp bed.

She saw we were hot and switched on all the fans. The blast cooled us instantly, then made us cold. It was eleven o'clock. 'So, niece,' she said, touching my hand. 'I haven't seen you since '54. And this is your husband?' She was bubbling over with curiosity. 'What a handsome man! How lucky you are! But is he *good*?'

She was large for a Vietnamese woman and wearing the customary loose satin pants, white blouse and plastic slippers, her teeth black with a natural lacquer which would never come off. Her long grey hair was rolled up under black velvet in a coil around her head. She looked healthy and exuded warmth. We were exhausted and hungry. 'Ah, I haven't kept food for you.' She was suddenly distraught. 'I didn't know when you'd arrive.'

Her daughter-in-law, Ly, appeared from inside and guided us to a soup place round the corner – a modern woman in fashionable baggy shorts and shirt, who shared a room with her ten year old daughter. The street was wet and dark, the stall a series of low tables on the dank pavement. We sat on stools and ordered *chao* with fish in it, declining the speciality of pig's intestines. The rice porridge was good, full of ginger and hot pepper, but the squalid surroundings made my stomach squirm.

It was midnight when we got back. 'Make yourselves comfortable,' said Bac, gazing at us for some moments. 'This is a good-sized house nowadays, you know.' A pause. 'We also have a Western toilet and a hot and cold shower.'

Justin was given the cushionless couch while Bac took me beyond the partition to sleep with her. Our bed was a kind of low polished table which I recognised from childhood – a precious antique of dark brown wood with elaborately carved legs. I remembered rolling on it in panties, relishing its coolness at hot siesta times. Now it pressed like rock, bare against my back. I lay in my clothes, a wooden support under my neck until I discarded it. Fans whizzed at full speed. I changed ends to escape the blast. Bac did the same to keep me company. She coughed and spat into a spittoon. I drifted off.

'Niece.' She touched me. 'Let's be sentimental about the past.'

'Uh huh.'

'Your mother was very good to me. I used to look after you all. I went on many holidays with your sisters... *You* were different. Your grandmother used to say you'd been swapped in hospital as a baby.' She rubbed my arm gently.

'Mother disliked me.'

'She didn't love you as much as the others. I think it was incompatible natures. You were the fourth girl in a row, you see. She wanted a boy. Also you were fat and healthy while your sisters were sickly.' She cackled. 'You were naughty too. Stubborn.' She was silent, seemingly asleep. I had no such luck. A fluoro tube, bright as daylight, was on in one of the other rooms and it hurt my eyes.

I was also thinking about her remark. How could it be incompatible natures? Isn't it a child's right to be loved? Tears pricked me for a moment and I felt surprise that it still hurt, even though the grudge I had carried for so long had gone.

The phone rang. It was Ly's husband from Italy where he was doing a PhD. The conversation lasted twenty minutes. One thirty. Another light was switched on, this time in Justin's area. Bac asked me to tell him to turn it off.

'I can't sleep,' he said. 'The couch is too short.' He had tried with his sleeping bag on the floor, squeezed between furniture and motorcycles. Cockroaches and mosquitoes had pestered him, also a mouse. He had rigged up the net but still could not sleep. When the phone rang, he had had to move to make way for Ly and was now planning to do some writing.

'I'm sorry,' I said, persuading him to go back to bed.

Now Bac could not sleep. She clutched at me, asking questions. What's it like in Australia? Do we have a big house? Do people eat sheep there and doesn't it have a rotten smell? What would we like for breakfast? She went through her list of specialities, from *pho* (rice noodle soup), chicken and vermicelli soup, steamed spring rolls with pork and shrimp stuffing, to young scented rice cooked in coconut milk, or glutinous rice with stewed pig trotters and peanuts. It was two thirty. I turned away, firmly closing my eyes against the light.

'Oh God, oh God,' moaned Uncle Ngo. Then he shouted out for one of his sons. Bac lay still, as though asleep.

I dozed on and off. Then it was six o'clock.

Hoan Kiem means 'Restored Sword' – the name of the lake in Hanoi's centre. Legend has it that in the fifteenth century, Heaven sent a golden tortoise to bring a sword to Emperor Ly Thai To, with which he defeated the invading Chinese. One day while he was out boating, the tortoise came to the surface again, grabbed the sword and disappeared into the depths.

An arched wooden bridge, painted red, leads to an island on which is the small *Ngoc Son* (Jade Mountain) Temple and a museum. Preserved in a glass case we saw a magnificent five hundred year old turtle which was caught in the lake about thirty years ago. Its tawny patterned shell was polished like a mirror.

In my childhood's eye this lake was huge and magical with emerald green water and fairy-like weeping willows.

On the planks of the red bridge I was walking once when everything became illumined and clear – the skin on the warm adult hand I was holding, the grain on the banisters by my head, the rippling water – and it came to me with a buoyant joy, It's me who's seeing this. It's I. I must have been about three years old.

We found a small clean room in a hotel near Bac's house and moved our gear later in the day. It was raining and we stayed inside, relishing the privacy.

'I'll tell you a story,' I said to Justin. 'One of the legendary emperors of what is now the area of southern China and Vietnam had many sons, of whom the youngest was the favourite. When he came of age, his father granted him a land in the barbarian South to rule over. He lived there alone, a warrior and poet.

'One day, chasing a deer in a forest, he came upon a poem freshly carved on a tree. He replied with his own before going home. Next day on another trunk he found a second one, to which he also responded. The ritual was repeated seven times. Then one evening he caught a glimpse of a beautiful maiden, weaving in and out of the mist. He followed and at last met up with her. "I'm the Being of the Land," she said.

'They married – Lac Long Quan, the dragon's son, and Au Co, the fairy maid. In due course she gave birth to a hundred eggs which hatched into a hundred boys. Half migrated with their mother to the mountains, the other half with their father to the coastal plains...'

'Out of whose descendants one day was born a chubby baby called Thu,' Justin added. But I knew the fairy tale images spoke as much to him as to me – the dragon's son, wilful representative of a new spirit, leaving the ties of the past to unite with the mysterious soul of another 'realm'. The Vietnamese are fond of referring to themselves as children of dragons and fairies, perhaps with good reason, considering their martial spirit and (at times) other-worldly grace.

The following morning I went round to see Bac who looked tired and old. She seemed touchy about our having moved out and told me how my brothers and sisters had slept on her floor whenever they visited. The comparison brought up the familiar feeling of guilt that lies just below the surface, for having been different. 'What does she expect?' I exploded to Justin later. 'How could we have stayed? I've had enough. I'm ready to leave.'

'Come on. There's something in you that keeps resisting. Why don't you spend a day being Vietnamese and enjoying Bac?'

I went to bed feeling lousy. The room was stuffy, the weather prickly and hot, the bed too small, the net too low. And I seemed not to belong anywhere.

I turned to my journal. 'What is nationality? I live and work in Australia, travel on its passport, pay tax and have rights like any other citizen. I also love the land, its space and light. Its spirit is part of me. I've chosen it. Vietnam is the country of my heredity. I've grown up with its culture and ways of thought. I still retain its essence in my bones.

'Like many others I carry the wish for a citizenship of the world. For this there is no outer procedure, only the inner one of uniting with what is human in all races and cultures. Yet I still hold back from Vietnam. Do I fear its power to bind me?'

Justin seemed to be heading for sickness. I took his advice and went off alone, stopping first to see Bac. She was stronger now and more friendly, and bustled around preparing something special to eat. She showed me a photo of her son in Italy – dark glasses, an immaculate suit and shining shoes. If I had not known I would have assumed he was Italian. Yet this same man, at the age of eighteen, had been sent to the South as a soldier. For four years his family knew nothing of him. 'News filtered back about the terrible losses at the DMZ,' she said. 'We called it the "mincing ground". Our neighbours lost four sons there.'

She paused, eyes fixed in memory. 'Then one day after the war, can you believe it, he was there at the door, right there, in the uniform of a captain. I thought I was seeing a ghost! Goose pimples went up to my head and my teeth rattled as if there was an earthquake.'

I wander through the old quarter, the busy commercial centre from the central market to the lake – a labyrinth of streets, lanes and crescents, small shops and stalls overflowing with goods. Vehicles, bicycles and food pedlars mingle in profusion with voices, horns, amplified music and the refuse and mud that accumulate from the daily deluge.

Street names bring back memories of wonder. In the past each had been devoted to a single trade, expressed in the name – Copper, Iron, Paper, Salt, Plate; and farther on, Key, Lampshade, Fish Paste and Grilled Dog Meat. The most magical for me had been Cross and Peach streets, with their lantern processions and dragon dances at the autumn festivals. People everywhere, lights, drumbeats, the terror of getting lost or squashed, the thrill of buying a miniature rabbit made of coloured dough. Back home, risking a scolding, I would sneak up to the roof to watch the full moon and sing with my big cousins:

On the silver moon is a big banyan tree.
The old hobo lies dreaming under its green leaves…

Near the hotel, a woman stands at a crossroads tending to a basket on her bicycle. I tiptoe over through the muck. It is filled with red roses, rain drops lingering.

Like dew.

9

At noon Thu and I went in search of food. It was a mistake. When finally we found a place in the cluttered back lanes, my stomach turned. I ordered plain rice porridge. What came was a grey colour with bits of red in it. The pyjamaed girl said she had cooked it with pig bones and lungs. I paid her the thousand dong it cost without touching it and headed back to the hotel, leaving Thu to explore the city uncluttered by my foreignness.

I was ill. And I knew it was connected not only with food and water, but the whole gamut of sense impressions from our way of travelling in Vietnam. I had had enough of the poverty and the grime. Thu had had her fill as well, but she reacts differently. Her stomach can take it, her soul cannot. There was a darkness in her eyes which I recognised from her crisis of exhaustion years before and it concerned me.

I stayed in exile for two days eating nothing, with the red roses Thu had bought in a glass by the bed. By the third day I felt cleaner though still delicate. As we walked along the street towards Bac's house, the smells, sights and sounds put my nervous system on edge and my stomach trembled anew.

We stopped at an air-conditioned restaurant where I ordered yoghurt, a boiled egg and toast. For once we were grateful for sterility and made no protest at paying extra for aloofness and comfort. The egg came in a blue china bowl. The lady placed each thing with care, plates and cups of the same set. The walls were white; there were lace curtains at the window and a pink geranium near our table.

Bac's youngest son, Thang, was back home at last from watching the World Cup with friends – good-looking, unusually tall, a lecturer at the university. 'Italy and Argentina are in the semi-finals,' he said with gusto. 'It'll be a good match.' He said he enjoyed his work and appreciated the facilities to which he had access. 'It's good to see Vietnam in the modern world,' he added, feeding a video onto the large television screen. A flickering Michael Jackson in pink pants appeared, body and face contorted as he screamed. 'This is forbidden, of course,' said Thang, with an easy smile, 'but there are ways of getting anything.'

The following day we visited the mausoleum of Ho Chi Minh. Getting in was a serious affair. We got personalised tickets from an office for foreigners and presented them to two guards in red and white uniform, who marched us along the majestic boulevard to the building. One of them, without turning his head or interrupting his stride, asked Thu how much she earned in Australia. They passed us on to other men in khaki, who took us in relays through the door, across the hall, up the stairs and into the silent darkness of the tomb with soldiers standing to attention a few metres apart the whole way.

The body was in the centre, below the viewing walkway. Head and hands were brightly illumined and from the waist downwards it was covered by what appeared to be a lead blanket. I stopped, and was prodded to keep moving. The accepted way of paying one's respects, it seems, is to file in and round without pausing. It left a lugubrious feeling. Since Marxism denies the spirit and soul becomes a unit of economy, all that is left of the person is the corpse, which belongs in this case not to nature but the state. It was not a place where I felt the presence of holiness.

The paths led to the simple two-storey house by the lake where Ho lived and worked from '58 until his death in '69. From the crowded viewing platforms we looked into rooms kept meticulously clean, the simple furniture and possessions as they were when he died. We were allowed to pause this time but not stray by a footstep from the designated walkways.

Outside we bought a copy of his will, published in complete form in '89, when Mr Nguyen Van Linh was general secretary. It was a brave step to take, for in it Ho asked for his body to be cremated. This part had been left out in earlier publications, allegedly because the people would not have been able to bear to let his body go. He continued:

> Let my ashes be divided into three parts, to be put in three ceramic boxes: one for the North, one for the Centre, one for the South.
>
> In each part of the country, let the box of ashes be buried on a hill. Let no stone stele or bronze statue be erected on the grave. Instead there should be a simply designed, spacious, solidly built, cool house where visitors can rest.
>
> A plan should be worked out to plant trees on and around the hills. Let visitors plant memorial trees. With the passage of time, the trees will form forests which will benefit the landscape and agriculture. Care for the trees should be entrusted to local old people.

Mien phoned from Ho Chi Minh City to say that Luke was ill. His school mates from Australia had arrived and the three of them had been flat out since. They had met some fellow musicians and even played at an open air concert and a night club, Luke with a wet towel over his head against a fever. She said they were planning to join us in Hanoi. We asked her to persuade them to come by train. It was a question not of comfort only, but safety.

Since being ill myself I had sensed something lacking that I needed to be strong again, yet could not identify what it was. We rented bicycles, a wonderful way to experience Hanoi, but not without peril. It required a heightened sensitivity to what drivers and machines veering at one from any direction were going to do – and whether to dodge, slow down, speed up or shutter one's eyes and continue. There was also the challenge of not getting separated from Thu. She at least, riding behind, could see my hat above the other cyclists.

The streets were wide and lined with tall trees in the French way, many of the buildings stately and with the old-world charm of colonial times. Though the Vietnamese fought to be free of France, they have respect for its culture; and one of the things that makes their country fascinating is the interweaving of West and East.

By the White Bamboo lake, one of many in the city, was a memorial to the shooting down of an American plane. A local person had jumped in and rescued the pilot who was held in prison until the POW exchange at the war's end. Now a senator, he had recently returned to look for the person who saved his life – and the one who shot him down. I understand that a similar spirit of reconciliation prevails in the tours for foreign soldiers who fought in Vietnam. The idea is for them to visit their places of combat with guides who are veterans of the Vietcong or Northern army.

So we found our way to the street of the Darling Cafés. Whichever the original one was, it was such a success that others of the same name were spawned nearby, each with a different prefatory word like Real or Only or True. Here was backpacker-land – pancakes, potatoes, boiled vegetables and ten different foreign languages. Such haunts are nodal points on the travellers' grapevine.

I began to feel nourished, in the part that had been empty. I am a Westerner and a backpacker, I had to admit, as well as one who has deep connections with the Vietnamese.

Suddenly too the idea of visiting Dien Bien Phu, scene of France's darkest hour in Vietnam, became a possibility; prices for a jeep were on a different scale from those in the conventional agencies. At a pinch we could squeeze six of us into one – a driver, ourselves and the three gangling boys. Once they made it to Hanoi.

As our time in Vietnam drew towards its end, I gave thought to the follow-up letter I had promised to write to Mr Nguyen Van Linh. It became another marathon, fourteen pages long. I wrote it on one of the islands in the bay of Ha Long – a place of mythic proportions in Vietnamese culture where over two thousand peaks rise like dragon teeth from a limpid sea, reminiscent of Chinese paintings. The French called it the eighth wonder of the world.

I wrote of the goodwill we had found and the poverty – also of the dangers as the stress of competing with wealthier nations grows daily stronger. 'Now at peace,' I suggested, 'Vietnam faces the same threat as the world does – being smothered by materialism. What can counteract this?' For Thu and me, I said, 'part of the answer lies in an education that develops a strength of heart as well as head.'

As in the conversation with Huong and Van in Dalat, I mentioned a third economic option besides capitalism and communism. 'It is sometimes called "associative economics", because it is based on policy-making associations between producers, consumers and people in the middle. The criterion for production becomes what is needed rather than what can yield the fastest profits. And though this may seem a long way off, I wish to let you know that it is happening already in some parts of the world, even if only in small groups of people.'

The day following we rented a boat with some other travellers to explore the wonderland of islands. As the owner tied up by a jetty to buy seafood for our lunch, a launch drew up alongside and a stubby man in singlet and shorts proceeded to unleash a tirade of abuse at him. It ended with the handing over of no less than forty dollars (the price we had paid for the boat). He said it was the penalty for taking tourists without a licence and that it happened about once a month. 'It's how we provide for each other,' he added with a shrug.

It was a scenario I had referred to in my letter to Mr Linh. With most salaries far below what was needed to keep a family, it was normal to seek other ways of supplementing income – by means of bribes, fines, tips, paybacks, gifts, whatever one likes to name them. Westerners call it corruption; for locals it was a matter of survival.

Misty rain alternated with sunlight. At one place we swam through a natural tunnel, twenty metres long, into a lagoon secluded by rugged cliffs, the water the colour of jade.

Legend attributes Ha Long's origins to a dragon who plunged into the sea, gouging out the depths and flinging up the peaks. Many of the islands have their own myths. In the *Grotto of the Virgin* is a rock formation resembling a woman with flowing hair. A girl in a local village fell in love, but her parents tried to force her to marry someone else. She ran away, waiting for her loved one to return from war. By the time he did – too late, alas – she had turned to stone.

In the end Luke and his friends opted for the bus after all because it was cheaper than the train. Its cost in other ways was a good deal higher; and thoughts about their safety knocked at the doors of our minds. After forty hours Luke phoned to say they had got off at Danang exhausted the evening before, and were hoping to come on by train.

We visited the family of one of Bac's daughters and were welcomed with characteristic generosity into a tidy, two-roomed house. The husband was a journalist, a gentle person with a keen mind. He was also a Party member and over cakes and tea, he told us why. 'Ho Chi Minh has shown us that socialism works,' he said. 'While he lived, we were almost a classless society.'

'Wasn't it the war that drew people together?'

'Of course. But why didn't it happen in the South? Because what ruled there was self-interest and the grabbing of power.'

I suggested that the collapse of the USSR had shown the impracticality of Marxist theory. 'Our ways are different,' he said. 'Even from China. Maybe again it goes back to Uncle Ho. He enabled us to go beyond our normal selfishness. And he was one of the only leaders in the world who remained on good terms both with the Russians and the Chinese.'

I asked then what the motives had been for the offensive across the DMZ in '72. Had it not been a mistake, coming out in the open like that with tanks and soldiers at the mercy of US air power? It had seemed to me an indication of the callousness of the leaders.

He laughed. 'Do you really think that's what happened? Is the Western press any more accurate than ours? Most of the tanks were either captured from the other side or fakes, to lure in the planes. That's when we started to use Russian missiles and the US lost many pilots.' He said it had broken the uncrossable barrier and many units from the South changed sides. 'From then on it was only a matter of time.'

At nine that evening Luke phoned again. They had missed the train and hired a car. One of the rear wheels had fallen off. They were now in a second one, near Vinh. He reckoned they would reach Hanoi around two in the morning. It sounded optimistic.

We had drunk too much tea and did not sleep well. I woke up at three. No sign of the boys. When we got up at seven they were still not there. At seven thirty they appeared, tired but cheerful, three woolly giants amidst the thin people of the streets. Their journey of eight hundred kilometres had taken sixty-four hours.

They vied with each other to tell the story. The bus had kept stopping for no apparent reason, sometimes for hours. Their seats were in front of a speaker through which music was piped at full volume. 'We asked them to give us a break,' said Luke, 'but they kept repeating the same stuff again and again.' In the darkness they had wedged a peg into it to stop it vibrating. 'That was the best moment,' exclaimed Jake. 'They just couldn't figure it out.'

North of Danang the bus had stopped yet again and, to the driver's amazement, they got out and walked off. They hitched back to town and found a hotel. Early rising was never their strength and they got up too late for the train; hence the car.

They had cut it fine. Our jeep was due early next morning to take us into the rugged hills near Laos and China. They had the rest of the day to get some sleep and in the evening we went to Bac's for Luke to meet his relatives. She beamed her goodwill on us all and filled us with spring rolls and sticky rice. 'What a beautiful grandson,' she cooed. 'Such a big nose.'

It took us two days of driving on winding battered roads to reach Dien Bien Phu. The country we passed through was as beautiful as any I have seen – hills of all shades of green, brown, blue, mauve, interspersed with lush valleys, flowing water and paddy fields glinting in the light. A similar tapestry of light and dark was in the sky and clouds above. Eventually, I thought, like the Mekong in the south these uplands must connect with the Himalayas. There was the freshness of mountain air.

As we got farther into the hills, the bright colours of tribal clothes became more frequent. Amidst tall silky bamboos and tropical forest growth appeared wooden dwellings with smoke seeping up through the roofs. Villages and terraces were orderly and clean – likewise the unpretentious restaurants where we stopped for coffee or *pho* or lunch.

Our driver Cuong, who spoke Vietnamese with a strong regional accent which made it hard for me to follow, had learnt his profession the hard way: in trucks on the Ho Chi Minh Trail. 'I thought everything was carried by foot or bicycle?' I said, amazed.

'That was earlier. In the last years we had better equipment for shooting down planes, so took more risks. Still there was only a twenty per cent chance of surviving.'

He had driven eight-wheel drive Chinese trucks, often with trailers, at night and without headlights. During rainy seasons the tracks were mud and sometimes they had to unhitch the trailers and push them up the hills. Suicide squads would drive in front, drawing the bombs onto themselves and setting off mines dropped from the sky. He said they knew of air raids before they happened, the number of planes and the target. They became masters of deception, camouflaging the vehicles and setting up false targets.

Now he was in his forties and married with four children. For all his war experiences he looked healthy, his face round and cheerful – and he drove with sensitivity for the pressure of metal against squashed limbs.

We spent the first night in the small town of *Son La* – 'Mountain Song'. In the square outside our hotel was a parade of local people in honour of the UN's World Population Day. Army khaki mingled with the blues, reds and greens of traditional clothes. The theme was family planning; the message, from loudspeakers and banners, to stop at one or at most two children. The women stood out (young and elderly), their long hair in buns and ringlets with lavish head-dresses. They wore shiny black skirts with bright belts, their tops tight-fitting and of a single rich colour, embroidered around gold and silver buttons.

The hotel manager prided himself on his broken English and insisted on translating for Thu when local people spoke. The boys got the giggles but this was put down to the rice wine. Toasts abounded – to 'many woman', 'many wife', 'many money', 'many life' and then to yet 'more many woman'. He fought hard to fill my glass but my time for that has ended and my will was stronger than my wish to please.

Later he took the boys to a karaoke dive – that din that grows rampant in Vietnam – where (we heard the next day) he sang pop tunes into the microphone and watched himself on the screen, but was unable to persuade them to follow.

We reached Lai Chau, the town near Dien Bien Phu, mid-afternoon and from the roof of our hotel looked over the lush remote valley where world history had been jolted.

The idea had been to make an outpost from which the French could flush out the guerrillas in their mountain hideouts and cut their supply lines. The valley was wide enough for the base to be out of range of all equipment to which the Vietnamese had access, except a certain 105mm Chinese howitzer. There is a poignant story about the French artillery commander who swore that it was impossible for such a thing to be dragged up the steep rugged slopes. When months later shells started crashing in, putting the airstrip out of action, he declared himself responsible for what would follow and committed suicide.

He was not the only one, however, who had deemed the network of hillocks, tunnels and bunkers protected by barbed wire, artillery, mines and planes to be impregnable. Visiting French and American generals had come to the same verdict and a quarter of the colonial army was garrisoned there, including paratroopers and legionnaires.

They had overlooked the power of the human will. They called it fanaticism and put it down to indoctrination. No doubt there was truth in both charges, but there was another element they refused to acknowledge – that in trying to shore up a decadent colonialism they stood against the spirit of the time, and that the fire of a cause worth dying for was with their enemy, not them.

Maybe they also feared death more than their adversaries did – not, as is so often said, because in the West people value life more and care for their neighbours, but because one is more alone. In places where the old ways still live, the pain of passing is made lighter by the thought of joining one's ancestors. What I learnt at Dien Bien Phu was that this inner security even survived communism. I realised then that the embalming of Ho's body had this aspect of ancestor worship to it, for to all who followed him he was both uncle and grandfather.

All this came into clearer relief the next day. As we went down into the French command bunker, I thought of the journalist Bernard Fall who had been here often, and whose books had been so important for me when first in Vietnam. It was a cross between a prison and a tomb – mud, metal and sandbags and the eerie feeling of a place where people have known the closeness of death, four dank rooms on either side of a corridor.

We walked to a neighbouring hillock and the cluster of bunkers called Eliane, the most strategically placed of all the outposts because of its vista across the plain. A local person walking with us said that near the end the French controlled only two-thirds of the hill. From inside their bunkers they heard the relentless tap-tap of spades against earth as the Vietnamese literally dug their way towards them. And it drove them insane.

In the museum were the human details – bicycles used to carry rice sacks and weapons through the jungles, and the famous 105mm gun; photos of the Viet flag being carried onto the command bunker's roof, of columns of POWs next to bone-thin guards half their size, of the French officers and General Vo Nguyen Giap who masterminded the siege.

On a large relief map of the valley were shown the forty-nine components which made up the fortress. A recording was played with the sequence of events, day by day, hour by hour. As the French positions fell, green lights would be replaced with red. The lines of red-flashing trenches grew like slow-motion missiles, homing in inexorably on the centre.

The speed of the penetration was incredible. We saw this again later in a video with live footage. It showed glimpses of how the artillery pieces were dragged up the hills by teams of people, mostly barefoot, pushing and pulling in rhythm. When planes swooped they either shot at them with rifles or froze, then carried on. When the attacks began they no longer even froze as shells crashed around the trenches. As one man dropped, another was there. Soldiers on the other side saw it as a supernatural power and their surrender was actually a mutiny.

Two opposite experiences lived in me at the end of the day. One was the obsessive recollection of a pile of stinking human faeces that had been in the bunker at Eliane; the other, humble amazement at what can be achieved when the stakes are high and people are united in a common enterprise.

10

'It's going to get rougher today,' says Cuong, as we set out for Sapa, a town famous for the H'mong hill tribe – Justin and I in the front, the three boys wedged behind. It is touching to watch the pride with which he cares for the jeep, even though it belongs to an agency. 'I know what needs fixing the minute a problem starts,' he goes on, giving the dashboard a pat.

'It's not only jeeps you like,' says Jim slowly. 'What about the women you seem to know in each place we visit?'

The road became bumpier than ever. We passed a work gang, mainly tribal women with colourful clothes and head scarves, languidly splitting rocks with long-handled hammers to create the small stones used for fill. Some were carrying them in deep baskets on their backs, held by bands across their foreheads.

At the top of a long rise we had a puncture. Cuong refused to let us help and we walked on, breathing out into veils of blue and green, interspersed with glistening leaves and distant plumes of white foam. Birds warbled; all around was peace. People passed with enormous bundles of faggots on their backs and heads. They seemed shy at first but when Luke asked if he could take a photograph, they held out their hands for money.

The jeep caught us up and we came to the Red River, so cherished in Vietnamese literature. Flanked by forested slopes, its rich chocolate waters swelled beneath in giddy whirlpools on their turbulent way to Hanoi and the China Sea. We crossed and followed one of the many streams cascading into it. 'Hey, unreal!' shouted Jake. 'Can we have a swim?'

Cuong was not sure. It was the first time anyone had made such a request. 'Why not?' he said finally and we clambered down through wild undergrowth. 'Be careful, though,' he hollered. 'It's dangerous.'

It was.

> Pale drenched torsos
> Battling the torrent;
> Above, the misty mountains.

Somewhere in these mountains my parents lived before I was born. It was my father's first post in the civil service and the place where my mother lost her first three sons.

People in the lowlands generally believe that the high country is the home of evil spirits. I had heard that one night my second eldest brother had had a fever and was sleeping in my mother's bed, while my father was away. In the greyness of pre-dawn, something opened the mosquito net and tried to snatch him out. 'Mother, they're taking me away,' he shouted and she awoke in horror to find a dead child in her arms. He was five years old.

In the main street of Sapa next morning we were surrounded by women and children who had come from outlying hamlets to sell their wares of silver jewellery and woven cloth, their embroidery intricate and playful. They wore enormous necklaces and ear rings, with bangles on arms, wrists and ankles. Their clothes were a stunning indigo with glimpses of black, purple, green and red. They had turban-like headdresses, embroidered tunics and leggings criss-crossed with coloured strings above bare feet. Their smiles were broad, their teeth strong and white.

The language had a quality of song and wind. It sounded closer to Mandarin and made me realise how clipped Vietnamese is, the vowels tight, words abruptly ended. We understood none of it directly but immersed ourselves in the lively process of bargaining – basking in the goodwill and ending up with more things than we wanted.

An Irish girl, who had recently crossed over from China, joined us as we hiked into the valley and swam in the river and waterfalls at the bottom. She spoke of the difficulties she had had in China. It brought home to us that in less than a week we would be there too. 'You feel such an outsider,' she said. 'It wears you down. But I want to go back.'

We came to a village through neat terraces, irrigated by streams. Here and there were levers for pounding rice. Water would flow into a bowl at the top end of a seesaw, at the other end of which was a weight pointing down. As the bowl filled, it descended and pulled up the heavy end. When it touched the ground it released its contents, shooting up again and letting the weight thud into a bucket of grain. So the cycle would resume.

The houses were of mud, wood, bamboo and straw and were dark and smoky inside. Families squatted by cooking fires on bare earth floors, while the lofts were kept for faggots and grain. They spoke little Vietnamese. Outside were large vats with the indigo dye from *cham* leaves, soaked in water until fermented. White froth bubbled on the surface and freshly dyed cloth in purple and blue was spread out nearby. Small children played on the ground, their arms and legs stained like the hands of their mothers.

Back in the market place, a Vietnamese stallholder was throwing stones at a group of H'mongs. A dog got hit and yelped piteously. Luke shouted at the man to stop. 'They're thieves, all of them,' he hurled back. 'Dirty, too.'

In the restaurant – mud walls, stone floor, windows with bars and shutters but no glass – was a black and white television on which the British comedian, Mr Bean, could be seen struggling unsuccessfully to hold back a sneeze in church. Under the icy stares of neighbours he shuffled his snot-saturated handkerchief from one pocket to another, contorting his face in disgust to the background of soaring hymns. Cuong and some local boys, though they understood no English, were hooting with laughter. It started to deluge on the bare tin roof.

Luke's cough was getting bad again. He was angry at what we had seen in the market, and generally low. 'I can't deal with racism,' he said in our room, 'or the poverty.'

I felt disturbed too – not only because of his turmoil, but the imminence of our departure from Vietnam. I was concerned about his health and, like Justin, wished he would join us in China.

'Dear God,' said Bac, rubbing my arm when we got back to Hanoi the following night. 'I'm so relieved the evil spirits didn't get you.' She paused, then added, 'It's lucky you're back, you know. Thuc wants to take you to *Thay* village tomorrow.' He was her second son, also a lecturer at the university, and was taking time away from his work for the occasion.

It was raining when he picked us up in a hired minibus and it was drizzling still as we reached *Lang Thay*, 'Village of the Master', two hours later. A large area dominated by a limestone peak with weather-beaten mud and brick houses, trees and an abundance of temples in the Chinese tradition, it had been the home of my family since the land was granted to them by an emperor many generations back.

Once they would have been venerated by the villagers as if they were their ancestors; and there were still shrines to them in the temples. In weakened form this continued up to '54 when the land was redistributed. My father's name was said to be on the list of landowners to be denounced, though this could have been a ruse by certain people to get him to leave his property. Bac and her family continued to look after the shrines – something that remained important even under communism.

The narrow paths were slippery with red mud and cow manure. The boys, as always, were wearing their patterned beach shorts, T-shirts and chequered Vietcong scarves. A young woman with a pink umbrella appointed herself as our guide, greeting Thuc cordially. It seemed not possible to decline. 'Don't tell her you're a relation,' he whispered to me. 'You'll be fleeced.' It turned out she was the daughter of a distant cousin and one of her jobs was to get donations to keep the place up. Such requests were not confined to relations, as we were to find out.

She took us to the lake bordering the village, with a temple on one side and what looked like a shrine with no gate or floor in the middle. 'It's a stage for water puppetry,' she said. 'The emperor began the art here in the eleventh century.'

We had seen a performance in Hanoi, the bulky wooden puppets being moved on the water by long rods from behind a screen. The orchestra consisted of a sixteen-stringed zither, a mono-string violin, bongos and bamboo flutes, the sounds strident and melodic, with the haunting nostalgia of a time long past. At the end the puppeteers had waded towards us, waist deep in water and clapping with the audience.

We went into a temple on the lake's edge: dark and musty, floors creaky with age, ornate columns and doors, with an opening into a cloistered garden. As we wandered among the brightly painted figures, rich in Confucian and Buddhist imagery – the former large-bellied, the latter inward and thin – an old man indicated that we should make a donation and Justin put a note in the box. 'Not there,' he said. 'You should have given it to me to look after.'

In continuing drizzle we climbed the peak. Stone steps wound past shrines and caves potent with elemental power. At the top was a natural rock table and two 'chairs' where, as legend has it, fairies used to play chess on moonlit nights. My great-great-grandfather spent two years up here, writing a history of Vietnamese culture, economy and politics. He slept in one of the caves and his wife sent up food daily from the village. It is said that he conversed with the supernatural beings that dwelt there.

We lit candles and incense in a shrine. Wisps of smoke meandered up through shafts of muffled light. Water dripped from the overhanging roof onto mud and moist leaves. A memory stirred of sharing a bed with my younger sister in a room with a looming altar. In the morning gloom, waiting for Bac to wake, we peered through a gap in the shutter into a green patch of garden – golden sunlight on wet leaves, huge in our tiny peephole. The feeling was intense and joyous. The sunlight, it is me...

An old woman nudged me, muttering that it was time we gave some money.

Down in the village again, Thuc led us past a pond covered with watercress to my family's ancestral shrine. On either side of an altar, large paintings of four generations of mandarins looked down at us – imperial officials and masters of literature, wearing long loose robes of mauve, turquoise and red. 'Hey, dig these guys,' exclaims Jake, delighted. 'How can they have produced a veg-brain like you, Luke?'

'How come they're still here?' says Jim in his easy drawl. 'I thought communism destroyed this sort of stuff.'

'Whoever they are, I'm grateful they lived.' It is Luke. 'Is one of them my grandfather?'

'No. He never dressed like this, and his father died young, so it wouldn't be him either. His mother brought him and his brother up on her own.' She had been an only child in a tradition of warrior mandarins and was fond of telling the tale of how her father had been away at court when rebels attacked their town. She put on battle clothes and jumped on the wall with a sword, directing the soldiers and saving the day. Her dominating nature, however, had had a crippling effect on my father's will. 'You know, she caned him when he was thirty for not obeying her. She claimed to have done it more than once. For smoking opium.'

I sense a sadness when I think of my father, which is partly a consequence of the time at which he lived. He was a cultured person who mixed equally with artists and business people – but no longer with the stature of a mandarin and not yet having found his right place in the new world created by the West. When he fled south, he lost not only his fortune but his spirit. My mother became the breadwinner, as well as looking after her enormous family. In the end she even took in the four children he had by his second wife.

That too came out of tragedy. Vivid is my memory of a thunderstorm one evening when I was fourteen, and of someone appearing out of the darkness at our house shouting for Mother to come immediately. Father was out and she took three of us in a taxi to the other house, where we were greeted with wailing and screams. The maid had been taking washing off the wire which hung across the yard when lightning struck. Auntie had heard her cries for help and rushed out to pull her away. She must have grabbed hold of the wire herself. Her body was riveted to it, electrified; while the maid, still alive, was twitching on the ground in the drenching rain.

Mother sent us inside to look after the children. I sat on the floor in the dark bedroom, trembling, with a whimpering baby girl in my arms. The two older ones and a boy were crying on my sisters' laps. We took them home while Mother stayed to sort things out. As our taxi pulled away, I saw my father, pale-faced, hurrying inside...

'Did he smoke again?' Luke asks, hesitantly.

His voice shakes me back to the present and I look up at the dignified portraits. How would they make sense of all that has happened since their time?

'It killed him.'

It was the last day in Hanoi – and Vietnam – for Justin and myself. With a nagging anxiety about leaving Luke and about China ahead we went to breakfast at Bac's. I gave her some roses which she arranged on the altar. She lit candles and joss sticks, praying to Buddha and the ancestors to protect us. The day before, we had said just the three of us would come, as family, alone. 'But I've cooked for five,' she said, distraught, then looked at Luke and cackled. 'I like your friends, a frizzy bear and a giraffe. You go and fetch them, grandchild.'

I had the feeling of being about to laugh and cry at the same time. Bac had put so much into preparing her *pho* and she served it with gentleness, cheeks pale and puffy, eyes watery. It was exquisite, a dish she knew better than anyone else how to cook. She was also famous for her bamboo toothpicks. After splitting and smoothing each one, she would steam them until they were soft, resilient and clean.

It made the picking of teeth into a fine art and often in days to come we blessed her for the supply she gave us.

The time came. 'Go well and strong, niece,' she said, putting an arm around my shoulders.

'Permit me to go, revered Auntie.'

Luke's plans were as uncertain as ever. He wanted to be free and cope alone but also recognised his fear. He was torn between the excitement of coming with us to Tibet and loyalty to his mates and the band they had formed together in Australia. His cough was dreadful. 'I hate myself,' he said, 'for being so confused. Sometimes I feel I can't cope.'

It was then that I shared with him the darkest experience of my life. It had been when I was nineteen studying in Australia, and going through my own turmoil of trying to sort myself out.

I had been brought up a Buddhist. Like my whole family, I prayed as a child and went to the temple at New Year and other festivals. I learnt scriptures and chanted verses but knew little of what they meant, even when studying philosophy at university. I believed in Buddha as the great teacher who achieved enlightenment and taught us the path of self-purification, but could not relate to our being reincarnated as animals or going round eternally on the wheel of death and rebirth. It had no point.

All is illusion, the teachings seemed to say. But life was real and I was in the thick of it. I became immersed in suffering, mostly my own, and although I longed to be free of it, I also had a feeling that I had to live it through. In my first year away I hardly spoke to anyone at all. I was buried in my own world of confusion.

Then my mother died. She had not wanted me to stop my course and rush back for her funeral, and it was six months before I heard the news. I went to pieces. Although our relationship had been dreadful, she was still the anchor of my life. Invariably I had measured my own actions in the light of how she would view them. Now she was gone and I felt suffocated by the feeling of being alone. Utterly alone. I had no wish for my future. No ambition, no direction. For months I did little more than sit in my room and cry.

Late one night – it was autumn and the air was cool – I resolved to put an end to it. I walked down Bondi Beach and into the ocean. I could not swim in those days and there were no shark nets. Water and seaweed were all over my head. A blank. An eternity. Then a great wave crashed me back onto the sand. Even in death I had failed. I ran back to the boarding house sobbing hysterically. From then on I had no alternative but to live.

'How did you get through?' Luke asked quietly.

My image of the Western world had been only of material well-being. It had not occurred to me that there might be anything spiritual there. Now the thought came that there was a culture too and I forced myself to take an interest in it. I went to art galleries, listened to music; I made myself open up to people and to nature. At first I seemed to get nowhere. I was exhausted by the effort, but I kept at it and slowly a new sensitivity began to dawn. 'I guess I learnt to be more objective,' I went on. 'To take an interest in things for their own sake without constantly relating them back to myself.'

Luke was silent for a long time, then got up and hugged me. 'Youth,' said Justin dramatically. 'The agony and the ecstasy.'

Luke hugged him too. 'Old age,' he pronounced. 'The wisdom and the bald head.'

The five of us had a farewell dinner after which, in the bedlam of downpour and darkness, Justin and I wedged ourselves into a cyclo with our bags while Luke, shrouded in a poncho, followed on a bicycle. Our last glimpses of Hanoi were through the plastic cover, water streaming everywhere. It had all the cloak-and-dagger mystique of the old Orient.

We were soaked by the time we got to the station and located our train. The place was flooded and packed with people, sombre and dishevelled like cast-offs from a wreck. Lights were dim and, in the waiting room, completely out.

A guard tried to stop Luke from carrying his bicycle onto the platform above the crowded heads of passengers. Then we were through. We talked in the sheeting rain for a few minutes, and it was time to go. Would he find his way back in the dark? Would he get through the maze of possibilities in front of him? How was he going to get rid of his cough? We embraced through wet ponchos. 'I love you, boy,' I heard Justin say. 'God be with you.'

Inside the dimly lit carriage it smelt of paraffin and wet clothes. The floor was covered in mud, the overhead fans not working. It was humid and hot but mercifully not full and most people were stretched out over two seats. We lurched forward with a jolt – our first and last train journey in Vietnam.

We reached the tiny town of Lao Cai at six in the morning and were driven the last four kilometres to the border on the back of Hondas, on a trail of deep ruts and thick red mud. The old paranoia hit me. Would they find something wrong with our papers? Would they say we could not cross here?

Another metal bridge across a river – empty but for two pedestrians and the armed guards in uniform at either end. We stopped in the middle, poised between the excitement of what lay ahead and the taut string binding us to what we were leaving behind.

Then together, no word spoken, we walked into China.

Part Two

In the new mysteries the whole earth becomes a temple. The hidden tragedy and triumph of the pupil begins to become external fact. Our own friends become for us, though we may know little of it, the terrible and wonderful actors in the ceremony of our initiation.[3]

---

[3]Sometimes attributed to Rudolf Steiner.

China – South

1

The border between Vietnam and China is more than a river and a bridge. For all the cultural connections between the two nations and the shared communist ideology, Thu and I had the feeling of moving from one world into another – from one in which life and passions abound, to one where there was a kind of stillness in the air. Or was it an emptiness?

We were treated with calm but distant cordiality and directed to a room with a sofa, to wait for the lady official who spoke English. All notices were in Chinese. The impersonality of symbols we could not understand heightened the sense of remoteness; but with one exception it was a gentle introduction to China we received that day. We found the station and, though we had to wait until midday for the office to open, succeeded in getting sleepers for the train to Kunming. The exception was the toilet in the square outside. Thu emerged pale and on the point of vomiting. 'Never again,' she muttered hopelessly. 'How are we going to survive this?'

On the train it was cleaner and our companions in the compartment, two lady teachers and a child, were hospitable and friendly. They offered us tea from the large jam jars that all the passengers seemed to carry and which they would replenish at intervals from the coal boiler at the end of the carriage. Using our phrase book we took our first steps into the language that would surround us for the next three months.

'*Women Aodaliya ren*,' I ventured, telling them our nationality.

'Ah, *tai shu*,' came the reply and there we got stuck. They repeated it several times, but without any gesture to indicate they were referring to kangaroos. They looked questioningly at Thu. Throughout our travels it was assumed that only I could really be Australian, Thu being bound by her Asian heredity.

In a neighbouring compartment we met Rachel who had been in China before. She had a sunny disposition and had experienced all four grades of train travel, from wooden hard seats – 'cattle class', she called it – to soft seats, hard sleepers and the elitist soft sleepers. She said that foreigners were charged two or three times the local price, but that one could counteract this with a student or teacher's card, available from dealers in most cities. 'The whole thing's a scam anyway,' she added, sensing my hesitation. 'Foreigner prices breed student cards. We suffer the same discomforts. Why should we pay more?'

Towards evening two cleaning ladies came through our carriage with brooms and mops, the floor thick by then with paper, plastic, nut shells, fruit skins and bits of food. They shovelled the waste into bulging bags and neatly tied them up. Then they opened a window and flung them out. By the side of the track was a trail of white polystyrene containers.

We practised the art of climbing in and out of the bunks. There were three on each side, ours the middle ones; and despite their designation as 'hard' they were padded. It was a tight fit but the confinement became a security. We could hide there and draw the fragments of our selves together. As teachers, our lives had had purpose. In Vietnam there was the goal of retracing roots. What use could there be in lying in a tiny space on a Chinese train, ignorant of the language and the people?

'A young man receives a "call",' I read in Bruce Chatwin's *Songlines*, about the archetypal hero and his Road of Trials. 'He travels to a distant country where some giant or monster threatens to destroy the population. In a superhuman battle, he overcomes the Power of Darkness, proves his manhood, and receives his reward: a wife, treasure, land, fame. These he enjoys into late middle age when, once again, the clouds darken. Again, restlessness stirs him. Again he leaves: either like Beowulf to die in combat or, as the blind Tiresias prophesies for Odysseus, to set off for some mysterious destination, and vanish...'[4]

The seventeen-hour journey hardly made any inroad into China on our map. We were beginning to experience its size. It was partly this that made it seem empty after Vietnam. Yet Kunming is a city of three and a half million, as big as any in Australia. Our first impressions were of row after row of apartment blocks.

None of the drivers at the station seemed interested in taking us as we stood with our baggage, like islands in a flood, at six thirty in the morning. The lack of hassling was startling. Eventually we found a willing *pedicart* driver – a single-wheeled cycle attached to a wood and metal cart on which we balanced precariously. A hush was over the wide tree-lined streets, unmolested by the terrors of motorbikes, cars and karaoke. Most people were walking or riding pushbikes and the prevailing sound was the swish of rubber against road. The pavements were clean, the air cool. We were nineteen hundred metres above sea level.

---

[4]Reproduced by kind permission of C.B. Chatwin and Jonathan Cape, an imprint of Random House Ltd.

After two nights on trains, Thu and I were spaced out and let ourselves be drawn along in Rachel's wake – to a government hotel of eight storeys, where we took a room together for nine dollars, looking out into the foliage of plane trees on the street below.

A lady in a lab coat brought in thermoses of boiling water. She entered without knocking and we were given no keys. The door could not be locked from inside. 'You'll get used to it,' said Rachel. 'There are more bizarre things in China. Have a look at the toilets.'

I ventured across the corridor with caution. They consisted of a sloping tiled trough with space for three people, separated by waist-high walls and with no doors. From time to time water would gush from the cistern at one end, swilling away what was in its flow.

> Squatting in fume-fog
>   from piles left by others.
>   A window...
>   Ah! the sky.

Showered and free of burdens, we headed out into the day's adventure. On the hotel steps a woman with a wrinkled brown face was embroidering a bag, her clothes as colourful as her work. 'You buy?' she ventured cheerfully. 'This, Bai. Me, Bai.' It took a moment to realise she was referring to the name of her people. China encompasses about sixty ethnic groups, the Hans being the largest. More than twenty of them – including Bais, Mongols and Tibetans – are represented in Yunnan Province, of which Kunming is the capital.

Most pedestrians in the street were wearing Western clothes, many in miniskirts. Here and there were older folk in the caps and baggy blue suits previously prescribed by

Mao Zedong. We passed a row of people in white coats standing behind chairs, on one of which was a man having his head put through the contortions of Chinese massage. The practitioners were wearing dark glasses and we realised they were blind. Farther on was a man having his ears cleaned out with a minute copper spoon attached to a toothpick-thin handle. There were fewer children than we were used to in Vietnam.

Following Rachel's long hair and wispy frame, we ventured on to a jam-packed tram, then walked through an older part of town. The few hawkers who approached took no for an answer. People peered, as from a distance, in a kind of dreamy numbness. 'Is it so surprising?' said Rachel. 'After forty-five years of communism and the chaos of the Cultural Revolution?' Maybe it is also a legacy of the old way of valuing the 'negative' imprint of life. For the Taoist the essence of a bowl lies not in its design and shape, but the emptiness it encloses. The secret of success is *wu wei* or not-doing – to allow events to unfold out of their own wisdom.

Past narrow cobbled alleys, stalls and the hushed bustle of a market, we came to the old wall of the West Pagoda. Tin-roofed awnings lined the streets, above the green shutters of shops and vertical plaques of Chinese characters. Men in blue sat in clusters, staring, chatting, drawing in smoke through fat bamboo pipes or playing chess. Even the language was quiet, compared with Vietnamese. It swished and flowed, like bicycles and the breeze.

The pagoda with its red tower and branch-like roofs pointing to the sky was a reconstruction and the buildings by its garden, once lived in by monks, a tea house. It was pleasant and quiet – the click of *majiang* pieces, the music of conversation, goatee beards and blue clothes against the green shrubs and red paint. But it was no longer a place of devotion.

To get back into our room each time we had to present our receipt to one of the floor ladies whose moods varied from moderate cheerfulness to downright sullenness. Once, one of them came in with a bucket of water and proceeded to march her mop up and down the floor, leaving it wet and no less dirty. I had my feet on a pillow. She grabbed it and flung it onto the bed without giving away any sign of recognition that we were in the room.

On another occasion someone burst in at ten minutes to midnight shouting, 'Telephone!' Who on earth could know we were there?

It turned out to be the receptionist. 'You have not paid today,' she said. 'You must pay before midnight.' The lift was not working. Having walked down the six flights of concrete steps, I decided to reserve a smaller room for the next day since Rachel was due to leave. 'Not now,' came the reply. 'Reservations only in the morning.'

China's history over the past four thousand years is like the tides of an ocean. Woven between the many periods of prosperity – the Han, the Tang, the Song, the Ming – are times of chaos and contraction. Like the ocean too, it has had the ability to absorb. Tobas in the third century, Mongols in the thirteenth, Manchus in the seventeenth, one after another those who invaded merged with its ways. Even the religions that took hold were influenced by Chinese thought (a notable product being Zen, which began as a confluence of Buddhism with the Tao). So it was, at least until the last two centuries when the Western doctrines of capitalism then communism sounded the end for most people of the old ways.

In traditional thought, the ebb and flow of dynasties was accepted as naturally as the passing of the seasons and the interplay of opposites, of yin and yang. Heaven's mandate belonged to those who were morally worthy and, as corruption set in, would pass to others. Change was an intrinsic part of reality; yet the philosophy which could see life in this light itself resisted change. So, in the strangest of ways, China within which events of such drama have taken place – droughts, floods and famines as well as revolutions – has been profoundly conservative. And over and again there is reference to a golden age, long before the time of the first recorded emperor, which was seen as the source of its culture...

Rachel was intending to go to Dali in the mountains to the west. We were tempted to follow, but more important was to get our bearings in this new world. Our hope was to go as far east as Shanghai, north to Beijing, west to the desert of the Tarim Basin, and from there into Tibet. Chengdu was a priority on the way east because we intended to visit the lady who had been at the heart of the book *Wild Swans*, the mother of its author Jung Chang. The gorges of the Yangzi River beckoned too. So did Hong Kong, as a possible rendezvous with Luke and a place fraught with memories from my time there twenty-two years earlier. The rest would resolve itself with time's passing.

Making plans brought clarity and gave me a feeling of being in control, however illusory that may be for we both knew that events have their own ways of coming about. Part of what we had set ourselves was to learn to accept, more of a challenge for me than for Thu. In tight spots – like in those dreadful buses in Vietnam – I have tried to think in a matter-of-fact kind of way, Yes, it will be interesting to see how *this* one works out!

I focus too on the thought: I am in my body, in the thick of things; I am also in the events and people that meet me – and at the same time somehow above, looking on. It is in similar vein that I think of one's angel. Far above, but connected, attentive.

Before leaving that evening Rachel introduced us to a young man through whom we could get train tickets. 'Can't we buy them at the station?' I asked naively.

A traveller, his nose dripping into a flamboyant moustache, leant over from a neighbouring table. 'I vent today,' he said, with a triumphant snort. 'I not get neargh ze vindow.'

'Because it was so crowded?'

'Zey not vant me. I am thrghown out by ze voman, vaving brghoomsteeck. Zey're mad, I tell you. Cuckoo.' He snorted again and returned to his beer.

'Even I not get tickets at station,' said the Chinese man, more calmly. 'I buy from police. They not sell foreign people.' He told us that the commission he took helped him pay for university, adding that he would only be able to get the tickets on the day of departure.

'What if we check out of the hotel and you don't show up?'

'You foreigner, worry. I get, no problem. I meet you three days.'

'You can trust him,' said Rachel blithely, as we saw her into her night bus. 'And remember, if you take things too seriously in this country it will kill you.'

Memorable during our time in Kunming was our visit to Yuan Tong Temple, with its origins over a thousand years ago. By now we were familiar with taking buses, even if our powers of communication were as stilted as ever and we had to get a friendly waitress to work out which numbers to look for. Increasingly I had a sense of how it is to be dyslexic.

It was athrong with worshippers. Whereas in Vietnam joss sticks are lit individually or in threes, here they were burnt in great clumps, often with sweet-smelling herbs, and the air was thick with smoke from small fires. We entered the musty main hall with its three giant Buddhas – of past, present and future – above altars cluttered with incense, candles, fruit, rice, flowers and pictures. There was the festive bustle of a market, people walking from shrine to shrine, kneeling, bowing, striking cymbals or gongs, making offerings, praying or meditating. High above were two mighty dragons, their carved scaly bodies entwined around the tall red pillars, heads facing the Buddhas. What happened to this devotional energy during the time of Mao? I wondered.

Behind was a new pagoda given by the King of Thailand, gleaming with polished metal and spotlessly clean. Into the inner sanctum with its placid bronze Buddha we could only peep. The atmosphere was empty, untainted by dragons, almost sterile.

On a high place beyond, beneath a sheer cliff, we looked back over the two buildings, old and new, and I tried to comprehend the changes through which China has been catapulted this century – from a culture going back beyond history to an atomic superpower.

The extent of its trauma, the devastation and massive reconstruction, is in part a measure of its resistance to change. When the West started battering at its doors in the eighteenth century, it tried to ignore it as always before and rejected the bitter pill of scientific materialism. And because it refused to recognise goodness in what was coming as well as evil, the touch of the West became poison.

Time passes however for all people and the civilisation that once illumined the East was degenerating from within, with an effete imperial system and rituals that had lost their essence, when the British forced the opium 'trade' on it in the nineteenth century, and Japan and the West tried to carve up its land between them. When Mao took power in '49, kindling the hopes of millions for an age free of tyranny, it was the death knell of an era that had already died.

Our student friend was true to his word. On our last morning he handed us tickets for the evening train to Chengdu, made out in two Chinese names. The writing on them was beyond our deciphering skills, but he assured us they were genuine and that we would be able to get out at a station close to Emeishan, the sacred mountain, on the way.

'What if the inspectors don't accept them because we're not Chinese?' I asked.

'You foreigner, worry. No problem. They okay.'

They were – but our faith in them was to be sorely tested. We reached the station in good time, to find it crowded beyond anything we had imagined. There were thousands of people milling about, sleeping on benches or newspaper, eating, chatting, dreaming, spitting, arguing and playing cards, as we gingerly walked over them or squeezed past, struggling to keep calm as the press of bodies and baggage grew steadily stronger around us. About twenty minutes before departure, a voice spoke rapidly on the loudspeakers, doors were opened at the far side of the room and we were swept forward in the torrent, grasping each other's arms to stay together and fighting to protect our chests from having the breath squashed out of them.

'We're going to suffocate!' Thu shouts, her voice close to panic. Being shorter than I am, she can see nothing of where we are being drawn to.

'Head for the edge,' I shout back more confidently than I feel. 'Let the crowd go ahead. Our berths are reserved.'

We shove and slither sideways, all too aware of being enmeshed in a will that is not our own. As we reach one of the walls of the corridor into which the flood is being channelled, a set of doors opens in front of us and a second river merges with the main one, the current truly dangerous now. We press back against the wall, while the tide flows on past, waiting for as long as we dare before plunging forward once again, running now to reach the train in time.

There were seventeen carriages. With how many thousands of people were we to spend the night, so close, yet in such different worlds?

*

For the bearers of Chinese culture in the past, the earth in all its details was a reflection of the heavens. Just as there were constellations in the sky and dark areas in between, and just as there were phases of the moon and every kind of gradation of light from the sun to the dimmest star, so on earth there were places where heaven's power was strong and others where it was not.

Inaccessible, steep, wild, reaching high through the clouds towards the majesty of the universe, sacred Emeishan was for those who sought to curb worldly ambition and commune with the spirit behind the 'ten thousand things' of creation. Undergoing long periods of seclusion in such surroundings was a stage on the path of almost all spiritual disciplines, from martial arts and painting to philosophy.

For Thu and me the climb was a kind of pilgrimage. We also looked forward to the physical exertion and to being in nature, for the summit is over three thousand metres high; and we were fascinated by the thought of there being steps the whole way up.

Our intention was to spend the night at Baoguo Monastery, near the beginning of the ascent, but no one at the station responded when we mentioned it. 'You come with me. I take you,' said a young lady in English. She was wearing a yellow *chong sam*, the traditional high-collared, sleeveless, hip-hugging costume, which we were to see nowhere else in China. 'One yuan,' she added enticingly, and we followed her to a motor rickshaw – a scooter van like a Vietnamese *xe lam*.

'Twelve cents! There's got to be a catch,' I said to Thu. 'The monastery's twenty kilometres away.' But we clambered in meekly, glad at least to be going somewhere.

The catch was that we did not go near the monastery, but to a hotel a few kilometres from the station. 'No can stay Emei Mountain,' said the lady gaily and the receptionist nodded agreement. 'Sleep here tonight. Good hotel. Tomorrow, bus.'

We were at the steps by eight thirty. Already there was a crowd of people with straw hats and knobbly sticks, some with baskets on their backs. Coolies plodded up and down, loaded with bricks and household goods, or in pairs carrying reclining pilgrims on stretchers. Many were old and a good deal thinner than their human cargo but the bulge of muscles on legs and arms revealed their familiarity with the work. Those who were spare pestered us in vain to let them carry the pack – or Thu.

Whoever laid those steps, it is a remarkable achievement, at times rising almost sheer against the rock face. We baked in the sun on the bare concrete and stone, grateful for the shade of firs and cedars and the intermittent temples and tea houses. Everything in them would have had to be carried up by porters.

We paused at the prosperous-looking Wanniansi – Temple of Ten Thousand Years – and browsed in the coolness and tranquillity of its gardens, courtyards and fine buildings. Pilgrims prostrated before inward-looking Buddhas, while the monks on duty sounded their bells. The central attraction was a massive bronze statue of the bodhisattva Puxian, the legendary guardian of the mountain, who is said to have ridden a white elephant which could fly.

Higher up, on the edge of a sheer drop into a valley far below, was a shack of timber and bamboo with a single bench. An elderly man brought out two glasses and filled them with green tea from a charcoal-black kettle. We climbed on into cloud, earth becoming mud, steps slippery, water drip-dripping on leaves and stones and the ubiquitous plastic.

At moments the swirl of veils would withdraw, revealing a fragment of peak or a sweep of tree-clad slope – the stuff of Chinese paintings. Then it would be gone. I saw why mist features so often in Zen and Taoist art. I had thought of it representing the emptiness out of which the manifest world appears. Now I experienced it as an element of that world itself, ethereal but no less real than roots and rocks.

Or monkeys – of which there were many, well versed in the arts of snatching. I saw, too late, the wisdom of carrying a stick. Most pilgrims were well armed with peanuts which they would throw into the air, to watch the animals scrap. They taught us the language of showing one's empty palms, which the monkeys respected with remarkable gullibility.

We spent the night at the monastery of Xixiang, a rambling place of stone, wood and iron, with ornately tiled roofs, secluded courtyards and long dark corridors. Its name means 'Bathing Pool of the Elephant', presumably the bodhisattva's. The man in the creaky reception hall quoted us a foreigner price. 'That can't be right,' I protested, innocently showing our guidebook. 'Look what it says here.'

'I understand. You are cheap travellers.' And he cut it in half, then ushered us along a sloping floor past jagged window panes to a room with naked wires in place of a light switch. From a large and ancient boiler, an old man allowed us a bucket each of hot water with which to shower in the stone-cold wash area. The toilets were foul.

At dusk the clouds cleared enough to reveal a momentary swathe of orange light and piles of rubbish on the cliff face. Glimpsing our environment of tall green crags, it was as if this motley spread of buildings had risen out of the rocks – or been dropped from the sky on to the narrow shoulder on which it perched. We had climbed over a thousand metres.

The following day we climbed as high again, through pine forest, fog and rain. How close were we to the edge? Both the danger and the beauty were hidden from us.

All at once a wooden building appeared, then another, then the strident sound of horns and engines and suddenly we were at a road. We gaped in amazement, then walked on past shops to a bus park as big as a city terminus and packed with vehicles. Music blared, raucous through loudspeakers.

On the steps leading farther up, slippery with mud, was a solid mass of people pushing and shoving in all directions. I plodded on, feet wet, sweating beneath plastic, while images of Dante's *Inferno* churned through my mind. On both sides were stalls selling food, umbrellas, trinkets, fans, paintings and medicinal herbs. Then, out of the fog and rain there loomed a high structure of iron and cement, awash with bodies. Another temple? We sat beneath a covered walkway, eating apples and chocolate and feeling the gloom. The crowd became a river. The penny dropped. It was not a temple – at least not of the old kind – but a cable car station for the summit.

It was cold. Maybe since half of China was lining up here, the steps would be less crowded. They were – on the way up, at least. At intervals we passed women squatting on their heels, devotedly sweeping the rubbish into scrub and ditches on either side. At times the smell of excrement was nauseating. The rain was heavy now and Thu was falling behind.

What is it in me that desires to go on to a summit? According to our guidebook, there was a shrine to the Ten Thousand Buddhas at the very top, an hour's walk beyond the Golden Summit Monastery at which pilgrims and tourists end their trek. I was keen to go the whole way, but by the time we reached the monastery Thu had had enough. 'We're soaked and exhausted!' she exclaimed. 'And I feel sick.' Neither of us knew she had altitude sickness. We saw it only in retrospect, when we reached the really high country months later.

It was not hard to find a hotel and Thu passed out on the bed. I lay down too but my mind was restless, and within minutes I was up again. No one seemed to know anything about the summit. From the edge of a shoulder I peered out into the billowing whiteness as the fog swayed, licking the mountain and tempting me to entrust myself to its cotton-wool softness. For an instant it opened and there was the peak, bare, dark and glistening with water, deserted but for a triangulation point; and between, a gaping chasm.

I asked again for the path. This time the recipient of my few words and ample gestures confirmed at least that it existed. 'But you cannot go,' he added. Why? I searched our phrasebook. Broken? No. Dangerous? No. Narrow? Still no.

'How long will it take, then?'

'Three hours.' It was four thirty. It would be dark by seven.

'I'll try.' He was still reluctant to help; then, like so many Chinese when giving directions, made a vague gesture that included about ninety degrees of the compass. One small path after another I followed, but they petered out at garbage heaps or toilets in nature. I got my foot caught on a plank with a nail sticking out and at last accepted reality.

When is it appropriate to push through with one's will and when to give up? One of the many beautiful aspects of the science of old China was its relationship to time. What mattered then were not cause and effect but the *qualities* of each moment with all their circumstances – on earth, in human hearts, in the elements, the stars. People lived *within* time's recurring rhythms and sought to reflect its hidden currents even in the smallest details of life. Thus there were times for action and inaction, times of 'thunder rising', times of the 'still lake'.

The script of this science was nature and the universe. Confucians tried to imprint its patterns into society, from the emperor as sun through the planets of warlords to the star dust of the people. The way of the Tao was to flow outward into the world in each unrepeatable moment and allow the world to flow within. Outer and inner were a single essence, ever in movement and eternally still. 'Am I a man dreaming of being a butterfly?' asked the old sage Zhuangzi. 'Or a butterfly dreaming of being a man?' Am I a Westerner stubbornly following his will – or a dragon mountain, shrouded in white breath, itching with people-fleas?

By evening, Thu felt a bit better and we went to the monastery, the sky suddenly clear. From its outer walls we looked over a vertical drop of a thousand metres and more, then farther down over rolling hills to a miniature world of rivers, roads, rice valleys, vegetation and towns. Beyond were other dragon teeth, sheer and sharp, but lower than ours; above, the sky, indigo and salmon pink against mounds of yellow-specked fleece. Once hermits would have lived here like eagles, at one with the elements.

The temple is a fine structure, several storeys high with orange tiles, red columns and massive doors embellished with calligraphy. In one of the halls a service is taking place and we stand at the entrance, pressed against others, by the bronze tripods in which people place incense. A hand touches my waist. I look down, expecting to see a child. A fragile lady in Maoist blue, eyes bright, face tanned and deeply lined, gestures that she wants to go past. I squeeze out a space and she slips nimbly through, taking her place among the kneelers.

She bows low, grey hair against stone.

2

'That *can't* be her,' Justin whispers in disbelief, as we wait by the guardhouse to the block of state-owned apartments. A woman is coming towards us, energetic and smiling broadly, in her mid-sixties, short hair permed and dyed black. She is wearing trousers and a T-shirt with large flowers. Meigu, our young interpreter, talks with her then introduces us. 'Welcome,' says Mrs Xia Dehong. It is our second day in Chengdu, capital of Sichuan Province, renowned both for its culture and spicy food.

We shake hands; and putting her arm round my waist, she steers us along the corridor and upstairs into a tastefully decorated apartment with a modern lounge suite, book shelves, rugs and pot plants. The sight of them brings to my mind Jung Chang's description of how grass and flowers were declared bourgeois in the Cultural Revolution, and how she and other high school students had to dig them up. But people loved their plants, she wrote, and some survived.

We sit on the settee while Mrs Xia makes tea. Reading *Wild Swans* had been an excellent preparation for China. The idealism Mao inspired in the early days of communism and the benefits it brought to the poor were as vivid as the insanity of destruction he unleashed later. The story spans three generations – a grandmother with crippled bound feet; a mother, who committed herself to the revolution with all she had, even at the expense of her family, and who was later victimised by it; and Jung Chang herself, now a modern woman of the West. Mrs Xia, the mother, went through terrible suffering and torture, and her husband died from it. I had expected to see a thin woman with a tired spirit.

'*Cha* – tea.' She puts down the lidded bowls of hot liquid with green leaves settling at the bottom and sits in one of the armchairs, Meigu in the other. 'The custom of tea offering has many meanings,' she says. 'It's an offer of friendship. Drinking it means you've accepted.' The host keeps your cup filled with hot water, she explains, so it never grows cold – a symbol of an ever-warm friendship. Traditionally, a man proposes marriage by offering tea to the girl he chooses, who answers by taking or refusing it. She invites us to sample roasted seeds from a lacquerware dish. 'You have to break through the shells to find the heart,' she goes on, smiling as Justin struggles to open them, often crushing the soft kernel.

On the phone the night before, she had said she would discuss anything but politics, so we asked about her life. She said it had been good, for all its hardship. The government left her alone now, though there were people in power who disliked her. She was happy that the book had helped others understand China and the revolution. Her life had served a purpose, and she proudly showed us a library with translations in many languages.

I asked her what had kept her going. She was silent for a while, then words flowed out without interruption for six or seven minutes. By the end Meigu, who until then had been chirpy and a bit pushy, was visibly moved. She said our hostess had been asked the question before, so had had time to think about it. Ultimately what it came down to was love – for her husband and family, colleagues, friends, country and ideals.

She spoke of her current work with poor people in the province. She had slept little since hearing that one of the ladies working with her had been taking bribes. 'Still the same problems I've had to grapple with all my life,' she added. Nevertheless, though most of her children lived overseas, she was quite clear her place was in China.

Justin told her of our work and when he spoke of educating the heart, she touched her own and said, 'In China too, that is what we long for.' We took photos on the balcony, among the luxurious pot plants. She spoke again to Meigu and hugged me goodbye.

In the taxi back, Meigu asked many questions about the book, still banned in China. She said she knew little about Mao, only that he had done glorious things for the people's revolution, followed by a lot of damage with his Red Guards. She did not understand why his statues and pictures were still around. The three of us shared what we knew.

Back in 1912, when China became a republic and Sun Yatsen its first president, the nation was destitute, split between warlords who were bleeding the peasants, and threatened with invasion by Japan. Though Sun achieved a degree of order, the country was still crippled by division when he died in '25 and the leading place in his Kuomintang (Nationalist) Party was taken by General Chiang Kaishek.

Chiang saw himself pretty much as a new emperor and had little interest in reform. Though the Communist Party, formed in '21, initially allied itself with him, it was but a marriage of convenience; and six years later he tried to eradicate it in a massacre in Shanghai. It was after this that

Mao Zedong, who had been training peasant leaders under the auspices of the Kuomintang, took to the hills of Hunan with the beginnings of a guerrilla army.

'We learnt that at school,' said Meigu. 'And about the famous Long March.'

It had lasted a year and covered five thousand miles in incredibly harsh conditions. As they moved, the Red Army seized land and redistributed it to the peasants, arming thousands and organising guerrilla groups. Although only twenty thousand out of ninety thousand made it to the end, it proved Mao's point that the revolution could be based in the countryside; and it brought together people who would later hold key positions in the People's Republic, among them Zhou Enlai and Deng Xiaoping. This was in '35.

The civil war dragged on until '49 when Chiang fled to Taiwan with the country's gold reserves. The decade that followed brought dynamic change as Mao roused the people to catch up with and overtake the world outside. They nationalised factories, set up farming cooperatives and built new railways. And to begin with, the results seemed awesome.

But behind the scenes, a catastrophe was in the making. The forcing of farmers to abandon their traditional ways; the obsession with isolated aspects of industry, such as steel production, to which everything else had to be subordinated; the misreporting by officials who were terrified to admit falling short of the quotas set by Beijing; low incentive for work and the stagnation of a system that rewarded political allegiance more than experience or training; all this combined with nature's harshness to produce a famine in which tens of millions died.

Cracks started to form in the leadership, but Mao remained the most accomplished in the art of power politics. The mistakes were blamed on others, while he fanned the embers of idealism in a new generation with his credo of perpetual revolution. The bureaucracy had become 'revisionist', the nation in danger of slipping back into its 'feudal and capitalist' past; a cultural revolution was needed to set it right, with Mao's thought as its guiding light.

It ignited a nightmare that even he could not control. It was during this that Mrs Xia and her husband – who had both been on the Long March, she pregnant at the time – were denounced and tortured.

'It's incredible!' Meigu exclaims. 'All this and she's so gentle.'

'Who knows?' says Justin. 'Today's meeting may have been as much for you as for us. Perhaps you can see her again?'

'I've already arranged to.'

The night was muggy and my mind had a will of its own, stirred by so many images of violence. That volcanic power of destruction that erupted during the Cultural Revolution, do I not know it in my own depths, in Justin too? He is normally a kind person and people who know me say I am neither bad nor mad. What happens then when dark emotions break through like lava, obliterating our ordinary way of being?

All at once, it was as if a trapdoor opened and a black swamp began to swell upwards from below, like a monster with a hundred writhing heads. Its power was of the ocean and it took all my strength to keep myself, in horrified silence, from falling in. I could barely breathe until at last, in agonising slowness, it withdrew.

It must be there all the time, I realised, but normally beneath consciousness – the quagmire of resentments, anger, hatred and all the other discarded and unresolved elements of my human nature. Something that one denies at one's peril. And the thought came: had not the imperial system in China, as it became decadent, done just that in its attempt to shut out evil and suffering from its midst? While the few lived in lofty refinement, the masses toiled, unrecognised; and beyond was a world of 'foreign devils'. Then would come the backlash, such as tore the country to pieces during the Cultural Revolution.

'It's tranquillity month,' Justin announced gaily the next morning, as we plunged out on bicycles to explore the city. Accepting the day's events with equanimity was the third in the series of exercises we were undertaking, following on from concentration of the mind and control of the will in the first two months.

Along wide streets, lined with flowering trees and shrubs and the unceasing flow of cycles, were tightly packed shops busy with customers. Hawkers and food stalls crowded the pavements, people squatting at the kerbs with scales and baskets of rose-pink peaches. Everything was in abundance, from areas with whole streets selling just one commodity (spices, eggs, soaps, lanterns) to supermarkets with televisions and refrigerators. In a narrow alley, bustling with fortune-tellers and beggars, were stalls selling joss sticks and firecrackers. We rode past an open-air clothes factory with rows of women behind old-fashioned Singer machines whirr-whirring against the background of traffic – and a colossal statue of Mao.

We came to the university, a spacious campus with clean white lanes for bicycles. Although on holiday, a number of students were around, seemingly relaxed and purposeful. Were the ghosts still there of a generation before?

The 'Red Guards of Chairman Mao' had their origin in '66 in a group of youngsters from a high school attached to one of the universities in Beijing. Many were children of officials, brought up in the religious cult of Mao and the militant doctrine of class struggle. They began by smashing up the system which 'treated pupils like enemies', unleashing their hatred against anyone in authority. Schools were closed, then universities and offices, as they roamed the streets, joined by older people, and set up courts of denunciation in one part of the country after another. Their actions received 'most warm and fiery support' from the Chairman and his wife, and the arms they used often came from the police.

I was studying in Sydney at the time. Like many other students, I felt excitement at the changes sweeping through the world, bought Mao's *Red Book* and had idealistic discussions about the struggle to break away from tradition. Blissfully unaware of what was actually happening, I saw Mao as a symbol of the modern quest for freedom.

The violence spread – against tea houses, temples, libraries, antiques and anyone with wealth, even friends and parents – fired by slogans such as: 'We can soar to heaven and pierce the earth, because our Great Leader Chairman Mao is Supreme Commander!'

In the end, factions within the Guards were fighting as well. China was on the brink of civil war and Mao had to call in the army to restore order. The fire was out, but society gutted.

And the human heart withdrew behind veils of blankness as its only way of surviving.

At a restaurant in town the following evening, we asked for tea to accompany our chilli-hot meal. '*Bu cha* – no tea,' said the waitress, taking away the food we had not finished. She ignored our protests and brought the bill. So it was that we moved to Lyn's Burger, a backpackers' café we had been avoiding for its crowdedness. 'Hi, I'm Hal,' said a Chinese man who joined us over ice cream. He was about twenty-five and owned the café. His English was good, though he seemed frazzled by the demands of customers.

What amazed me most was that he had his own ideas on everything from economics to politics, philosophy to education. He spoke of the tension between individuality and the state, personal faith and organised religion. He scorned empty tradition, yet paid tribute to the ideal of serving parents and country and to the extended family system which I had found so suffocating as a child. In college he had joined a Christian group, then become disillusioned by the history of atrocities done in Christ's name and moved to Buddhism. 'But I still can't believe in reincarnation,' he said, embarrassed. 'I'm at a crossroads.' And he was suddenly silent.

So were we, as we struggled to take in all that he had shared with us. 'I feel something in me that wants to express itself,' he continued with new emphasis, making a vertical line from above his head to his chest. He said that politics still controlled many aspects of daily life, even though there was much more openness as regards business. His dream was to become a teacher – but outside the current system with its political bias.

A young woman walked towards us. 'Ah, the lady of the café,' he said affectionately. 'We run it together.'

Her face was gentle, with strength in the cheekbones emphasised by short hair. She said she was a teacher of small children. 'We sing about sun, moon and stars,' she went on, in halting but clear English. 'I tell stories.'

'Is that the normal way here?'

'Oh, no.' She shook her head a few times and paused. 'I get trouble sometimes. Not enough science and politics and exam work.'

From then on we took most of our meals at Lyn's. Often we would find them poring over the brochures about education we had lent them; and they gave us lessons in Mandarin.

One afternoon Hal treated us to a ritual of bitter tea made in a terracotta pot, the size of a small apple, which he poured into cups little bigger than a thumb. Three sips of it sent my head spinning. He now suggested the four of us go to a tea house, or *chadian*, where one can sit and drink endlessly, play chess or, in certain places, watch performances of storytelling or singing, for almost nothing. He said it would be a better place for conversation.

The one we chose was a family chadian with a large room and outdoor area. It was filled with people back to back on bamboo armchairs, eating boiled peanuts, empty shells covering the floor. Sounds wafted out – of talking, arguing, laughing, babies crying and the thudding of billiard balls. Tobacco smoke swirled in the air, mingled with smells of sweat and jasmine. Children squatted on the concrete while tea pourers shuttled between the seats with enormous kettles, filling up cups with spouting liquid from half a metre above.

Braving the mosquitoes, we settled for a table beneath a willow outside. Two beggars stood beside us, hands reaching, faces mournful. 'Don't give,' said Hal, seeing us vacillate. He spoke to them harshly, mirroring their gestures, and they shrugged and walked away.

Jasmine tea mixed with three other kinds was brought in small bowls with lids and saucers. A kettle man came by and filled them to the brim. It is said that a skilful waiter can make the water higher than the edge of the cup without it spilling. 'Now,' said Hal, after our third round. 'Tell us more about this education.'

We spoke of children growing up and the tendency today to look on them as little adults, forgetting how we ourselves once thought, felt and behaved. It is a different world.

The golden key in kindergarten is to recognise that small children learn by taking their surroundings into themselves, even the mood and tone of our thoughts and feelings, and by acting out over and again what they have absorbed. 'They are the thunder and the trees, the caterpillars and stars,' I said to Lyn. 'And the angry or loving adult beside them. That's why it's such a responsibility being with them. They are laying down patterns for their lives.'

The key in the primary years is that children think in images and are much closer to their feelings than adults are. Therefore the content needs to touch them in a personal way, to speak to their hearts. Art in its many forms is a medium for doing this, for it brings life to what is otherwise abstract. So too, the relationship with the teacher and others in the group. 'How one teaches is as important as what one teaches,' Justin put in.

'*Wei ren shi biao*,' said Hal. 'Confucius. To be a teacher, you must be a model.'

Though dictators may wish it otherwise, independent thinking must be an aim of any healthy education today. Its vitality and strength depend very much on what has taken place before it emerges in adolescence. 'It needs nourishment,' Justin went on. 'Just as our bodies do. Dry facts in the primary years are like stones. They come alive only through imagination and the warm interest of the heart – which become the free spirit of thinking later on. It is this we need to awaken in the secondary school.'

It was twilight when we walked back along the river. The pall of pollution was heavy overhead, as muggy as a greenhouse. In the night, a storm blew up – piercing lightning and thunder that shook the building. Tension dissolved; it cascaded rain, showering my face through the open window in sharp fresh lashes. I floated away into the vast super-earthly rumbling.

Was I the thunder – or the tired body on the bed?

It was on our last day in Chengdu that we got through to Luke by phone and confirmed we would meet in Hong Kong in two weeks. What a relief! His voice was stronger; he seemed to be finding his way.

Our train for Chongqing on the Yangzi River was due to leave that evening and we had arranged to share a last meal together at the Burger. We found Hal absorbed in composing a letter to teacher training colleges we had recommended in England, the US and Australia. He read out what he had written of his life. It began:

> *During a rare October typhoon, a couple of poor villagers were rushing to town in a cart pulled by an old water buffalo. The man whipped the animal repeatedly to get his wife to the hospital in time. But it was too far and the buffalo too slow. My original name, Che Sheng, means Born in a Cart.*
>
> *I spent my childhood in the village and on the land, growing vegetables and rice, herding buffaloes, geese and ducks. I was sent to the local school when I was eight. The reason was that I needed a 'holiday' from the fields. My parents had never been to school and that was what they thought schools were for.*

Then Lyn gave me a last lesson in Mandarin. For the first time I had an experience of that elusive wind-like 'S' sound, for which one has to curl back the tip of the tongue against the palate. As an adult I had to watch and listen from the outside, then try and copy it consciously. Were I still a small child, tongue and larynx would move out of an inner participation in the other person's action, in a spontaneous empathy of will.

★

'In the old mysteries,' I read to Justin, from an article called 'The Michael Impulse' by Ita Wegman, 'those who were to be initiated were recommended to undertake great journeys, so as to come to know the manyfoldness of the world; to feel the contrast between regions of coldness and moisture, on the one hand, and dryness and heat, on the other, and to take into themselves all intermediate conditions.'

In the heavily polluted air outside, it was forty-four degrees and as humid as a sauna. In the air-conditioned café of the Chongqing Hotel we were in icy paradise. Around us, smartly dressed customers lunched on fish and chips, sandwiches and beer, attended by staff in red and white uniforms. A couple were holding hands across a white tablecloth adorned with a red rose and ice cream cocktails. We had two more hours to wait for our boat on the Yangzi.

The train from Chengdu had disgorged us at seven thirty that morning into a huge industrial port with belching chimneys and no bicycles. It had puzzled us, until we joined a minibus headed for the river and experienced the steep hills that make up this partly ancient city. At the dock the streets were lined with ticket offices vying for tourists. Young men with salesman smiles called to us in English and pointed to billboards with pictures of luxurious cabins. Our instinct was to go for one of the less ostentatious establishments.

We found one and relaxed on the sofa under a pelting fan. The ticketing lady was smartly dressed in a suit, her gestures brusque. Justin was appalled at the prices and wanted to economise in a dormitory. Since our journey would last three nights I felt the need for privacy and comfort. We took a second-class double for eighty dollars each. 'I bet the Chinese pay twenty,' he said, grudgingly.

'Anyway, it's done. Let's enjoy it.'

We left our packs in the office and went out to explore. In the street we met a group of Italians who invited us to share a six-bed cabin for forty dollars a head. We declined, explaining our situation. 'There's no such thing as a double in second class,' one of them said, a tall man from Milan. 'You've been hoodwinked. I'd get a refund if I were you.'

It spun us into a turmoil, Justin in particular. We checked at another agency and were told that second-class cabins had four beds. The tall Italian came back with us to the booking office. 'Don't give in,' he said. He seemed to take a delight in the thought of vengeance and his insistence played a part in the ugliness that followed.

The brusque lady now said our cabin would have three beds and showed us a picture of it. 'So why did you tell us there were two?' Justin's voice was hard.

'Only one more person,' she replied. 'What's the difference?'

He said he wanted the money back, at which she blanched. 'No refund,' her voice high-pitched.

'Tell her you'll call the police,' whispered the Italian. 'See how she reacts.'

A man walked in and sat down at the main desk, looking at us enquiringly. He talked at length with his colleague, seemingly scolding her as a boss would. 'I'm sorry for the misunderstanding,' he said reasonably. 'We cannot refund. If you want a two-bed cabin, you can upgrade to first class.'

Justin dug in. He seemed as stony as the lady. It took fifteen minutes to reach a settlement in which Eastern face was saved and Western righteousness soothed. We got a discount of twelve dollars.

'And you're sure there are only three beds?' Justin said, as they shook hands.

'I guarantee.'

There were not three but four. And in the cabin, as we came in, were five people smoking and drinking, the television blaring. We stayed long enough to register that the air-conditioner was barely working, then plunged back into the corridor. Justin demanded in unspeakable Chinese to see the 'boss' and we were admitted into the refrigerated lounge next door by a timid lady who said, 'You wait here,' and locked us in.

We began to freeze. The door opened and a young man in uniform entered, locking it behind him. He greeted us politely and as Justin began to offload, the door was unlocked again and another man came in. They spoke together briefly then the first one left. Next to enter was a woman and before she finished the ritual with the key, I escaped into the heat of our cabin, in which peace now reigned as the visitors had gone and only the couple who were to share it with us remained. They were sitting on the beds by the window – she plump, pretty and pushy, in a satiny pink petticoat and black nylons; he older with an open face and smiling eyes.

It was a small neat room with clean white walls and ceiling, and a reasonably new carpet but for the chewing gum and hair stuck to it. I unpacked what I would need and sat on one of the beds by the door, staving off the heat with a paper fan and settling in to the boat's gentle sway. We were moving. It was a moment we had looked forward to.

The Yangzi is the world's third longest river, reaching all the way from Tibet to the China Sea. It waters the heartland of China and yet, true to Chinese thought, it has its shadow side too, for the huge volume of water can swell into floods that wreak mayhem on vast regions and imperil the lives of millions. What was drawing us were the gorges through which it passes, to the praise of generations of Chinese poets...

'Well, at least I didn't get angry,' said Justin, suddenly standing by my bed, shivering with cold. 'Even if I didn't achieve anything else. Except banging my head against a wall!'

His presence made it easier with our companions, who gestured us over to share their rice wine and sweet things. 'China love Australia,' said the man in English when we told him where we came from. 'America, no. Now, yes. Money.' He shrugged. 'Me, Shung. Lady, Wei.' Our conversation for the next few days would be an exotic hybrid of our two main languages.

We managed to ask him what he did but, as so often, could not grasp the answer. 'Mercedes,' he tried again. 'Rover, Nissan. Good.'

'Mechanic?' He raised his head in the gesture that looks like it is going to be a nod, but then freezes in negation. 'Sell cars?' Same gesture. 'Driver?' He beamed, relieved. And we raised our glasses.

Wei fiddled with the knobs on the television like an excited child, speaking rapidly in a petulant tone, then lay on her bed and fell asleep. Shung took out a photo of three children from his wallet. 'Me, father.'

I glanced at Wei.

'Wife, Canton. She, flend.'

Wailing songs poured from the address system, then a female voice speaking at length. Our companions insisted on taking us to the scrummage of the restaurant three decks below to show us how to order. The harsh clamour of voices mingled with the press of bodies and the smells of sweat, food, fishy water and garbage. The large round tables were covered with dishes. As people left, the waiters scooped up the half-eaten food and threw it into the river.

'These, for you,' said Wei, putting down a plate of 'thousand year old' duck eggs by the other bowls of food that had accumulated on our table. Pickled in spices and buried in straw and lime (though not exactly for a thousand years) they have a jelly-like texture and look like transparent green and yellow eyes in black sockets. Next to us were three men washing down their own meal with beer, intermittently throwing back their heads in laughter.

As we ate, Shung said we were passing a special place. 'Bad-bad,' he emphasised, screwing up his eyes, then when we still did not catch on, pulling at his mouth, ruffling his hair and smearing chilli sauce over his cheeks, to depict the devils for which the temples of Fengdu are famous. 'Now we sleep,' said Wei with a giggle when the food was all gone.

Justin and I lingered on the lower deck, gazing at the turbid water and the bobbing plastic. As we watched, full garbage bags plummeted into it from various positions on the boat. At intervals we passed towns against the backdrop of brown-green hills and smoggy sky – identical apartments with clothes hanging outside, and in various degrees of disrepair.

Then I attempted a shower. It had been out of action the day before because the knob had been removed from the cold tap and the hot water was scalding. It was apparently the opposite in the men's, with the hot tap missing. Shung thought it was to stop people wasting water! A crew member turned the tap on for me with pliers and the temperature was perfect. But it took a while to find someone to shut it again and I wondered what would have happened if I had not done so.

I got the answer soon enough – a steaming flood on the carpet outside the cabins.

We stopped at a place with a temple nestling among trees against a cliff. Two ships as large as ours were already there, and our contents merged with theirs in a river of heads and bodies in the evening light. There must have been close to a thousand people and we were virtually carried up the steps by the current.

It consisted of a maze of rooms, balconies, courtyards, passages and traditional tiled roofs saturated, despite the Revolution and the crowds, with the culture of centuries. Shung said it used to be a centre for martial arts. On the walls were lacquered boards of calligraphy and classical paintings – pale-pink blossoms with a green and yellow butterfly; a sprig of bamboo; chrysanthemums; a misty lake against cliffs with two ink blots for boats. The stones in the courtyards were rutted and worn smooth; the crimson banisters, cracked with age. In the master's room were a carved upright chair and a table with a miniature tea set.

I grew up with stories woven around places like this, in Chinese classics such as *The Water Margin*. In the Confucian tradition prevailing in Vietnam then, girls were discouraged from reading, especially fiction. It was said to corrupt morals and turn us into bad wives, so I used to hide under a bed or in a cupboard with these enormous volumes.

There were endless legends about the wise old masters and I used to identify with the young men and women who came from far away to be admitted as disciples. For years they would be put to work in the kitchen or yard, as a moral preparation for the powers they would later develop. Each further stage would depend on their diligence, patience and centredness, in a process of learning that continued until death.

They made journeys through forests and over mountains in search of adventure and the opportunity to do good, in the ever-varied struggle with evil. Only later did I realise these were descriptions of initiation. As in the legends of Arthur or Parsifal, danger, sorrow, joy, courage, failure, love and death were the threads in the tapestry of their lives. Mistakes too.

There is a Zen story that goes like this:

A monk lay dying in his old age, attended by a disciple.

'Master, if you had your life again, what would you do differently?'

'Make more mistakes.'

'Why?'

'Because then I'd learn more.'

'You know I seem to have lost some money,' said Justin quietly as I was about to fall asleep that night. 'Maybe someone took it in the crowd.' He had found the zip on his waist belt open. 'It's what we got back from the ticket people,' he went on. 'What is that saying to me?'

We woke to the thudding of feet and the droning of the loudspeaker. I realised we were more sensitive to its chatter because we could not understand what was being said. Normally one tunes into the meaning and ignores the sound.

The ship was nearing the first of the three gorges and we followed the stream of people onto the deck, which had until then been firmly locked. The chocolate-red water was a flood now, a torrent, the wind fresh in our faces as the canyon walls drew close and we raced, seemingly out of control, into their daunting shadow. Dark cliffs, half a kilometre high, threw back the surge and the throbbing echo of our engine. In days gone by, riding these waters would have been heroic, especially when going against the flow, hauled up by hundreds of people with ropes. A few sampans were being pulled even now; but the larger boats and barges, which we scattered with our siren as we washed by, had motors.

The second gorge was longer but wider and less sheer. By then, however, our allotted half an hour was up and the officer in charge approached us with a peremptory, 'Finished. Down.' And the door was locked again.

The ship tied up near a concrete town, and the crowds filtered into rows of narrow long boats with outboard engines for an outing up a tributary river. The water was low but the current strong against us, its bed a carpet of many-coloured pebbles, and several times we had to get off as men with bamboo poles strained against the rapids, muscles bulging, motors screaming. Higher up, it was deeper, jade green and crystal clear, swirling in vortices, sliding over rocks. Cliffs towered upwards to dizzying heights with here and there a red curved roof and calligraphy on the rock. Shung pointed to caves high as eagles' nests, saying they were the tombs of emperors from two thousand years ago. He acted out the process of lowering the coffins from above and then removing all traces of their location.

We asked him about the regular square holes cut into the cliff face a few metres above the river. He said there had once been a hanging wooden road, attached to the rock. Had it been on such a perilous highway that ancient heroes in flowing robes had once ridden, fast as the wind?

In the evening we were allowed onto the front deck again while the ship passed through the third and longest gorge. By now the cliffs had become dusty slopes as we came closer to the vast eastern plains. Twilight descended, the breeze cool and pleasant. Jupiter appeared, that much closer to Venus, but a brown shadow hung over everything.

It was dark by the time we reached the lock at the Gezhouba Dam. There were at least twenty boats, several abreast, and the water took half an hour to go down. It was a weird festive atmosphere with three tourist ships close together, garish with lights and music. The massive metal gate, half a metre thick, slowly opened, controlled by invisible computers. The dripping walls gleamed in reflected light, our cruiser a toy by comparison. The wonder I had felt beneath the cliffs of nature became fear at the might of technology.

The bigness of China hit me. Those mighty gorges and turbulent waters were moral teachers for people of old. They taught humility and inspired courage and one can see this still in the old paintings – humanity a dwarf against nature's brush strokes. Century by century the human being has grown bigger and the landscape smaller until, in the art of Maoist China, the whole canvas is taken up by smiling faces, cheeks pink as apples. Nature's power becomes our slave. Who is left, then, to teach us?

Our last night on the boat. From Yueyang, we would head south to Yangshuo in the direction of Hong Kong. As we exchanged addresses, our friends gave us two medallions, one of a laughing Buddha, the other of Guanyin the compassionate; then two stones. 'This is you,' I understood Shung to say as he placed the red one on the bed. 'You are the earth that goes round. This white star is me. It circles, falls and collides with it.'

He also wrote down in Chinese a small verse which means:

> We have loved each other.
> Now we go our way.
> We will miss each other.

*

Yangshuo. Through rain-splattered windows, fairytale peaks beckoned in swirling mist, stirring up memories from my childhood hideout in the cupboard. We had been moving for five days and nights and the anticipation of being in one place for four days was exquisite.

When the rain cleared, we ventured out into uncrowded streets, colourful with cafés, restaurants, art galleries, clothes and souvenir shops. An artist was creating a landscape with a few quick movements of fingers and hand, dipped in black and green ink. A repair man glued some tyre rubber onto Justin's sandals which were wearing thin. At Lisa's Café, its tables spread out on the square, we celebrated with mashed potatoes and salad.

We walked to the river, the Liyang, flowing placidly through the town to the backdrop of limestone pinnacles, bare or bearded with foliage. A solitary slim boat floated by, the boatman a still dot.

> Like water is the Tao!
> For water brings life to all things
>   and does not compete.
> It flows where none would deign to be.

So speaks the *Tao Te Ching*, 'The Way and its Virtue' – a collection of verses and sayings attributed to the 'Old Master' or Laozi, two and a half millennia ago.

The Tao speaks not to the intellect but a state of being at one with the world, as a small child is. For the ancient Chinese it was the foundation of all existence, of heaven and earth, yang and yin. It was the Way, the creative sound in the universe, comparable to the Veda of ancient India and the Logos of the Greeks. It was as real as the air and as essential for life. 'Fish live in water,' sang the old Zhuangzi. 'Man in the Tao.'

If the Tao existed then, I thought, it must still exist now. But how can one find it?

Before I saw his face I saw his hands, the sight so unexpected it repelled me. They were covered with warts, even on the palms, and seemed no longer fully human. He told us later he had them all over his body but the worst were on the hands. I turned away and ordered tea from Lisa, the owner of the café. She had organised a boat to take us upriver to the village of Xingping, from where we planned to ride the twenty-five kilometres back by bike. We got up to go. The traveller with the warts and his girlfriend got up too.

We were all four in pretty poor shape, Justin with a cough, Anna with a bladder infection, me with an unsettled stomach and Will the worst off of all, for what he suffered was long-term; and during the tranquil three-hour journey he told his story. Light shone radiant on the peaks on either side of the water, their reflections like giant emerald flowers, pointing to unknown depths. Swallow-like birds flashed among the reeds.

His ordeal had begun at the age of five with a kidney infection which necessitated long stays in hospital. By his early teens he relied on dialysis treatment, first with a machine, then learning to change the bags himself four times a day. 'I felt weak and unclean,' he said. 'I had to force myself to take part in life. Then my mother donated one of her kidneys.' He paused. 'It was the first time I had known what it was to feel well. But after that the warts started. It's because of the drugs to stop my body rejecting the new organ.'

We glided on, past pinnacles with names like 'Paintbrush' and 'Cock Fight'.

'It reached a point when I felt I had no worth.' He had tried everything – radiation, surgery, homeopathy, spiritual healing. 'The healer told me it didn't work because my "window" was closed. It's true I'm cynical, but there it is. I even went to a sorceress in Turkey.'

I asked how he had been treated in the East. 'Sometimes like a leper, sometimes okay. The best was in Arab countries. They accepted me as one of them.' He added that he knew such things were taken as predestined in Asia. To him it was just a defect he had to live with. 'I'm working on my scepticism, though. At least I believe in love.' He was convinced it was his mother's love which had kept him alive, as well as her kidney. And there was Anna.

We had lunch in Xingping, then headed out into the sun and wind and landscape. For two hours that day China revealed herself in her beauty.

The empty lane wound through villages of mud walls and shingle roofs as we raced or meandered, or stopped to chat with local people. On both sides were rice fields and peasants in straw hats bending over new shoots or beating grains from sun-bleached stems. The tall peaks stood like guardians behind – 'colourful and in different postures and making you feel intoxicant,' our tourist brochure informed us. But there was something else that was different which I could not identify at first. It was the first time the sun had shone for us in China. Yes, of course. The shadows!

We came to a small town with dusty streets and smoking chimneys. 'The Heartiest of Welcome, Far-Sighted Personalities! Come to Fuli. Set up Shops and Factories!' proclaimed a banner in English. And all at once the sky was black, thunder rumbling, zigzag lightning. The wind came up so strongly it threatened our balance and we took shelter in a lean-to by the road, shivering in the near-darkness. The wind tore off leaves and whipped them into vortices in the air, on the tarmac, in the air again. Rain fell in buckets.

Nothing else existed. 'God, the power,' said Will, in a hypnotised whisper.

Anna spoke then, almost for the first time. She had been inward with her illness but the storm drew her out. 'I guess Will and I are looking for a direction. We've been through a lot together and it's been good travelling, but there's something missing.'

She asked what our book was going to be about; Justin had mentioned it earlier. 'You're not the only ones at a crossroads,' he replied. 'Nothing is certain any more, even the future of the planet. Fear and darkness can easily overpower us, but we can also see it as a process of initiation, of being jolted to wake up, worldwide. That's what I'd like to write about.'

It was still raining the next morning when we met for breakfast and there was talk of floods in the direction of Canton which was where we were all heading – Anna and Will in a few hours, Justin and I later that evening.

We hugged each other. And I held Will's hands.

The sleeper bus is an exotic creature which had only been introduced, we were told, that year. Inside were twenty-five almost horizontal chair-beds plus a few ordinary seats, separated by two aisles. The air-conditioning did not work and I was alarmed by the smoke and lack of space. I took heart from the thought that if I slept for twelve of the fourteen hours the trip was meant to take I would be in Canton in no time.

The first of the hold-ups began within an hour. The rain had not ceased all day and a truck had skidded onto its side across the road. Its cabin was empty but people were squatting in the dark nearby. There was no sign of any emergency services. Next stop was at a café; after which the road deteriorated to mud, gravel and potholes. Then at eleven we stopped decisively behind the black shapes of vehicles, illumined ghoulishly from time to time by distant headlights. 'You realise this country has atom bombs and satellites?' said Justin.

An occasional truck passed by from in front, but there was no movement in our line. We lay in darkness. Midnight came and suddenly our driver was in action, bypassing the stationary vehicles until we came to one, deep in mud in the middle of the road. Memories flooded of Africa, of trucks buried to the tops of their wheels in mud holes as large as our Kombi. A cable was attached to our bus and we revved in reverse, wheels burning. Several times we tried and in the end the leaden beast had moved barely a metre.

But it was enough. One by one, lumbering shapes roared towards us, lights blazing. Way beyond, I could see headlights as more traffic joined the flow that was against us. The hardest thing was to hold in my will and not let it waste itself on something over which it could have no influence. This was for the driver to deal with; our role was to wait.

At last the tide turned, and as we inched forward we saw the second bogged truck behind the first. The only way past was to wriggle between.

I slept, intermittently jolted by potholes, and woke at six to find ourselves stationary again by a violent river, brown and swollen. In the grey dawn I clambered down. The line of vehicles stretched on as far as I could see, a number of them loaded with pigs in bamboo cages on top of each other. The day's heat was growing and pathetic grunts came from their bodies as we saw bits of snout, ears and trotters sticking out between the struts. By the wheels was a pool of their fluids moving sluggishly into the ditch.

'Accident,' a boy indicated in gesture and Chinese. 'Rain. Taxi. *Kaput.*' There had been a mudslide. He acted out bulldozers and ropes. I needed desperately to relieve myself but there was nothing to hide behind, and despite Justin's prodding my shyness would not let me.

I went back to bed, feeling a fever coming on. The two men next to me, having chain-smoked much of the night, had started afresh, talking querulously. Below was a young couple wearing shining wedding rings. As the girl tenderly wiped her partner's brow with a handkerchief, he turned his head, scraped loudly and spat out a blob of phlegm on the floor between their bunks. She waited for him to finish, then resumed her stroking.

It took five hours in terrible heat to get through. An hour of breeze and we were on another patch of red mud pulped by tyres, with piles of stones packed tantalisingly by the side. We were held up at another accident in which two people had died. A man's body was lying by the road, his face beneath a newspaper. Then at last – the tarmac.

But our relief was short-lived. Our driver, so patient hitherto, was now a maniac. For a while I watched in horror as we wove in and out of traffic; then I closed my eyes and prayed, committing myself and those with me to the protection of our angels. It is something the buses of Asia have taught me how to do. And when, months later in another country, the bus that Justin and I were in went off the road and turned over during the night, the presence of something higher in our midst was as palpable as the mangled metal, the shattered glass, the noise of the engine still running in the blackness, and the groans of those who were hurt.

We reached the port at Canton just in time to catch the overnight boat down the Pearl River to the 'Fragrant Harbour', better known as Hong Kong. Our journey of fourteen hours had taken twenty-six.

Red and white uniformed hostesses welcomed us into the spacious carpeted interior. Air-conditioners purred softly. We were in a dormitory of over a hundred bunks, as neat, clean and comfortable as a luxury hotel on the mainland. Showers and toilets were spotless, rubbish bins lined with fitting bags, everywhere signs of 'Keep the ship clean' and 'Do not spit'. As I was about to pass out, I saw Anna and Will in another part of the room. But I was too far gone to greet them.

Hong Kong

Light was gaining fast, the city across the water sparkling with sunrise and wealth, as Thu and I stood on the deck. Twenty-four years before, how I had longed to leave. Now, after our month in China, how good to be back. We felt the breath of freedom and realised the strain under which we had been. I had the feeling of having been in a kind of inner wasteland – akin to the deserts we would be entering in coming months in the far west of China.

Everything depends on where one is in one's journey through life. As a young man I had left this place in disgust at colonialism and the self-interest of business. I longed for an alternative to material values. In the ensuing years I realised that the spirit works in many ways, not just through ideals. And now thoughts came that I would have treated with contempt before: for all the materialism there is a spirituality in Hong Kong.

It is connected with its lifeblood, trade – of anything with anyone, initially opium forced on China. It is not a place where the morality of trade has been much considered, but it is an organ of the world where currents flow together – and there is freedom and life. On one level, what Europeans did in their colonies was violent, racist and egoistic; on another, one can equally say that what has emerged in Hong Kong, through the combination of British planning and Chinese ingenuity, on a previously deserted island, is a kind of miracle.

Good flowed with wrong in what the British brought to the world. Beyond the racial arrogance and plunder, there entered a spirit of internationalism and of human rights. For all its distortions in practice, the essence of the law they spread is equality.

'So all this is to be handed over to China in '97,' Thu said as we steamed into the heart of the harbour. It seemed to me then that, though Hong Kong's wealth had depended on Chinese labour and business with the mainland, and though the British had no option but to hand it over, what Beijing was to receive was nevertheless, in part, a gift.

At the post office in Kowloon, on the mainland side of the harbour, was a casual note from Luke suggesting we meet at McDonald's, that ever-spreading representative of Western culture in Asia. 'Cheapest place to eat,' he said breezily, when the hugging was done. 'Gunk,' said his dad.

He was relaxed and happy. Had only a month passed since that haunting goodbye in Hanoi? 'What of your future?' Thu asked.

'It's okay. University, I mean. Just so long as it's not all theory.'

'And before that?'

'I'd like to come to China with you. But not yet. There's a girl I met...'

We wandered through the gardens of Kowloon Park – packed, but with no trace of litter – as Luke let the memories of the past month flow into our midst. Notices by cages of colourful birds announced fines of five hundred HK dollars (about seventy US) and fourteen days in prison for anyone feeding them. Elsewhere were warnings of five thousand dollar fines and up to three months' imprisonment for littering. By the harbour the figures were twice this.

We walked on in the sultry heat through a maze of old streets bustling with restaurants and shops. Vegetables and fruit spilt out onto the pavements; dried fish, squid, octopus and crimson fat-strewn sausages dangled on hooks above barrels of spices and roots. The smells were as rich as the colours – warm, musty, putrid, exotic – all intermixed with the clatter of buses and fumes of trucks, the cries of hawkers, the street games of kids. Piles of golden paper, gifts of 'money' to the gods of prosperity, blazed in small fires while women with plaits prayed softly, raising and lowering the joss sticks clasped between their hands.

A goldmine with zero unemployment, Hong Kong was not a good place for cheap accommodation. The best deal we could find was a windowless box in a grotty high-rise building, with an air-conditioner we could only use at night because of the heat it belched out into the corridor. No fresh air or natural light, toilets and showers communal and tiny but clean. For this we paid the cost of luxury accommodation in China.

Luke befriended a young engineer from the UK in a neighbouring room and as we squeezed together in our cramped space (about the size of two double beds), he told us of the antipathy between Beijing and London over the coming transfer of title. He said the Hong Kong government was reinvesting its surplus in construction, while what Beijing wanted was cash. Also that, despite China's assurance that nothing would change, many people were trying to leave. One of the most vulnerable groups were the local Indians, who were not being accepted as citizens by Hong Kong's new masters.

He spoke of legislation being passed to enshrine democratic voting despite the colonial method of government practised hitherto. 'Hong Kong will not only be a money mine,' he added, 'but a wedge of the West in the side of China. Foreign poison, like opium, but far too tempting to be turned away.' It gave me a glimpse into the dark side of the 'gift' I had envisaged that morning.

The visit to my old place of employment on Hong Kong Island, across the ever-bustling, light-glinting water, churned me up a bit. The company now had its own high-rise building and I recognised nothing except the emblems and photographs of old steamers and modern tankers and container ships. None of the people with whom I had been close were still there, but there was a Chinese man whom I remembered with affection and who was now a director.

'Ah yes, Justin,' he said, welcoming us into his luxurious office. 'I wouldn't have recognised you, but I remember how you were. An idealist, hey?' He looked scarcely older than before, a little rounder, more stooped and mellow, but with the same beady-owl look and benign humour. 'People here are more pragmatic,' he went on. 'We don't put energy into ideals. We accept reality and turn it to our own advantage. That's business, you see.'

A lady brought us tea in a set of deep-blue china. 'I do now,' I replied. 'I guess you need to be able to take risks and make hard decisions. No doubt patience and a clear head come in too. All I could see before was selfishness.'

'Greed confuses the mind,' he said, with his contented twinkle. 'A business person must learn to be detached. Your son looks just like you.'

'More hair,' I replied, and he touched his own immaculately combed and similarly balding head with good grace, saying, 'Old age has its beauty too. For us Chinese, growing old is a virtue. *She* knows that.' And he beamed towards Thu.

On one occasion he and his wife had taken me out to the so-called New Territories, the land on the mainland leased to the British years after they had seized Kowloon and the island of Hong Kong. It was surprisingly rural – streams, rice paddies, orchards, villages and small temples gleaming with red and gold. The place of our picnic was the family tomb. 'Here there's peace,' he had said. 'Where the old ones live.'

'And after '97,' asked Luke. 'Will you stay?'

'Of course. China knows the value of this place. They'll make changes but business will go on. It's as unstoppable as water. Besides, they need big companies like ours.'

I shared the thought I had had the first day about the element of gift in the handover. 'Ah, Justin,' he replied. 'You're still an idealist. I'm sure your wife knows better. Imagine that someone kidnaps your baby and brings it up to become a brilliant person. Would that compensate for the loss you suffered? You must see it from China's point of view. All children return to their mother – and she receives the bad and the good they bring back.'

As we stood to go he said with his expansive goodwill, 'I haven't seen as much of the world as you have; but I've cultivated my garden, if you understand what I mean. You know, Justin, if you'd stayed, you might now be sitting at this desk yourself.'

His words echoed on, arousing the many-headed demon called 'what if?' It was at twilight on the Kowloon waterfront, looking back across to the tall towers on the island, many newly sprung since I was there before, that thoughts started to move in answer. Around us on the spacious benches, residents and tourists were chatting in the gentle breeze. A little boy, feet not quite touching the ground, struggled to get off the seat to take an empty carton to the bin nearby. As the day withdrew, the skyscrapers glittered and garish neon colours danced and splintered on ripples and black swell, awash with tugs and ferries and piers. How good that after twenty-four years there could be friendship still between a businessman and an 'idealist'!

Until that moment I had thought of my time in Hong Kong as having been simply a forerunner to going to Vietnam. Now I recognised it as having a teaching in its own right. And though I ran from it, it nevertheless worked on in me, as all experience does. It was not only 'out there', this place I used to hate and now could respect. It was inside too, like a friend – or enemy – from an earlier part of one's life.

'I like your friend,' said Luke. 'Do you wish you'd stayed?'

'How can you ask? You wouldn't be you, if I hadn't left.'

But it was more than that. It was as though I could see now with the objectivity of distance what had tormented me as the need to go to Vietnam – something incomparably stronger than mere wilfulness. I glimpsed that freedom is doing what we must do, consciously and in full acceptance. We can wriggle and curse, but we cannot destroy the power in us which moves our lives. And if we do not work with it, slowly it changes from a force of creativity to one of destruction.

'We'll come back to it, Luke,' was all I could add. 'There'll be time in China.'

Luke met Chen in the lift the next morning. 'Strange guy,' was his comment. 'He's Chinese but doesn't dare leave his room. He hasn't even been to the island. He asked if I'd show him round and said he'd pay me.'

'Is he all right?' Thu asked with concern. 'I mean, can you trust him?'

'He seems really gentle, almost feminine. I said I'd have a drink with him.'

'Aunt Thu,' said Chen in Vietnamese when Luke brought him back later. 'I'm *so* relieved to meet you. These

Hong Kong Chinese terrify me. Nobody smiles and they're really aggressive. Luke says he'll take me to the island. He's so brave.'

His voice was high-pitched and he spoke rapidly, with stylised hand movements. Though Chinese – from the island of Hainan off the south coast – he had lived most of his life in Vietnam. He had emigrated to the States as a refugee and done well, first as a cook, then in a trucking business, and was here on holiday. He said he had come for the shops and restaurants. But perhaps there was a more hidden reason.

We had lunch together in a fast food plaza and he insisted on paying, though he hardly touched his food. 'They don't know how to cook here,' he said scornfully. 'Next time I'll take you to a *real* restaurant.'

Then he told us he had escaped from Vietnam by boat during the anti-capitalist purges in '78, of which the ethnic Chinese, who controlled much of the economy, were the main victims. It had been one of several reasons for the deteriorating relations with China, which culminated in the Chinese army's 'punitive' incursion across the border in '79 at terrible expense to itself. Chen's boat made it to Hong Kong. His first experience of the place had been from behind barbed wire. But he was one of the lucky ones; many were still there, refusing to go back, and with no country willing to take them. 'Will you visit the camps?' Luke asked.

'Oh no,' he said, wriggling in horror.

I no longer knew any of the staff at the magazine for which I used to write. The company had changed hands and was owned now by people whose profession was money, not writing. We were welcomed into a room with a magnificent vista over the harbour, and into the library where they kept copies of past issues.

Looking through my articles, I was surprised to find ideas I had thought belonged to a later time in my life. It brought home that our development is a process of deepening and ideas can be far ahead of our inner state. They light things up; but to understand something we need time for it to sink in, to be pondered and weighed and, for a while, forgotten.

Luke asked why I had not stayed with the magazine. It was another 'what if?' The staff had been supportive when my Vietnamese visa was withdrawn with no reason given. I was invited to cover the whole region of Indochina; there was even a chance of visiting Hanoi. The truth is, I was exhausted. I needed distance to take it all in. 'Why don't you write something now?' he said suddenly. 'About Vietnam.'

We were introduced to a sub-editor, who outlined their current interests. What they were after were facts and informed analysis. What I had to offer was more subjective, but we agreed that an article about the massacre site of My Lai might be relevant. 'It's a matter of where one's focus is,' I said to Luke, as we left. 'I guess I'm more interested in trying to see world events as symptoms of what's happening in human evolution.'

'That's fine. But it doesn't mean the details aren't important too. In their own right.'

It was mid-afternoon, the peak clear of cloud for the first time. We opted to go back to Kowloon and lure Chen up there in time for sunset. By the time we were on the island again it was evening and traffic was at its height. As we waited for the bus to take us to the peak tram, my mind raced on ahead and I became irritable.

'Hey, crazy light,' exclaimed Luke suddenly, taking out his camera. 'Look at that building.'

High up, its glass side was a flame of bronze – the drama in the sky which caused it hidden from our sight. Idiot, I thought to myself. Who was going on earlier about seeing events as symptoms of something greater? What need to reach the top? Sunset is everywhere.

Twilight became night and on the top at last, we looked down over a jewelled harbour sparkling with man-made light. Chen was not interested in the view, rather in the shops and trinkets. But he was also happy simply to be – with us, with the buzz, with himself. Part of Luke's chaperoning involved taking his photograph in each place they visited, and he would look on in benign bewilderment as Luke focused with his own camera on a mere neon sign or rock, or a stranger's face or foot.

We stood by a display of coloured lights and fountains – spurting up or resting, high and low, fast, slow, separate, together, in a kaleidoscope of patterns, electronically controlled. It was another kind of beauty, based on technology and wealth, and self-contained, not dependent in any way on the daily drama of earth and sky.

All at once I felt tired. 'I'm ready to go back to China,' said Thu.

'Me too.' It was extraordinary how sudden was the change.

We decided our way out of Hong Kong would be by boat up the coast to Xiamen, halfway to Shanghai. Now the time had come for making reservations Luke started to falter. 'You guys are always in a hurry. I might stay and get a job for a few weeks.'

We held off another day and Chen invited us to breakfast at a tea house full of the Cantonese delicacies for which he had come to Hong Kong. It was a feast. As the ladies wheeled their trolleys to our table, loaded with plates or bamboo steamers, he would peruse the contents and exclaim enthusiastically, 'Yes, *this* you must try!' or wave them on.

'Did you see that?' Luke exclaimed.

'What? The prawns?'

'No. That waitress smiled. It's the first time I've seen such a thing in Hong Kong.'

'They're nice to you because you're foreign,' said Chen in his conspiratorial way.

'You call it nice?' Luke replied. 'Being treated purely according to how much money you're going to spend? The other day I was told to leave a store selling cameras simply because I was looking around and not buying.'

'They despise me,' Chen went on, 'because I'm a different sort of Chinese. I can feel it. Ah, *this* is special.' He selected a plate of brownish chicken claws, a delicacy for its spicy sauce and tender cartilaginous chewiness. Each dish was so varied, colour and texture as important as taste, and without grease. At the end were the sweets and lychees.

On the way back, Chen ducked into a shop and came out with a box of exquisite French pastries. 'For you,' he said, presenting it to Thu. 'You are my family.' He declined our invitation to come to the History Museum though. 'History is dull. I'll go and sleep.'

Hong Kong's 'story' was cleanly presented in writings, artefacts, photographs and models. Free of smells, textures, noises, insects and heat, we entered into houses, junks and streets from the beginning of the century. I have come to appreciate the teaching our bodies give. In our minds we can go anywhere, but bodies are heavy things and the laws that rule them inexorable. Wherever they are, we are *there*, and they draw our souls back to face what has to be faced. In the real Hong Kong of 1900, what emotions we would have encountered!

So much has changed. Up to '49 when China became communist, the culture, dress, beliefs and superstitions on both sides of the border were much the same. Westerners were but ships in a Chinese ocean. Since then, the old ways have passed – again on both sides – and what has sprung up between has been the monumental divide between poverty and wealth.

In the fifties the tallest buildings were only a few storeys high. Massive growth began in the sixties, but more radical was the change in lifestyle. Early photos show men with heads shaved in front and a plait down the length of the spine. They reminded me of the cobras often depicted behind images of Buddha, symbols of the central nervous system and of the old clairvoyant consciousness.

In the West, I thought, as in the East, has come a new world order, in many ways uglier and more dangerous. The plaits have been cut and we are loose on an uncharted sea. But it is from that cutting, inside each person, that we have the potential for evolving further – into a clairvoyance, no less spiritual than before, but based on independent reason.

First thing next morning I had a further encounter with a 'what if'. It took the form of the fan, low enough that if I stood on the double bed it could chop off my head. The room was so small that I had to walk on the bed to cross it. Groggy from lack of air and light, I stood up.

It happened in a second, the body's reaction so fast I could not control it. Yet I was aware of every detail – the slicing of the iron sword through my hair, within a whisper of the scalp, then being hurled back down before the moment of contact. Is not this the lightning action the martial artists of old strove to master?

Luke was still not ready to decide and I became impatient. He muttered again about our speediness but came with us to China Travel; and once he had decided, perked up. We had three days left.

On one of them he and Thu went off with Chen to visit Lantao Island, and I shut myself up in our box with a hired typewriter and memories of two months before. In a hard-headed magazine read by diplomats and business people, could I write of forgiveness? How could I know that was what had really happened at My Lai anyway? Was it not just my own subjective feeling?

Perhaps it is an appropriate moment to clarify further the words 'soul' and 'spirit' which have appeared at intervals in our story. Within the soul are all the feelings, emotions, impulses, images and thoughts that characterise our inner lives. Our tendency is to move between likes and dislikes, and this filters and colours what we perceive and the conclusions we make.

Perceiving with the spirit means allowing that which *is* – within and without – to reveal itself. Whether I like or dislike something is irrelevant – whether I judge it bad or good, beautiful or ugly. We attain to spirit activity in so far as we are able to still our souls and bodies through and through and use them as an instrument unclouded by bias. An eye which is in pain and therefore preoccupied with itself is failing as an eye. Its task is to be transparent, selfless. It is not similar with the soul? When its own voices and demands die down then it too can become an organ of perception. Is this not the essence of poetry, science, art, Zen – indeed of journalism itself?

I did my best with the article, then headed off to explore the park by the seventy-storey tower of the Bank of China, my thoughts still engaged in the question of objectivity. In how many different ways must this reflective triangular obelisk appear to people? To one as a place of work, to another a travesty against nature, to a third a sublime expression of lines, angles and equilibrium. How varied are the experiences of a tourist, a local, an engineer, an artist, a hater of banks, a lover of China, a window cleaner, a child, a New Yorker or a person who has never been in a city!

Does it matter that each one perceives through personal colouring? The intellect says it does and in its attempt to get away from the subjective reduces everything to abstrat mathematical concepts. The heart speaks differently: imagine being able to encompass all possible perspectives, even those which are opposed to each other! Is this not also reality?

I see my shadow and that of the building. This helps; the sun unites us, relating to each without favour. Yet with what different results – the mechanical effects of warmth on glass and steel, compared with all that I can experience through a human body and soul! I walk on. Stillness in traffic's ocean; rainbow on a dragonfly's wing.

Twilight on swallows and concrete.

On our last night in Hong Kong we had a farewell dinner with Chen. He wanted to take us to the night market for a seafood extravaganza. We had glimpsed it before – trays of fresh fish, squid, eels, crabs, prawns, winkles, whelks and many other shells, cooked on the spot and eaten at bare tables in a blaze of electricity and a surge of shoppers. But we had packing to do and I felt the pressure of time, so we ended up in the usual food plaza.

It was a sombre occasion. Words seemed to run dry and the silences were solitary rather than uniting, each one perhaps thinking on what the dawn would bring – for Chen too would be leaving the next day. 'I wish aunt-uncle could taste the seafood,' he said sadly, his plate untouched. 'At least let's go and have pancakes and ice cream.'

We did and it felt better. There is an art in being able to honour moments when the heart needs to speak but has no words. With my dullard sense of duty and orderliness I nearly ruined his way of saying, 'I'll miss you, for you're my family.'

He barely looked at us when we parted and only absently shook our hands. For it was in the delight of exquisite things shared together that we had encountered each other; and it was in those moments that we had already said goodbye.

China – East

3

Five minutes before departure time Luke, Thu and I were still at customs. 'Don't worry,' said a middle-aged American man. 'This is China. The boat won't go until everyone's ready.'

It was a modern ship, clean and spacious. Our cabin was twice the size of the room in which we had spent the past nine nights. Outside our window was a large pile of bulging garbage bags. As we drew away from Hong Kong – the island a silhouetted peak in the haze, the sea air blowing strong and fresh – a member of the crew came and threw the whole lot overboard. 'Damn!' said Luke. 'The oceans are bloody choking.'

The sun set over the water, red and distant in the mist. Then the moon rose, huge and hazy, and I realised how out of touch we had become with the night sky. Three moons already since Australia. Even in moonlight we could see plastic every time we looked over the side.

'It must be possible to do *something*,' Luke went on. 'Can you imagine if every government in the world agreed to a clean-up week?' We have the technology but we lack the will – or rather the recognition of a crisis to activate it. We also lack the heart. 'Third World' blames 'First World' for its hypocrisy in advocating environmental awareness while producing most of the waste. 'First World' looks down on 'Third World' for its primitive methods of disposal and lack of education. 'Imagine!' he continued. 'Military ships, fishing boats, tourist liners all sweeping the seas and rivers. Ships from all nations. It's worth thinking about.'

We went below with Thu and played cards in the freezing air-conditioning of the bar. I lost thoroughly and enjoyed it. Now *that* is progress. Luke was still in full spate at the end. In Hong Kong we had seen a film about the oil fires in Kuwait after the Gulf War. It was in the domed cinema of the Science Museum and the fire fighters, projected huge across the ceiling, would have seemed like gods to the many children there. The message was the atrocity of Saddam Hussein and the power of goodness when people pull together. Teams had come from many nations and a task that could have taken ten years was completed in nine months.

We spoke now of another form of heroism, the humble one of giving up something for the sake of others before one is compelled to. Were the fires caused by the evil of one man? Or were they equally a consequence of a world economy based on self-interest, in which some have abundance and others barely enough to survive? Is it not this that spawns dictatorship – and the technology that produced the fires in the first place?

We reached Xiamen around eight in the morning. It could have been such a good night, we had everything in our favour – calm sea, distance from the engine, comfortable beds, right temperature, no karaoke or canned music. But my chest was welling catarrh, its source too far down to reach. I understood with a trace more sympathy why the Chinese preface their expectorations with such a violent scraping of the throat. No sooner would I clear it a bit, than it would be back, threatening to choke me.

With its proximity to Hong Kong and Taiwan, Xiamen is a 'special economic zone', in which a more flexible attitude has long been accepted towards free enterprise. Prior to '49, like other ports on the east coast, it was under colonial rule and much of the architectural finesse and general well-being stem from these factors. The streets we walked along were clean and orderly and shops well supplied, though without the super-abundance of Hong Kong. There was a quality of light clearer than in any place we had yet visited in China – from the ocean and the openness in people.

A young man, tight and thin, approached us wanting to practise English. 'Where are you going, sir? Can I help you, madam? How do you like our city?' The questions streamed out in succession with little breathing space between.

'Do you know the Xiaxin?'

'Indeed, yes. Many foreign guests stay there. Will you permit me to guide you?'

Were there strings attached? I wondered even if he was a spy with his glibness and intensity. But he remained polite and helpful and when we reached our destination, simply gave us his card, saying his name was Hua and he would like to meet us again.

We were given a generous room with light streaming in through the windows. 'Right, folks,' I said. 'Let's clear the slate, okay? A fresh start in China.'

Luke assented with raised thumbs and a grin. Thu opened a window and took a deep breath. 'Ah! Light and air,' she said.

Did we have a presentiment of what was coming? It is easy, looking back, to fasten on symbols of doom – the redness of Venus through the ship's smoke, the sickly yellow of full moon, the awful clutter in the ocean. Maybe we had dreams but did not hear their message. And if we had known, would it have helped?

Our days in Xiamen were full and we were tired each evening, but we slept well and were happy. I look back with affection on our room where the sombre event began, with its white walls and cheerful red curtains.

We went first to the station to book sleepers for Shanghai. Floors, benches, stairways, steps, even the square outside, were jam-packed with people. Queues were the length of the hall and we did not know where to begin. We could wait for hours and find it was the wrong window or that they would not sell to foreigners. The atmosphere was sullen, on the edge of hostility. 'Forget it,' said Luke. 'Let's get out of here.' But he was torn by wanting to experience it too, and take photos.

A travel agent outside mentioned a boat, saying we would have to make reservations at the harbour. On the way I bought some medicine for my catarrh. It claimed to have won first prize in a pharmaceutical competition in Canton, as an answer for 'sore throat, phlegm, pneumonia, bronchitis, laryngitis, tonsillitis, back pains, anxiety, stress, sleeplessness and impotence'. Its main ingredient was snake bile.

We reached the office at four. A sign announced the closing time to be five but the girl at the window looked at us disdainfully, shrugged, then turned away muttering '*Mei you*' – that familiar phrase meaning 'not have' or 'no' which can turn Westerners into raving beasts. I asked why in Mandarin. She ignored me and I asked again. Still no reply, so I simply stood there in front of her, in the way I had learnt, confident *something* would happen.

It did. Luke exploded. 'Damn! Why do they make it so unpleasant?'

'Because we're a nuisance, I guess. If we're ignored enough maybe we'll disappear.'

'You come tomorrow.' The voice was from a neighbouring booth.

'Why not today?' I asked as we moved over; but I was asking what should not be asked and the lady did not answer. I tried again: 'When does the ship go to Shanghai?'

'Four days,' she said in English. 'Tickets tomorrow.'

Time was running out for us to get to the Himalayas before winter. Could we afford four days in Xiamen? What other option was there? We asked at the hotel but no one was optimistic about buses.

At two in the morning I catapulted to the end of my bed, unable to breathe. The ghastly noise I made woke the others and Luke was hitting me on the back in the instant. It was like being in a glass capsule. I was aware of Thu next to me and of Luke rushing out of the room and down the stairs – and of still not having drawn breath when he got back. I thought, To die now... It doesn't make sense. Only then did I remember the spiritual world and called inwardly for help.

As the breath at last came through, the others were as shaken as I was and insisted that we find a doctor. The night watchman appeared, calm and considerate, roused by Luke's knocking. He led us out of the hotel, round a corner – and there, lo and behold, was a hospital.

Along a drab corridor was a bare room with chairs and a desk. A lady in a white coat listened with a stethoscope and took my blood pressure. She seemed preoccupied with my heart. Two other ladies in white joined us and I was given a glass of fiery liquid, which briefly made me choke again, and two tiny pills.

They insisted that I sit in an invalid chair. It had no arm rest and a wheel that kept falling off when it was pushed, but I was told firmly to stay put while Luke and the watchman lugged and pulled me three floors up to a room containing two bare beds with wooden planks and rush matting. Another lady appeared and gave me a more thorough check-up. I was surprised she only listened to my main pulse, not the more subtle ones of Chinese medicine. She then wheeled in an old electro-cardiogram.

Luke started to mutter. 'What's that for? Heart no problem. Lungs.' And he acted out struggling for breath. She put the plethora of electrodes on my chest and looked at the screen, then moved them and looked again. She fiddled with the recording arm but it seemed to be dysfunctional. Why this concern about my heart?

Next came a nurse with a drip outfit, including two unwrapped needles rolling about on a tray. This scared us, Luke most of all. 'There's no way they're putting that in your vein,' he exclaimed and gestured for her to take it away. 'Look, it's his lungs, do you understand? He couldn't breathe.' And he repeated his imitation. I was as concerned about offending them as about having the drip. She looked confused, then left.

Our hotel friend asked why we had turned it down. Thu looked up the word for 'dirty' in our book. 'No,' he said. 'Needle clean.'

It was nearly four and I suggested Luke go back. First thing in the morning he would contact Hua, the man we had met in the street, and ask him to come and translate. I was given more pills and another cardiogram, this time with the paper register working. Thu was allowed to take the other bed. What was the message in all this? To my surprise I slept.

My father died of a heart attack and his father before him. During my twenties when he had his first crisis, a fear burrowed into me of my own susceptibility. What finally took me to a doctor in Sydney in my forties was my waking up at night, drenched in sweat, with chest pains. To my astonishment, though he diagnosed weakness of kidneys and liver, toxins in the blood, chaos in the relationship of one organ to another, imbalance between nervous system and metabolism, he said my heart was strong.

For years I had worked with the thought that the heart is far more than just a pump and that the blood is moved in ways that are infinitely more subtle and diverse than in the mechanical model that prevails today. I knew, from science studies at university, that the circulation in a chicken embryo is active before its heart has been fully formed. It comes naturally from the surrounding warmth – and, I believe, a deep will towards life which we share with the animals. Steiner connects our circulation with the power that moves the planets. To embrace such a thought one has to go beyond the concept that the human organism is self-contained, like a motor, needing only fuel to make it work.

The heart is an organ of rhythm and balance; that much I could see. When we move and stimulate the circulation, it responds; when we are still, it responds again. It is sensitive even to our thoughts and emotions, forever equilibrating the extremes. To begin with I grasped this only in the mind, but more recently, as a result of working with children and through the crisis between Thu and me, it sank in more deeply. I felt horror at the thought of a mechanism that *drives* in my chest, and began to experience a new loosening there, like ice melting in the spring sun. The result was pain as well as relief. But little by little I was learning to listen, not only *to* the heart but *with* it.

Luke came at eight and shortly after, our friend Hua. It was as we had suspected – the staff were more concerned about heart than lungs. 'My heart's okay,' I said valiantly, but submitted yet again to a cardiogram.

'Now we test your lungs,' I was told and was dispatched to a dingy room with a bored-looking official. All the patients I passed in wards on the way were attached to drips; all the staff were wearing white coats, cleaners as well as doctors. Hua later told us that they are all considered 'medical workers' and have the same basic salary.

'Only one X-ray, please,' I say meekly to the man who mutters, 'Yes, yes', puts on special glasses and turns out the light. In the darkness comes a series of clicks, then his hand moves me roughly to a different angle, followed by more clicks. And in the end there is no photograph but a cartoon drawing of the lungs and a series of Chinese characters. It has been like the machine at our shoeshop through which I gazed so often as a child in fascination at the bones of my feet – before it was banned.

How much radiation had I absorbed to allow this surly man, who spoke no further word to me, to look into the hidden places of lungs and heart? Anger stirred. Was this what I really needed, with my proneness for cancer?

To the end, the doctor insisted the problem was in the heart. She expressed concern about our coming journey to Shanghai, saying there would be inadequate medical facilities on the boat. She respected my wish to leave however, and took Thu to get medicines – more heart pills plus some antibiotics.

Then at last, the street. The noise of traffic. What joy!

Our remaining time in Xiamen was spent largely in recovering from the hospital. I took the antibiotics but not the heart pills and threw out what remained of the snake bile. While Luke and Thu went to the telegraph office to phone the travel insurance company in Australia, I hid in our light-filled room. I had been so absorbed in protecting my heart I had almost forgotten the ailment that caused the trouble in the first place.

Luke came back radiant, almost crying. 'Take this, Dad. The lady *listened* to what I had to say! She even put me through to a nurse at their expense. They said you mustn't panic. Your body will get the breath in if you let it.'

He was less jubilant in the evening, when he returned from a meal in the small room Hua shared with his mother. 'All he wants is to get out of here. He claims there's corruption everywhere and no concept of people's rights. He even asked me to find a woman in the West to marry him, regardless of what she's like.' He paused. 'Do you realise his monthly salary as an engineer, working a sixty-hour week, is thirty-five dollars?'

4

From Luke's Diary

The image of Dad fighting to breathe, his eyes bulging out of their sockets, haunts me still three days later. I was on a top bunk on the boat from Xiamen and several times almost fell out in panic to get to him, when he cleared his throat or made a strange noise. I guess we're all highly strung. Mum has been snappy and I have times of dark despair. My cough is better but I feel weak and sometimes have pains in the chest. I know it's partly anxiety, made a thousand times worse by Dad's incident, but can't get rid of it.

There are things I need to offload. Some of it is restlessness about the future. I want to *do* something that's worthwhile, but I want to earn money too. Seeing so much poverty depresses me. When people have to work all day, like Hua, just to make ends meet, it screws them up, there's no joy in it. It makes me feel guilty – and I resent that. I feel such anger sometimes, almost hatred. Life doesn't have to be like this. It's because of mismanagement and greed. Here am I, free to travel anywhere, and these guys are stuck where they are, under a regime that seems to care nothing for them. I hate it.

But it's more than that. The way people behave also maddens me. From Hong Kong onwards I've been treated like dirt most of the time, without recognition that there's a person here. I'm just a thing in the way – from which, if lucky, they might extract some money. I know I'm overreacting. Why am I so sensitive? That too drives me insane.

Things seem to be coming to a head here in Shanghai.

Not that everything has been bad. There were some great people on the boat, from a different part of China. They approached us with broad smiles – big bodies, unshaven faces, darker than the Hans. Their language was different too, more guttural and passionate. They said they were from a place called Kashgar in the far west.

We were invited into their cabin – a real squash with eleven of us, Mum the only woman. They passed round nuts, sweetbreads and cups of super-strong tea, followed by rice wine which Mum and Dad obstinately refused. They spoke no English but we got by with the phrasebook and our scanty Mandarin, along with mime and laughter. That's the secret, goodwill and imagination. Interest too. It's amazing what can be communicated.

They were employed by an oil company and this was the first time they had seen the sea! They said they were Muslims, their language close to Turkish but with Arabic script; and told us of the market in their home town to which tribal people come from all directions. It made me long to go there – where there is *life*.

While we were talking two policemen came and checked their papers. Word must have gone around that the foreigners were with them. We did not then know of the long struggle for independence in their province of Xinjiang, brutally squashed by the army.

Later we looked up Kashgar on our map. What a place! To the east, the deserts of the Tarim Basin; west and north, magical names like Kyrgizstan, Tajikstan and Kazakhstan, formerly in the USSR; south, Pakistan and Afghanistan. Should I travel on instead of going to university? There's so much I want to see; and we're unlikely to get to Kashgar if we go to Tibet.

By the way, one of the men recognised Ho Chi Minh from my T-shirt. He apparently visited Xinjiang in '64. 'Good man,' he said. 'Very good man.'

We had a bad start in Shanghai. Anger and frustration seemed to be all around as we disembarked in the morning, though I enjoyed the run up the wide Huangpu River, filled with ships and boats of all sizes. The wharf was chaos, vehicles and pedestrians battling for the single shabby road out to the city. Motor rickshaws harassed us until we agreed to climb into one of them, which brought our driver into violent words with his rivals. Several times he was abused by cyclists, pedestrians and other drivers. He gave back as good as he received.

We got to our hotel, hot and frazzled. The two women at reception, in white coats and heavily made up, continued their conversation for several minutes; then one of them turned to us with a look of disdain. It seems their state salary remains the same regardless of whether business is good or bad. Guests mean extra work, especially foreign ones. Besides, foreigners are supposed to be rich and those who go to cheap hotels deserve the scorn they get.

As Mum and I were filling out the police forms, the lady pulled them from under our hands and finished them herself. She threw back our passports as if she was dealing cards. The woman in charge upstairs was asleep with her head on the counter. It was then that I snapped, waking her up with a start as I thumped on the desk. She asked for our receipts and I dealt them to her in the manner of the woman below. She looked back in bewilderment.

'No, I don't regret it,' I shouted at Mum in our room as she tried to calm me down. 'They deserve all the rudeness I can give them.'

It took the rest of the morning for my outrage to pass. I expected Mum or Dad to put in a few wise remarks about how if I hate *them*, it's because of something I hate in myself, but they held off. At least the bathroom's okay and there's water. Having showered and had something to eat I feel better. But my stomach is not well and my chest aches. Do I want to see a doctor? Will I trust what he or she says after what happened in Xiamen? I just can't *decide*.

In the evening we had a meal with an older couple whose address Dad had been given by a friend. The conversation plunged me further into gloom and played into the events of the next day when we reached exploding point.

Sarah, though English, had been brought up in China and works here now as a teacher. William, a university lecturer, was from Shanghai, but from a family so poor he had had to leave school in his teens and get work. He mentioned that he was imprisoned during the Cultural Revolution. He did most of the talking, mainly to Dad. I noticed too that at times he looked around to see if anyone was listening.

We asked about China and one of the remarks he made early on was that no one born outside can understand it, least of all Westerners. He criticised the Western press for its bias. 'Besides,' he said, 'what happens here is an internal matter. And whatever bad things the government may do, they're no worse than what the colonial powers have done.'

I mentioned the Tiananmen Square killings of '89 and he replied that there was no evidence of the scale of massacre spoken of in the media overseas. He spoke of his horror at seeing leaders of the demonstration wearing red bandanas and chanting slogans. 'No one needs reminding what those headbands signify. Better the army kills a few hundred than millions die in another cultural revolution.'

He spoke most vehemently when I asked about Tibet. 'Why did no one get outraged when the army put down riots in Xinjiang Province? It suits Western governments to use Tibet to manipulate us. They take no notice of the fact that it was still feudal when the Dalai Lama fled. And that's how the West wants it to remain.'

Beneath the surface of decorum emotions were running high; and we spoke more generally about East and West. He said a multi-party system wasn't appropriate in China. 'Most people prefer to leave the government to get on with its work, without wasting time and energy on party politics. They trust their leaders more readily than in the West.'

Dad, true to style, spoke of the lack of spirit in both capitalism and communism. 'You're wrong,' William replied. 'Communism *does* recognise the spirit, but that stage hasn't been reached. The first priority is socialism, which is far from complete; people still struggle for basic needs. Mao became big-headed and plunged on towards higher goals, with catastrophic results. True communism will not come about for five hundred years at least.'

Towards the end, Dad said he thought the main problem was China's size. I nearly choked when Sarah replied that there are many who look at a map of the country and see there's a part missing in the north. 'You mean Mongolia?' he said, incredulous.

I slept badly and woke up feeling irritable and ill. The atmosphere in our room was pretty tense. I knew I was partly responsible but could do nothing about it. I'm young, strong and fortunate. What right do I have to be depressed? Thinking this only makes it worse.

Mum insisted that Dad and I have check-ups; so we headed off, shrouded in cloud, to the Number One

Friendship Hospital. It was a rambling, chaotic, rundown place and we could not find a reception area. At last a quiet-spoken doctor told us it was not for foreigners and led us to a bus that took us to a new building, almost empty, funded with aid from the US.

The doctor there was a pleasant young woman who spoke some English. She attended to Dad first. He showed her the report from Xiamen, and she said his heart had been diagnosed as normal! The comments on the X-ray, however, referred to bronchial problems. He mentioned he was still having pains and in came a nurse wheeling a cardiogram machine! So he had his fourth wire-up in four days with the same result as before.

When it came to my turn, she refused to test my heart, saying I was young and didn't need it. She said the problem was overtiredness and put me on antibiotics. I felt relieved, but also a bit dubious about the speed with which she had come to her verdict.

Dad seemed ill at ease too. As we went out, he muttered something about being reluctant to take the antibiotics she had prescribed for him and about the money he had wasted on them. And suddenly Mum was in flames. 'I'm disgusted with you both. Here we are in a foreign country, the doctor was efficient and considerate, and all you do is complain.'

'In Xiamen they misdiagnosed but refused to admit it,' he shouted back. 'Don't I have a right to query what they say now?'

I kept silent, brooding in my own gloom. We were walking towards the centre of the city, grimy in the heat and exhaust fumes. Was there something from Shanghai's own past of repression and violence that was getting to us as well? It was in this city of dirt cheap labour that the foreign powers created their most prized 'international settlement' in the nineteenth century; here too, the Cultural Revolution was sparked off nearly a century later.

I seethed at the difference between the general hospital and this one for the elite and poured my scorn onto Mum. 'Where's the socialism William talked about? It's a lie, and I'm sick of it. I want to go home, get a job, make lots of money and forget about it all. Everyone's just interested in their own needs anyway.'

Dad had paused at a crossroads. As we came closer, I said, 'Why do I get so depressed when I'm with you guys? I'm not normally like this.'

It probably hurt Mum and she snapped at *him* something like, 'So what are you sulking about *now*? I can't stand it any more. Living with people who are so negative.'

'I can't live with this either,' he fired back. And suddenly he was crossing the road shouting that we could look after ourselves, he had had enough of being blamed all the time. Passers-by looked on with bemused interest as if we were circus animals.

Mum was distraught, but the lights had turned against us. 'How dare he!' she exclaimed, fighting back tears. 'What will we do? I've got no money on me. I don't even know what the hotel's called and Justin has the guidebook.' By the time we got across, he had calmed down a bit and was waiting. 'I want to go my own way too,' shouted Mum. 'I just need the hotel's address. And enough money to get back to Australia.'

We were over-hungry as well as exhausted. Dad suggested we walk towards the famous Nanjing Lu and look for a restaurant. It was somewhere Mum had been wanting to experience – reputedly like London's Oxford Street. They walked in front and I heard him say sorry; then she touched his hand.

Rivers of people surged around us in Western clothes, women in doll-like make-up and miniskirts. 'Here's your special place,' I said, patting Mum's back; and she smiled. Shanghai is so densely populated that the different trades have different days off to avoid total congestion at weekends. We ducked into a fast food joint which at least was cool and had a free table. There in calmness we spoke in turn, listening without interrupting.

We realised how much the event in Xiamen had put us on edge. Mum had been pinching herself awake at night and was fearful of what might happen in the remote places to which we were heading. She begged Dad to put aside prejudice and take any medicine that might help. For him the issue was of not being in control of what was done to his body. He felt under pressure from us both and was concerned the drugs might be counter-productive.

What had weighed most heavily on me was the thought of death. My fear was not about Dad only but myself, and all my thoughts were cloaked in negativity. I knew I was not through it yet, but speaking and being listened to brought solace to us all.

We walked on through the crowds in the awful heat past restaurants, beauty salons, hotels, shops and superstores crammed with every kind of merchandise. Though Shanghai has been at the heart of the Communist movement, it also seems to be thoroughly committed to capitalism. We stopped at Renmin Park, a dusty unexotic place with sparse vegetation; but in it our spirits revived, largely through the jollity of an eccentric old man.

'Honoured sirs, good madam,' he began, tapping his bulbous nose. 'May I have the honour of your acquaintance?' He was wearing a white shirt, baggy pants, sandals and a floppy sun hat. 'Welcome to the Park of the People. Not what it used to be, I have to say. Our government does not manage matters well, I regret. They feather their own nests, you understand. I know for I have worked with them for thirty years. Not as a high-class gentleman like you good sirs – and madam – just a small potato. But I did my work honestly.'

We sat with him at one of the many stone tables, most of them occupied by elderly men playing chess. I enjoyed the way he followed each sentence with a sucking sound and a laugh, baring his few remaining teeth. Each time he said sir or madam, he nodded his head and wiggled his bushy eyebrows in respect.

He told us he had been an officer in the navy before '49 and had travelled to many parts of the world; hence his fluency in English. By this stage we had quite an assembly around us, of people watching impassively or nodding their heads in thoughtful agreement. 'These are retired citizens, like me,' he added. 'Those who worked faithfully for the government have good pensions. We no longer need to earn our bowl of rice.'

He told us then of the English-speaking gathering in the park on Sunday mornings and of the acrobatic show farther up the street, which had toured the world. Being with him gave us the energy to attempt to get tickets.

It was there we met Sui.

If our queue seemed long we only had to look across the road to feel better. The one over there, several people thick, went for about forty metres and disappeared down a side street. I assumed it was for a cinema. Then I saw the Kentucky Fried Chicken sign.

'Can I help you?' said a genial man in our queue. He had a frazzled, somewhat sad look behind glasses, and his hair was thinning; but though his voice was slow and gentle, he took us under his wing with firm authority, organising our tickets and making sure we understood what was written on them. He said he was a physics and history teacher at the university and wanted to practise his English.

'Physics easy,' he went on. 'Everywhere same. History dangerous. Government decide and change. I not like.'

He told us he lived alone and that his hobbies were calligraphy, poetry and painting. He declined our invitation to come to the show, but said he would take us the next day to the Yuyuan Gardens. 'By the way, how come you were in our queue?' Dad asked.

'I, waiting,' he replied, looking vague.

The Yuyuan – or Mandarin – Gardens are in the old city, an enclave of China amidst the areas previously grabbed by the colonists as their 'settlements'. We had to change buses several times, but Sui was astonishingly patient and would let them go by if they were too crowded. We made our way through a maze of markets and cobbled streets. If one of us stopped to look at something, he would immediately check the price. 'People only think money,' he stated several times. 'You always careful.' He invited us to sample various drinks and cakes, each time hunting around for the best deal. I tried to be interested but felt as heavy as lead. There was activity and colour but it seemed lacking in joy and the crowds and heat were dreadful.

All in all it took two and a half hours to reach the gardens, but at least there was beauty. They had been built as gifts for high-ranking mandarins over four hundred years ago – red pagoda-like buildings with ornate carvings, set amidst lotus ponds, paths, bridges, shrubs and trees. The French apparently laid into them as a reprisal for uprisings in the last century and much of what we saw was reconstruction. There were goldfish in many of the ponds.

We could hardly get our bodies into the place where we had lunch because of the press of people and the surliness of those who were working there. The way of ordering was by buying tickets from the cashier, which meant we had to barge forward and shout out what we wanted – a problem, since we could not see the food. Even with Sui arguing and gesturing on our behalf, what finally appeared was not what we thought we had asked for. I guess I long for Western food. Every day, rice, rice, rice. Maybe I should go home. But where is home? The only family I have are tramping through China with backpacks.

Sui was eager to please, but his energy levels were not much greater than ours. What does it do to a person to live fifty years in a city as crowded as this? After lunch he took us to a tea house at the lake, its blue roofs curving like elephant tusks. It was surprisingly peaceful and we sat at our hundred year old table looking out over the lotuses, while our cups were filled magically with tea. But there was a distance between us – Mum, Dad and I because we could not talk through the things that still weighed on us, Sui because of language and the Chinese way of saying only what one thinks the other person would like to hear. It began to dawn on me that the bluntness of my questions to William that fateful night might have been offensive.

I realised too that Sui understood less English than he appeared to. His way would be to repeat what we said as though pondering it and it was only when we asked direct questions that we saw through this.

'Did this building survive the Cultural Revolution?'
'Yes. Revolution.'
'Where do we get the bus back?'
'Yes, the bus back!' And he got up to go.

Yet much did pass between us. We learnt that his father had owned a factory and shop prior to '49. When Mao's government took control of the banks, it had broken him inwardly as well as financially. He spoke of the fear under which people had been living. Until recently, talking to foreigners without permission would result in interrogation by the police; and he reckoned rooms were still bugged in high-class hotels.

He said he knew the Chinese were hated in Tibet and that Buddhists had been persecuted there. He added that he would have liked to visit but not under present circumstances. His way of coping seemed to be to let the world flow round him in a kind of dream. Perhaps he knew that if he ever expressed what he really felt, he would drown in the same black flood threatening me.

As weariness descended, the gardens and make-believe architecture became distant and there arose in me a sense of despair which expressed itself as irritation. Where was it coming from? Memory stirred – of a time when I was nine and became unaccountably ill. For two months the smallest movement would exhaust me and I hardly got out of bed.

We lived on a hill not far from the school, and I remember with special fondness a morning when I was lying on the terrace with my head on Mum's leg, while she read from *The Secret Garden*, by Frances Burnett. The rambling vibrant flowers of the girl in the story fused with the colours around and I felt a stream of strength surge from my feet to my chest, the autumn sun warming my body through and through. It was as if I had become transparent.

I loved to play the piano. It was almost the only thing I could do. My hands seemed to dance on the keys with a life of their own. Mum and Dad became concerned. They said my energy was flowing out through my fingers, making me fade away. But I did not feel morbid. It was more like being on a cloud and not being able to come back. Now it was the opposite: the danger of drowning...

We decided to take a taxi back – easier said than done. Sui stood calmly in the street bedlam, waving down drivers who either ignored him or shouted. At last a lady stopped. 'You know,' said Dad in the comfort of the cab, 'I reckon people are ruder to you, Sui, than to us.'

'Yes. You big shot. I nobody.'

'We've got to get to the bottom of this,' said Dad later. 'Your misery's driving us mad.'

'Do you think I don't realise it?' I flared. 'Last year, making the film, I had so much energy. I knew what I was doing. Now I don't know anything – what's right or wrong or good or bad. I only know I'm filled with hatred.'

'Let's talk about it then. Where is this hatred? What shape is it? What colour?' It was one of many techniques he and Mum had experienced with a counsellor when they almost split up. The man must have been good at his job, because he helped them through the swampland.

The intense feeling in me formed into a murky green ooze which I had to 'put' into a basin and speak to. Then I had to talk as *it*, telling Luke what it thought of him. At the end, Dad got me to 'pick it up' and 'throw it' out of the window. Some of it 'got stuck' and I had to 'scoop it up' again.

Next they said various words to which I had to reply instantly with whatever came to mind. It became a game. Among the words were China, Africa, sex, father, racism, mother, rice, pain, heart, Adelaide, music. The last two affected me most. To 'Adelaide', I replied, 'Place of my own where I can cook breakfast'; to 'music', 'Creating, working together, crossing the barriers of race and language.' I asked why Dad had mentioned Africa.

'Because maybe you picked up fear when we travelled there. You were only six.'

I felt lighter, as though something had started to move. As we lay in bed that night, he said aloud a kind of prayer he and Mum sometimes use to overcome anxiety. It began like this:

> Whatever the next hour, the next day will bring for me,

first of all because it is entirely unknown,
I cannot change it by any anxiety.
I await it with inner quietness of soul,
with perfect equanimity.
Through fear and anxiety our evolution is held up.
We reject through its waves
what out of the future wants to enter our souls.
The devotion to what is called the divine wisdom in events;
the acceptance that whatever happens must be,
and must have its positive aspect in one way or another;
the giving rise to this mood in words, feelings and ideas;
this is the mood of the prayer of surrender.

★

Well, today I achieved something – I didn't get depressed. Mum and I went to a Western-style restaurant, while Sui took Dad to get train tickets for Qufu, birthplace of Confucius, a full night's journey to the north. After a steak and chips, salad and a Coke, I felt as if I had glimpsed the sun through dark cloud; and there was just enough light left over to get us through what followed – the simple and fantastically complex act of sending a parcel to Bac in Hanoi. It took four and a half hours.

We met up with the others at the Jade Buddha Temple. 'You should see Sui in action,' said Dad, as we entered the familiar chaos of smoking fires, chanting monks and tourists taking photos. 'He's as fierce as anyone else and barges straight to the front, no doubt shouting he's on important business with a foreigner. Each time, he would cheerily say, "You not worry," then come back crestfallen.' The only tickets they could find were for soft sleepers at foreigner prices or bare hard seats, one extreme or the other. They had opted for the cattle class.

We went upstairs and were in a different world. The seated white Buddha, originally from Burma, is nearly two metres high and is said to weigh a thousand kilos. Its purity exudes tranquillity. Into the stillness came the creak of floor boards, the rustle of clothes and the cracking of bones as people prostrated before it.

'It's only a statue,' I said to Mum afterwards. 'They seem to worship it.'

'At least there's reverence. It's the first time I've seen it to that extent here. Devotion, even in the simplest things, was one of the virtues of old China.'

I thought about it as we threaded our way through the jungle of people at the Bund, the promenade by the river. How can anyone feel reverence and interest when they bump into ten thousand fellow bodies each day? And how can one possibly have the energy to recognise in each one a unique human being? Strange! I had never thought this way before, but if we strip these feelings away, we become like machine parts clanking against one another.

'This river leads to the Yangzi and to the heart of China,' said Dad. 'Imagine the excitement of standing here a hundred years ago, when the interior was still wrapped in mystery, and knowing *that*.'

Sui found a tiny restaurant farther on which we would have passed without even knowing what it was. We had to bend to enter, through a white cloth curtain. 'Here cheap,' he said, a common word in his vocabulary, synonymous with 'good'.

'Where can one find the spirit in China?' Dad asks him out of the blue.

'People no time for Buddha or God. Only worry money and price.' He says the temples are mainly frequented by retired people with pensions and time on their hands.

'Young people only pray get rich. "Make money, is glorious," so speak China president Deng Xiaoping.'

'And the heart? Isn't that like a temple? Where is the *heart* of China?'

'Yes,' replies Sui with enthusiasm. 'The heart!'

On our last morning in Shanghai, I went alone to the weekly English-speaking event in the park, hoping to see the old man who had revived us with his jolliness. He was not there, but many others were and they surged towards me when they realised I was a native speaker.

To begin with, rational conversation was impossible. No sooner had I acknowledged one man's greeting than I was saluted by another.

'May I be so bold as to approach you?'

'Good sir, might we know of your motherland?'

'Would you do us the courtesy of lending your ears?'

I told them where I come from and this produced a competition of compliments. 'Australian people are honest,' I learnt that day. The land is 'hot', 'large', 'rich', 'barbecued' and 'ebullient'. People made comments about kangaroos and crocodiles. I felt like an exotic flower on the ripples of a lake and let myself drift into the general goodwill. 'What do you think of China?' The question cut through the chatter.

'Difficult to say,' I said, struggling. 'It's so big. People don't seem very happy.'

'What do you know of our history?' He was an elderly man, skeleton-thin in a white Chinese suit. Other voices quietened as they waited for me to answer, but he went on. 'Our nation is not yet complete. Japan, Vietnam, Korea, Mongolia – all are part of China.'

Anger moved in my stomach and I could feel the unease of other people. 'I disagree,' I said. The word 'Tibet' flashed through my mind but I dismissed it. 'My mother is from Vietnam. They are a different people. And will remain so.'

'Nepal is part of greater China. So is India.' At this, some of the listeners started to protest – amazingly, still in English. But he had not finished. 'The Chinese empire is worldwide. America's strength comes from the Chinese people who live there.'

What warmed me was that there was now no need to reply. Others were visibly affronted and did the speaking for me. The circle disintegrated and I took the opportunity to leave. 'I'm catching a train this afternoon,' I said, trying to include everyone. 'Thank you for your conversation. Your English is very good.'

A number of them shook my hand and wished me well, saying they were sorry about what had happened. As I left, the man pressed his address on me, saying, 'You will see me again.' It disturbed me. I was glad I had not said more – but glad too that I had broken through the tentacles of etiquette and been direct in what I did say. Well done, mate!

Sui came with us to the crowded squalor and chaos of the station. He wrote a note for us to show to the ticket collectors on the train, requesting that we upgrade to hard sleepers. His advice was that if we could not change, we should get out at Suzhou, famous for its gardens, then go on the next day. 'You not worry,' he said.

We stood together, awkward, for a moment, Sui holding the big bag of goodies we had given him – teas and biscuits and other foods he would never have bought for himself. We shook hands and said goodbye, hesitated but could not find the words to say more, then plunged into the unbelievable scrummage of the carriage where we had to shove like everyone else to get to our seats.

He was still there as the train left, his face impassive; and he didn't wave. But I knew he was sad. As were we.

China – North

5

Within minutes our T-shirts were wet with sweat. Justin was being squashed against me by a woman pressing in on the edge of his seat. A man pushed people aside to spit on the floor, then gargled with lemonade. I watched with relief as he leant over his family to the window. It dawned on us that this was as comfortable as we would get. When the inspector eventually shoved his way through, he showed no interest in the note about upgrading. 'That decides it,' said Luke. 'There's no way I'm staying in this for sixteen hours.'

Justin ferreted out a book – Georg Kuhlewind's *From Normal to Healthy*. He even attempted to read some of it to Luke, who was sitting opposite, about how modern psychology has tended to focus on what is *below* consciousness with little acknowledgement of anything *above* it. By doing this, we give too much power to automatic patterns of behaviour and turn away from that part of ourselves beyond normal awareness, which is the source of our moral striving and, ultimately, our capacity for freedom.

We depended on our neighbours to tell us when we were coming into Suzhou and it was a mad scramble to barge our way out before the train started again. From the bedlam of hard seats we catapulted into the most expensive room of our journey. We could find no other option in the city that was famous, long before Marco Polo, for its silk, canals and beautiful women, on the stupendous Grand Canal which once linked the Yangzi with the Yellow River and stretched from south of Shanghai to north of Beijing. 'In Heaven there is Paradise,' runs a proverb from those times. 'On earth Suzhou and Hangzhou.'

Justin was angry when he saw Chinese guests paying substantially less than us and his negativity persisted as we came into our ice-cold room. 'Who's on automatic now?' Luke gently clobbered him on the shoulder. 'Let's enjoy what we've paid for.' I myself was looking forward to its comforts; but it was not to be. The air-conditioning was out of our control and though I piled on layers of clothing I could not get warm. I felt irritated at the stupidity of the situation. Images crashed around in my mind. I realised that I too was on automatic, and that this chaos of thoughts was doing nothing to solve the problem. It was a form of self-absorption – just as greed is, or envy or ambition – choking everything, like weeds.

I slept at last; and had a dream. We were cultivating a garden. Nothing fanciful, just a small square of rich soil. We tended it, weeding, planting, watering, and many things grew, vegetables and flowers of all colours. People came and went, young and old, picking, cooking, eating. Children started to make their own plots and a boy from kindergarten said he wanted to create one too. I took him to a corner and we dug together. It became a festival of gardening.

As Justin headed off to the station the next morning to try his luck with sleeper tickets, thunder rolled ominously and it started to pour. He came back soaked, saying he felt lower than at any time since leaving Australia. After two hours in queues, he had been told one cannot book sleepers or soft seats here. Our old tickets were still valid but without reserved seats it would mean standing for twelve hours. 'God, I hate this system,' he said, sinking onto his bed. 'How the hell are we going to get out of here?'

Checkout was at midday and time was running. It did not seem the right moment to remind him that in the sequence of exercises which we had begun on leaving Australia we were at the stage of positivity, finding what is good in every situation.

Still feeling the wash of well-being from the dream, I went out into the sheeting deluge with Luke to see what we could come up with. At least it was warmer than our room, as we waded through small lakes in cobbled lanes to a stinking canal where at last a pedicab driver, hidden in a glistening oilskin, stopped for us. Luke pointed to the ideograms for CITS (China Independent Traveller Service) in our guidebook, and we piled in behind a plastic curtain. The road became a fountain with each vehicle that passed, engines racing, cycle bells cawing. We could see but dimly through a crack – on pavements, under awnings – drenched figures beneath streaming plastic, staring.

The rain lessened and became separate drops beating hard against the hood. Luke was still trying to check the map. 'It's all right... No, it isn't... Yes, we're near. Oh no, why did he cross the canal? I don't think he understood.' We stopped in the driveway of the posh Gusu Hotel. 'Oh damn. I must have pointed to the next address on the list.'

The driver pushed back his oilskin and became a young man with a glint in his eyes. He seemed chuffed at having weathered the storm and insisted on taking us to the right place without charge. The woman inside was gentle and spoke fluent English. Her advice was to get to the platform at departure time; there were usually vacancies in sleepers or soft seats. The alternative would be to go back to Shanghai and start again. It was not much but her care and calmness gave us heart. She also wrote us a note for the ticket collector.

'You look happy,' said Justin when we got back.

'You're different too. What happened?'

'I've thought things over. We're here to see China. Whatever happens is part of it. It's all right. Now tell me your news.' So the darkness lifted and events were free to turn.

Suzhou's gardens are celebrated as a fusion of nature, architecture and art, many of them created by retired officials who sought solitude in harmonious surroundings after the hustle of worldly life. In the garden of Wangshi, the Master of the Net, is still a flavour of old China. The use of space is exquisite – courtyards, pavilions, halls and gardens, close together in a small area without any feeling of being cramped, their different worlds separated by walls and hedges, bamboos and frangipanis. We linger in the master's study with its dark but elegant Ming furniture and red paper lanterns, looking out over a rockery and pond with a weeping willow. Tiny heads of moss stick out between rain-washed stones. 'This is okay,' says Luke. 'I reckon I could live here.'

'I thought you hated China,' says Justin in his dry way.

My own feelings are mixed too – the love-hate between Vietnam and China going back centuries; my attraction for the ancient culture to which I owe much of my upbringing; the shock and sadness at what we have encountered. It seems at times so bereft of beauty and spirit and I am worn down by the sheer mass of people.

'It's so familiar, don't you find?' says Justin. 'Yet elusive, like a dream. As if someone from the past is looking out through my eyes, and seeing everywhere the destruction of what he once knew and loved.'

'Doesn't destruction also bring release?' I reply.

Zhuozheng, Garden of the Humble Administrator, is a large place with lakes, streams, bridges, bamboo islands, summer pavilions and ponds. Although there are hundreds of tourists, mostly Asian, it is extensive enough for peace to prevail.

The rain resumes and we sit on a verandah under the old dragon roofs, watching it collect in drops and glistening pools on the enormous lotus leaves. As the water becomes too heavy, one or another of the long thin stems tips over, releasing it onto a lower leaf then into the mother pond – and springs up again. Now and then a gust blows and all the stems tremble and bow at once, to the silent swish of ripples on the surface. I imagine the faces of little children and their laughter. 'This one's *mine*. *I* saw it first. *Now*, it's going over… *There*!'

*

Sunshine streams into our room, as we look over Kong Miao, the temple complex in Qufu dedicated to Confucius. People in the street below are cleanly dressed and cheerful. 'You realise,' says Luke, 'we've already seen more smiles here than anywhere else in China?'

We had also slept well on the train from Suzhou. Our note from the lady at CITS was a magic wand which whisked us out of the chaos of the hard seat area into the bliss of sleepers…

Until Mao, Confucius was perhaps the most influential person in China's history. Born during the 'Warring States' period in the sixth century BC, a contemporary of Laozi, Buddha and the pre-Socratic philosophers in Greece, he spent much of his life close to poverty. His teachings – largely a restatement of what prevailed at an earlier time – were little known until, three centuries later in the Han Dynasty, they became enshrined as a kind of religion. They formed the main content of the rigorous exam system through which state officials were selected up to this century, on the basis not of independent thinking but memorisation.

I know his influence well from my own upbringing. His teachings were even more prominent than those of Buddha, and my stern grandmother (the one who caned my father) seemed to have a ready quote from him for everything that might conceivably happen. One I still carry with affection is his recipe for conducting one's life: first improve yourself, then create harmony at home; after this you can stabilise the state and finally bring peace to the world.

The cornerstone of his ethic is acceptance of one's position and of the behaviour that goes with it. Young defer to old, children to parents, wives to husbands, with the emperor as supreme father commanding loyalty but also setting a perfect example. The 'superior man' has a sense of '*li*', of what is *appropriate* in each situation. It is one of five essential virtues, the others being compassion, justice, knowledge and trustworthiness.

For Confucius, *li* was a self-evident faculty which he sought to reinforce by rules of social conduct. He belonged to a time before the individual intellect and conscience had developed. People were still bound into the culture of their birth and had a deep instinct for community. As time went by and an independence of spirit started to take root in other parts of the world, the structure in China remained the same. It rigidified into a hierarchy of male dominance while the old morality based on duty, which was its quintessence, ebbed away.

Inside the extensive Kong Miao are temples and shrines, halls and courtyards, set among cypresses, pines and giant stone steles on tortoise-like *bixi*, the legendary offspring of dragons. Their calligraphy is renowned throughout China.

The central south–north walkway, over a kilometre long, enters through the Gate of Stars and leads through thresholds adorned with words of Confucian wisdom. As in other sacred sites, the physical path is a symbol of the inner one, each portal representing a stage of insight. At the Arch of the Spirit of the Universe, the teachings are represented as heavenly bodies, circling without end. Roughly midway is the Great Pavilion of the Constellation of Scholars with its three-tiered roof – and beyond, a small building commemorating the place where Confucius is said to have taught under an apricot tree. The climax is the ceremonial Dacheng Hall, with its ornate columns, lintels, windows and roofs rising from white marble steps and terraces. Story has it that its dragon columns were so finely sculpted, they had to be covered in silk when an emperor visited in case he was roused to jealousy.

We breathed in the tranquillity, but also the mustiness of tradition. Defaced statues here and there spoke of the deeds of Red Guards. 'How do you reckon Confucius would have coped in today's world?' asked Luke, seeing Justin's wistful gaze.

'I was thinking how everything has its time of youth, then grows old and dies,' he replied. 'That sense of the appropriate, the *li* that Confucius held so dear – you could say it's pretty remote from modern life, no?'

'Thank God too. Can you imagine living in a society where we all do precisely what we're meant to?'

'But the *li* is in you nevertheless; it's just that it's in a completely new form. Nothing's fixed any more, least of all when you're on a journey. What you do in one situation isn't necessarily at all appropriate in another. Agreed?'

'So?'

'How does one know how to behave? By finding, out of oneself in each moment, what the "right" thing is. No longer from instinct or prescription, but from one's own sensitivity and judgement. That's quite a transformation. I think Confucius would be pretty impressed.'

In a quiet street was a concrete building with ideograms on the front. Through the glass door we could see a receptionist in a pink and white uniform and a room with a tiled floor, bare except for three tables in a corner. She shook her head in bewilderment at our attempts to speak her language, burst into giggles and ran out through the curtain of bright plastic strips behind her – coming back with a man in a white coat holding a chopper.

They spoke rapidly in Chinese, the chopper coming dangerously close to Justin's scalp, as the man gesticulated with passion and the girl broke down into more giggles. Then he withdrew into the kitchen, the girl to her abacus behind the counter, while we took our place at one of the tables, wondering what was going to happen next.

Clack-clack, clack-a-tack. Now and then she looked up and smiled, then covered her mouth as a new wave of giggles threatened. Twenty minutes later out came the man again with a beautifully arranged and plentiful dish. It took a while before I recognised aubergine as the main ingredient, something Luke usually detests. He was eating with gusto. We all were. 'I don't know what it was,' he declared at the end, 'but that was a meal.'

The day was hot; and it was late afternoon before we felt ready to cycle out to Confucius Forest, where he and seventy-four generations of the Kong family are buried. It is a woodland park of cypresses and other trees surrounding the steles and tombs that mark the graves. The larger tombs have a 'spirit way' leading to them, lined with stone guardians in the form of panthers, goats, horses, griffins and people. But alive and well in this place of the dead were mosquitoes such as we had encountered nowhere else, so stillness and respect were not easy virtues to express. Also there, again a rarity, was bird song.

We cycled along the ten-kilometre perimeter until we found the graves of Confucius himself and his son and grandson – simple grass mounds with steles in front. Sitting nearby was a young man conjuring up bamboos and birds, phoenixes, butterflies and lotuses, with graceful and confident brush strokes. He had a number of techniques by which he could reproduce the same themes over and again: bright red, pink, orange, yellow, green and black, on white paper. He said he was a seventy-seventh generation Kong, and that almost everyone in the town was a descendant of the master (known locally as Kongzi).

Luke bought a set of paintings and got a dragon for free. Maybe they had a spell on them to dematerialise when leaving the homeland. When we reached Kathmandu months later they were still with him, but when we left there, they had gone.

It was dark by the time we got to the station, Beijing a full night away to the north. The waiting room was an inauspicious start. A drunk man lay on his back fondling his genitals. Near him on the floor was a woman with blood oozing from a cut foot. Everywhere was garbage, rotting food and sputum. And the only tickets we could get were for hard seats.

When the train came in and the stampede began, the carriages were so full we could not even put a foot inside. We ran towards a sleeper section and jumped on as it pulled out. We were in the corridor by the kitchen and could move no farther. Even the restaurant was packed – under tables, on top of cupboards, outside the toilets.

We parked at one end, Luke and I on our packs, Justin perched with others on the low finger-wide ledge running along the wall. People passed by constantly and we had to move our feet or stand up each time. An old man wandered around looking for a place. The train lurched and he hit his head. Angry words followed and a younger man, pressing a wad of tissue paper against the bleeding wound, led him towards the sleepers. A waiter shooed them back and they squeezed in next to Justin.

By midnight the activities had quietened down but the lights remained on. I realised I was the only woman. All the men on ledge and floor were nodding off, heads on arms or hands in various positions. Luke seemed to be asleep, leaning against a wall. Justin laid his book on his lap and closed his eyes. Many in the world are homeless because of poverty or disaster. Why do others, of their own free will, leave the comfort of their homes? What were we *doing* here?

I took out our book of verses and wise sayings. A man pushed past and it fell open on the grimy floor, at a verse from Martin Buber's work, *Daniel: Dialogues on Realization:*

> This is the kingdom of God... the kingdom of danger and risk, of eternal beginning and eternal becoming, of opened spirit and deep realization, the kingdom of holy insecurity.

★

Beijing, capital of the People's Republic of China. Exhausted but jubilant, we stepped out towards its highrises and expressways, unaware that a bigger trial lay just ahead.

Famous and infamous on the backpacker grapevine, the Qiao Yuan Hotel seemed spacious and clean enough, though the showers would only be open in the evening. We washed as best we could and headed out into the lively scene of small restaurants with tables across the sidewalk. 'You want student card?' A heavily made-up woman in satiny pants and blouse smiled ingratiatingly, then winked at Luke. 'Handsome young man. Many girlfriends, hey?' A man shuffled past, with a guttural whisper. 'Change money?'

Our priority was the post office; we had had no mail since Hanoi. On the steps of the hotel were some bicycles for rent. 'Fifty dollar deposit each,' we were told. It seemed a lot but Justin paid without question. He asked for a receipt and the man scribbled some characters on a piece of paper. The lady in satin stood watching, exuding her slippery charm.

The streets were wide and full of traffic, the smog so bad it affected our breathing and made our eyes smart; but at the poste restante we were allowed to look through the whole pile and each moment of finding something addressed to ourselves was a celebration. It was quite a catch. Included in it was a letter from the Hong Kong magazine informing Justin that his article had not been accepted. 'Are you disappointed?' Luke asked gently.

'A bit. Is the way I see things really so way out?'

We flowed with the river of bicycles to Tiananmen Square, a massive space of paving bordered by huge buildings – the Great Hall of the People, Mao's Mausoleum, the Monument to the People's Heroes – and dominated by a gigantic portrait of the smiling Helmsman by the Gate of Heavenly Peace leading into the old Forbidden City. The heart of Beijing.

Here, at the height of the revolution, Mao, wearing a red armband, presided over a million Red Guards. Another million jammed the square in '77 to mourn his death. Twelve years later, in the year of the collapse of the Berlin Wall, it came to fame again as the scene of anti-government demonstrations and the massacre of students that followed. Now the crowds milled around, posing for photos beneath the smiling face.

There was no sign of the people from whom we had rented our bicycles when we got back. We locked them up near the steps and went to our room to browse through the mail. Ten minutes later Luke went down to check and found they had disappeared. 'The owners must have put them away,' said Justin, strangely unconcerned. 'Let's go and get our deposits.'

They went out together and I ventured up to the sixth floor in anticipation of a shower. People were hanging around on the landing, scantily clothed, towels over shoulders, sharing their anger. 'They say nine in the morning, then six at night, each damned day,' one man was saying. 'I haven't had a shower for a week.'

On the wall behind them was a handwritten note warning about a gang of thieves, who rent out bikes and go off with the deposits. An uneasy feeling that had been lurking below consciousness broke now into clear certainty.

'You can forget the money, Mum,' said Luke when they came back an hour later. 'We've been bloody ripped off. How could we be such idiots?' He started rummaging around in his pack.

'What are you looking for?' I asked, realising what was about to happen.

'Clean clothes. I'm going to have a shower.'

'There's no water, Luke.'

He stormed out, slamming the door.

Justin told me what they had learnt about the gang. It was almost a daily occurrence. They would even follow people who had rented and steal back the bikes with a duplicate key. Police did nothing and hotel and restaurant staff were too frightened to interfere.

Luke came in. He said he had searched behind the counter upstairs and found the shower taps that had been taken off; but even that had not yielded water. 'Not a drop,' he raged. 'I hate this hotel. I hate the Chinese. I hate everything in this stupid country.'

'Is there no one we can trust?' I asked pathetically. Justin mentioned a foreign resident in the hotel, who had said, 'Speak to Mr Zhao. Ask anyone. They all know him.'

It turned out he owned one of the restaurants. The chirpy waitress said he would be there shortly, so we sat and ordered dinner, lonely and dejected. We felt conspicuous and strangely ashamed. 'It's as if *we're* the guilty ones,' said Luke, still simmering. 'All these people talking together and giving us looks. They know. Look, that's him over there.'

'No, it's not.' I held his arm. 'Our guy was taller than that.'

Justin pointed to someone else. We were becoming paranoid. We realised too that each of us had a different memory of what the people looked like.

A plump man with a Buddha face (full cheeks and kind eyes) came to our table. 'I've heard what happened,' said Mr Zhao. 'I'm afraid you won't see those particular characters for a few days. They'll go and do a job somewhere else until the attention has died down.'

'I wish at least we'd kept the bikes,' said Justin. 'Perhaps we could have sold them.'

'It's not that easy. They were probably stolen and unregistered. Even a new one doesn't cost as much as your deposit.' To our astonishment, he advised us to go to the police.

On the way to our room Luke asked the woman at reception when the shower would be working. She was watching a portable television and did not reply. He asked again to no effect, then reached across and switched it off. 'Morning nine o'clock,' she said without looking up and turned it on.

Day came, but no water in the showers. We moved to a multi-storey building across a courtyard at the back. Here for the same price we had our own bathroom with cold water all day, and hot for at least part of it. After a shower we began to feel human again.

The steps of the main hotel were deserted but for two rusty bikes. The one clue we had was the 'slippery' woman who had witnessed us paying. Mr Zhao said she lived in a shack round the corner and was probably part of the racket.

The dingy street was lined with small tin sheds, some with cycles for rent. People were sitting on chairs or beds along the dirt patch that was the pavement. 'That's mine,' shouted Luke suddenly, pointing to a bike chained to a sad-looking tree. He looked more closely. 'There's no question. Same saddle. And there was a scratch just like this on the handlebar.'

We became aware of someone watching and turned to see the lady, a few steps away. 'Who owns this bike?' said Luke truculently. 'Where is he?'

'Everybody know.' She shrugged. 'He come soon.'

'You tell your friend,' Justin said. 'He clever, we stupid. Okay. He keep fifty dollar, give back one hundred. No problem. Otherwise…' He clamped his wrists together and announced he was going to the police.

Two hours became three as evening drew on. Anxiety gnawed – what had happened to Justin – and paranoia about each person who passed by. 'Slippery Woman' was in and out of her shed, smiling ironically. Then a boy of about twelve in torn clothes and with intelligent eyes sauntered over, telling us calmly to break the lock and take the bike.

'Smart boy.' Luke ruffled his hair. 'You know who owns it, don't you?'

'He not here. I give you tool. Come.' Luke went with him to the street corner where he repaired cycles. His place of work was a cloth on the pavement on which lay a dozen spare parts and a worn-out metal box. With the pliers he lent Luke cut through the chain and we wheeled the bike in eerie silence to the hotel lift, then along the corridor to our room.

It was dark by the time Justin got back accompanied by a policeman and a lady in civilian clothes. The people at reception looked on with a touch more respect than the day before and a member of staff came with us to identify the bicycle. 'You can sell it if you like,' said the policewoman in English. 'The guard will look after it for now.' We were led to a security area, where it was padlocked to a post. She said they could do nothing further since the thief had gone. Then Mr Zhao appeared and agreed to make a statement.

At his restaurant afterwards, we met three Germans who had been through the same ordeal that day. They still had their bikes and we suggested they keep them in their room. Justin and Luke were happier now that they had at least done something. 'I no longer feel I've lost face,' Luke confided.

'Aren't you becoming a bit Chinese?' said Justin.

But the incident echoed on inside us. 'It's time for a pow-wow,' said Justin solemnly the following day. 'Either we accept the money's lost and get on with what we came here to do, or devote our time to catching the thieves. We each have to decide.' He and Luke felt split. On one level they wanted to forget the whole thing, on another to see justice done – and get revenge. Maybe face was still an issue too. I was for letting it go.

'I can agree with that in here,' said Luke. 'But when I see them ripping people off in front of me, I go berserk. It's cowardly to watch and do nothing.'

'Would you feel so strongly about protecting others if *we* hadn't been fleeced? Besides, what do you think the opposite of cowardice is?'

'Courage, of course.'

'Isn't it foolhardiness? Vengeance? All that stuff in action films?' I paused. 'True virtues are always a middle way. Not doing can be just as courageous as doing. It's a question of being true to what one sees as the right thing, regardless of what others might say.'

'The *li*!' Justin chimed in. 'The appropriate! People pay a fortune in self-development courses to understand such things. And it's coming to us for only fifty bucks each.'

'You two are nuts,' said Luke, but not unkindly. 'You get upset about being fleeced twenty cents and now you're saying you're *grateful* for this.'

Wisdom is one thing, the pull of one's will another. We agreed to have a day out to visit the Forbidden City, but during breakfast our attention kept being drawn to the gang's activities around us. 'I don't know if I can switch off from what they're doing,' said Justin. 'It gives me a creepy feeling. Like having lice.'

On the way to the bus stop we passed two men luring a foreign couple into renting bikes. Luke saw red. 'Don't do it,' he shouted across the narrow street. 'They're crooks.' He started taking their photos as the police lady had advised. One of the guys jumped on a bike and dashed away, covering his face; the other screeched at us and came forward with a stone, arm raised in the air. 'Why do you steal?' said Justin sternly.

The man let out a string of words and made as if to smash the camera. I came towards them, grabbed Luke's arm and steered him around, glaring at the man. He lowered his hand, muttering angrily and turned away. I was suddenly angry too.

'You think I should stand and watch them like a wimp?' Luke was almost screaming. 'They'll go on robbing people until *someone* has the guts to do something.'

'And get knifed for it too. Do you realise it's now unsafe for us to stay in this area?'

'It's strange,' said Justin. 'It's actually dangerous to be a victim.' He paused. 'You know something? That guy was genuinely indignant that we tried to interfere with his profession.'

We were still shaky half an hour later as we entered the Forbidden City – as thousands have been in centuries past, though for other reasons. Here was the domain of the emperor, screened off by high walls from the ordinary world. Over those whom he invited in he had the power of life or death. With eight hundred buildings and nine thousand rooms, it is the largest and best preserved monument in China, and attracts over three million visitors a year.

We were inside for four hours. We even found places where we could hear the wind rustling the trees; but most of the time were part of the unstoppable flow, treading a halting zigzag path between the thousand and one cameras and the smiling people on whom they were focused. Could emperors have conceived, even in nightmares, of such a desecration? I think not, for the outside world and that within hardly connected, except through fear and worship. It came to me then that beyond Buddhism and the Tao, the most widespread Chinese religion was the worship of the emperors which, in turn, was an aspect of ancestor worship.

Justin and I had dinner at Mr Zhao's, while Luke 'hit' the town with a backpacker from England he had just met. The evening light was gentle, the air cool, around us the hum of conversation in many languages. The girls working there spoke a charming broken English and seemed to have an international spirit. It was before peak time and one of them was flipping sulkily through the music tapes, eyes red with tears, while a Western man pleaded in Chinese. 'Boy flend,' said Mei, my favourite waitress, with a smile and a sigh. 'Fight-fight two days. Then kissing and more fight. Happy that way.'

At the centre was Mr Zhao himself. His education had ended with high school and he had worked in business before opening the restaurant. He had learnt English from travellers and spoke it well. He had also been a Red Guard. 'It's not as simple as people think,' he said that evening. 'Bureaucracy was terrible. Mao spoke of the need for continuous change and this appealed to young people... It's better now; it's good that we've opened up to the world. But greed and corruption have increased too. And children don't behave like *we* used to.'

Partly, perhaps, it is a consequence of the 'one child' policy. In all the cities we had seen parents with a single child, usually a boy. 'Little emperors' they were called, because of the way they behaved and the attention lavished on them in their extended families. We heard later that it has had a more sinister effect too. Because of the predilection for a son, girl babies are sometimes got rid of in one way or another, even sold into slavery outside China.

I told him of the incident that morning and asked if we should move hotels. My main worry was Luke's hot-bloodedness. 'Another Red Guard, hey?' he laughed. 'I'll talk with him.'

Tiantan Park, the extensive complex of the Temple of Heaven, dates back to the Ming Dynasty in the fifteenth century. For the second day in a row the sky was clear, the air free of smog. In the less frequented parts – by the moats, little bridges and red stucco walls with curled roofs of royal blue tiles – there was peace, and a magical play of light and shade. Small suns, some as large as a fist, danced on the paving – images from the universe cast through the pinhole gaps between persimmon leaves.

As in the Forbidden City, the main buildings are aligned on a south–north axis and it was along this that the emperor, the 'Son of Heaven', would proceed in ceremonial yellow at the winter solstice. On the outcome of the stylised rituals he performed – including the procession from the City in silence and full pageantry hidden from ordinary people who were forbidden to watch – would depend the good or bad fortune of the coming year.

Vermilion and round, with a three-tiered roof of blue tiles, the main temple, the Hall of Prayer for Good Harvests, is completely symmetrical. Inside are four central columns representing the seasons; around them, twelve more for each month of the year with an outer ring of another twelve to symbolise the day, broken into twelve watches. Each section is rich in red and gold and decorated identically with dragons and phoenixes.

Here had been a centre of 'dragon power', a nodal point of the old religion. The time was, thousands of years before, when as in Egypt the Son of Heaven was prepared by initiation to be clairvoyant priest as well as king – a mediator between spiritual realms and the earth. Further back still, he was worshipped as the actual dwelling place of a god. When he spoke, it was a god speaking and to question his word was unthought of. Such lofty states of being had long since passed by the time the Temple of Heaven was constructed and in its secret rituals the old power became autocracy.

Was it so different with Mao? Though esteemed as a poet, he swept away the beauty as well as the clutter of the past. The sparkle of the old dragon was gobbled up by the grey one of mechanisation. But the spirit of autocracy – and of secrecy – remained.

BE A MAN AND CLIMB THE GREAT WALL, proclaimed a poster in the lobby of our hotel. We chose to show our virility, however, in a different way from what its designer had had in mind. Mr Zhao had told us of a section off the tourist trail still in its natural state.

It involved taking a train, then walking along the railway track to a cutting from which crumbling steps and battlements rose on either side – steep and dangerous enough that we had to watch where we trod and help each other up. Luke was the first to the top. 'The *madness* of it!' he shouted exultantly. 'Like trying to fence in the ocean.'

On all sides were undulating mountain ranges, green and hazy blue, over which the line of stone twisted and meandered up and down like an organic being. 'A dragon path!' was Justin's comment. The steps were its scales, the zigzag its coils, its back punctuated with towers. It snaked so much it was hard to make out its direction. In the distance we could see the restored part at Badaling, gleaming with light and tourists.

No doubt, I thought, the plan was laid out by geomancers – those whose task it was to feel the land and sense its veins and arteries – as well as engineers. I remembered stories of the horror local people had had when railways were introduced by the 'foreign devils', not only at their noise and size but their *straightness*. Like the modern intellect out of which it arose, the iron dragon seeks the shortest way between two points. It pierces through mountains and flies across valleys, caring nothing for the pathways of nature. So the old art of geomancy was lost to the demands of a new age.

In Vietnam too it had once been known out of clairvoyance where a grave should be, a dwelling, a temple, and where one should never build. We make the same decisions today, but out of a different part of the mind and with very different results. Something was gained, something lost – but the way to find again what we had before, I believe, must be forward, not back.

We walked on, the sky clear again, sparrows above our heads. The stone blocks fitted precisely though they were eroded now, with holes through which wild plants were growing. As a barrier against the outside world the wall had not been a great success. It became instead an elevated highway, five thousand kilometres long and wide enough in most places for two horse carts, across the rugged terrain from the east coast to the desert.

Two thousand years old in parts, thousands died in its construction and were buried inside. According to one story, there was unrest among the conscripts because of a rumour that 'ten thousand' would die before its completion. Finding that one of the labourers was called Wan, which means 'ten thousand', the authorities hit on a solution. They had not counted on his wife. She lamented his disappearance so vigorously that some ravens showed her where his body was buried; whereupon the wall split apart, revealing the bones...

The noise from Badaling grew stronger, loudspeakers churning out music and words, cable cars wheezing. A tower of spanking clean brickwork blocked our way.

As we stood there between the old and the new, I realised we were in the process of saying goodbye to Han China. Our next destination would be Xi'an to the west, the beginning of the legendary Silk Road leading to Europe. Beyond, we would encounter very different people. The group we had met on the boat to Shanghai were an example.

To my surprise, for all the hardship and frustration of our time here, the thought brought a lump to my throat. It seemed as if through the turmoil of these decades people had been sucked dry, with little left over for creativity or interest in others; and I felt our journey had been tarnished, because we had often let negative thoughts outweigh the positive. We seemed to have so little to offer.

The sun was westering, highlighting the pollution over the hills. I turned to Luke and asked if he could see yet why he had felt such antipathy in China. 'I think it's a question of distrust,' he said, after a long pause. 'People don't seem to say what's really true. Least of all the government.'

'Isn't that because we can't speak the language?'

'Dammit, no. There's always a way of getting through if people want to. It's like they avoid contact. They don't want to show themselves as they really are.'

For centuries in China – in the Mandarin circles of Vietnam too – it was a virtue to hold back from saying anything that might offend. The British habit of talking about the weather is nothing compared with the subtle ritual of conversation in the East, through which meaning would be conveyed as much by what was not said as what was. It became an art of the indirect and it required a high degree of cultural refinement to interpret it.

'Doesn't that say it all?' Luke exclaimed. 'Isn't that hypocrisy?'

'Others would call it tact.'

'Or lack of courage.' It was Justin. 'It's hard being upfront. Much easier to say something pleasant. But that way we never really meet each other.' It had been an issue between us in the early years. I was happy to leave things as innuendoes while he wanted them spelt out. For him it was 'telling the truth'. What mattered to me was being allowed the 'space' to come to realisations in my own time and way...

The gate to the tower was locked but we found a way down to the ground and levered ourselves over the new ramparts on a stone drain spout. From there on it was a test of endurance, battling the din and the river of people, up and down.

That night Justin woke us, shouting in his sleep. For a few seconds I was back in Xiamen. 'I'm sorry,' he said. 'It wasn't that bad. I was simply asking it what it was.'
'What what was?' Luke asked.
'The shadow that was leaning over me.'

There remained a final act to perform in the saga of the bicycle. 'Slippery Woman' had twice approached Luke with an offer to buy it. Since Mr Zhao also had a hire business, we gave him the option of having it instead. But the guard refused to hand it over, saying that only the police could release it. Justin gave him their phone number and we followed into his room. Time was getting tight. We were due to leave Beijing in a few hours.

Inside were four important-looking men in suits. One of them dialled and spoke at length. 'Well?' said Justin.
'Not yet.'
We waited an hour, nerves tightening, while they steadfastly ignored us. The phone rang, followed by another conversation. 'Well?' he repeated, reminding them of our train.
'Wait.'
They played their hand to the full. Justin spoke more strongly and perhaps they realised that if it went on much longer, he would offend the rules of face as an unrefined foreigner; for suddenly it was over and we were told brusquely to take the bike and go.

By then it was too late to catch a bus to the station. Opting for a taxi meant we had time for a final pancake at the restaurant. I felt the queeziness that seemed to come each time before taking a night train. Would the crowds suffocate us? Mixed in there too was the wrench of another round of goodbyes; and a tingle of excitement.

We had been as far east and north as this journey would take us. A new chapter was beginning. The desert beckoned and beyond that the Himalayas – and Tibet. Had I known what awaited me there, would I have been so glad to be going? Would I have dared go at all?

China – West

6

Thirteen centuries ago the city of Chang'an, where Xi'an stands today, was amongst the greatest in the world. Its population of two million included a rich diversity of races and religions, including Buddhists, Muslims, Zoroastrians and Christians. It was the capital of the splendid Tang Dynasty and roads and canals connected it with all parts of the empire.

In the world beyond, it was known as the almost mythical starting point of the Silk Road which reached south through Himalayan valleys to the land of the Indus and west through the parched heart of Asia to Constantinople and Rome. Stories of these arterial trade routes have passed into the legends of many cultures, linking the imperial city with such names as Samarkand, Buchara, Baghdad and Damascus.

During the Han Dynasty in the third century, Chang'an was already three times the size of Rome and the crossbow, the compass, the wheelbarrow, the rudder, even an earthquake detector were in existence long before they became available in the West. Cast iron-making was widespread and there are stories of Chinese and Roman armies clashing swords as far afield as Central Asia.

Sites of human habitation in the Yellow River basin by the city go back to Neolithic times, six or seven thousand years ago, and the area is traditionally hailed as the womb of

Chinese culture. It was here that the warlord emperor Qin Shihuang, centralised his power in the third century BC, and it remained the focal point of the empire until the collapse of the Tangs in the tenth century and the subsequent chaos of Warring States.

It was into a cold afternoon, heavy with pollution, that Luke, Thu and I emerged from our long train journey; but it was here that a mood of warmth began to grow, partly from the feeling of history that still survives, partly from the presence of ethnic peoples, partly from the friends we were to make.

The first of them was Cameron. He had breezed into our compartment as the train was pulling out of Beijing with the words, 'Excellent. Made it', followed by a flow of Mandarin to the man and two women sharing it with us. He had studied in Taiwan where he was teaching English. 'Hope it's not too chilly in Xi'an,' he added. 'I didn't bring a shirt or trousers.'

With his help the next morning, we had got to speak more fully with our companions, who were involved in some kind of research in Xi'an. They had assumed he was our guide and were astonished to hear that it was possible to travel without one.

The carriage woman came by with bucket and mop, cleared up the rubbish and threw it out of the window in the familiar way. Luke asked what they thought of this. It aroused quite a discussion in which Cameron was totally absorbed until Luke tapped him on the arm. 'They recognise it's an issue,' he said. 'But there are many problems and they can't all be tackled at once. People are told they shouldn't litter, but they're used to throwing their waste on the ground. They haven't realised that much of what we use now doesn't break down.'

'Are our friends aware how serious the pollution is in the world?' I asked. It provoked another exuberant conversation.

'The answer is no,' he said at last. 'They hear something about how it is in China, but little about the rest of the world.'

The second wild and woolly person was Lucy – tall, black, irrepressible, hair in long dreadlocks; the third, her boyfriend Tom, a gentle giant who had been a merchant seaman and had such a strong Yorkshire accent I thought at first he was speaking a different language. They had been together in England before heading for China. Lucy, in her early twenties, was a flame that devoured each moment's experience; Tom, older, an unruffled lake in which everything was okay. They travelled everywhere on hard seats and loved China.

We met them on the platform at Xi'an and together checked into an old hotel with grotty rooms and putrid carpet but unusually cheerful staff. Outside were two restaurants spilling onto the street in fierce competition. We were assaulted by their owners as we arrived, each pleading for our custom and pressing business cards into our hands. 'How do we sort this one out?' I thought aloud. 'Why do they choose to be next to each other?'

'Do what's natural,' said Lucy. 'Just go with it.'

Luke needed to extend his visa, so I cycled with him to the Public Security Bureau, while Thu went with the others in search of train tickets for our next destination, Lanzhou. Despite the pollution, it was pleasant cycling in the bustling tree-lined boulevards – past the massive old walls with their battlements and towers, round the bell tower at the centre, and through the streets of modern China. We passed a soup stall with a giant wok of water mounted on a wood fire. While one man put fistfuls of spinach leaves into it, another, from about a metre away, was slicing snippets from a loaf of raw dough, directing them expertly and rapidly into the liquid. Farther on was a whole row of them. 'Hey Dad,' Luke shouted across the traffic, 'maybe China's not so bad after all.' I nearly fell off my bike. 'I just wanted to let you know.'

The thought was in me too – an acceptance that, no matter how it could be or should be or how I had hoped it would be, this was how it was. This was China and we were in it.

It was dark and the others were not back. I began to worry. Thu tends to fall behind when we cycle together; maybe she had got lost. She had no map and probably had not memorised the name of the hotel. She seems to navigate more by intuition than observation.

Is this a difference between West and East, male and female or simply two individuals? In a new place I look for the sun or some indicator of direction. Matching this with a map, I feel more ready for what lies ahead. With Thu it is different. Once we have decided where we are going, she allows herself to be guided and opens up more fully to the impressions of each moment and place. It works well between us because we do not vie for leadership. We each lead in our own ways. I guess hers involves more acceptance and trust, but she makes herself vulnerable. 'She'll be okay, Dad,' said Luke. 'I hope she comes soon, though. I need to eat.'

She did, without tickets but refreshed. It seems the combination of Cameron and Lucy's energy with Tom's phlegm was quite a mix and as they cycled round town after finding the station office closed, they had drawn crowds everywhere, doing acrobatics on their bikes, singing and calling to passers-by. 'Lucy never stops,' she said. 'She takes it for granted that others share her goodwill. And they do.' Luke was delighted.

They had elected for the original of the two restaurants, and were into their second beers by the time we joined them. Cameron was holding forth in Mandarin with Clare who ran the place, and Lucy seemed on the point of getting up and dancing. 'It's a shame for *them*,' said Luke, gesturing towards the other establishment, almost deserted.

'They'll be all right. Hi there...' Lucy waved to the woman next door. 'Here Luke, I'll shout you a beer.'

Her life had not been all merriment, however. Her Irish-Spanish mother had died while she was a child in England and she had brought up a brother and three sisters with her West Indian father. They had struggled to make ends meet, but somehow along the way she had shed the prejudices and inhibitions that skin colour provokes. She seemed to have no racial feelings and did not find them in others.

It brought home how much the experiences we encounter correspond with the attitude we carry. 'I'll tell you why people like this restaurant more than the other, Luke,' she went on. 'It's because of Clare. Look at her. She's happy.'

She joined us later. Though a single mother in her thirties with a small child, she was young at heart and quite radiant. Her parents worked hard too, doing most of the cooking on the wood fire beneath a clay surface with two holes, which was the kitchen. They had been going for ten years, their neighbours only a few months; and they felt piqued about it. 'They copy-copy. Our business still good; travellers like our restaurant. But her – we not speak.'

The air was fresh and Cameron was shivering. Clare looked at him and disappeared, coming back a few minutes later with some trousers and an old shirt. 'From my father,' she said casually.

'Hey, is there any night life in this city?' said Luke, perking up.

'Sure,' she replied. 'I take you now.'

The excavations at Banpo, east of the city, date back to the fifth millennium BC. From its kilns, artefacts, dwellings and graves, the picture emerges of a community of about three hundred, dependent on hunting and slash-and-burn agriculture. Their main food was millet and pork but they also grew mustard, cabbage and hemp for clothes. On the earliest of their beautiful red pots are paintings of fish and deer; on later ones, abstract geometric designs.

What had most impact on me were the skeletons – children in urns, adults on their backs. For a brief spell, life and consciousness had combined with matter as human beings on earth. For a much longer while the bones have lingered on, along with the imprint of deeds – shards of pottery, ornaments, post-holes, trenches. Then they too disappear, absorbed back into the earth out of which they were formed. Yet each of those whose remains lay in front of us would have once learnt to walk, to speak, to think.

What does it mean to walk? A skeleton in a biology lab falls in a heap without a rigid support to keep it in place, even if one wires it together and pads it out with the equivalent of muscles and skin. So how can it stay upright during life? One only has to be in the presence of a corpse to realise something is missing, which one normally takes for granted. For in truth each day's simple act of sitting up or walking on two legs is a miracle; it speaks of a force which overcomes gravity, a revelation of the spirit in the clear language of life.

We were ushered into a medley of new mud buildings in the style of the old, where people dressed as cavemen brandished spears, danced and wrestled. More eloquent was a concert by a group of youngsters, one on a zither, the others on clay instruments the size of goose eggs, with two holes at the back for thumbs, six unequal ones at the front, and an opening at the apex for the breath. The result was a mellow warm sound, luminous and amber.

For centuries, we were told, villagers in the area of the tomb of the emperor Qin Shihuang spoke of ghosts that lived underground. During a drought in '74 a well was sunk and what they found were remnants of a terracotta army thought to number eight thousand.

Though he initiated the Great Wall, built roads and established a single script for the various languages, Qin Shihuang was a leader who ruled by force. Obsessed with the desire for immortality, he sent messengers in search of its legendary elixir to mythical islands across the sea, and conscripted a workforce of seven hundred thousand to prepare his mausoleum and the army of clay that would follow him into the next world. His actual tomb is said to contain palaces and pavilions, with pearls as stars, mercury as rivers and oceans, and crossbows poised to shoot intruders. In it too, no doubt, are the remains of concubines and slaves entombed with him, along with its wretched builders.

We entered a hangar-like enclosure and pressed through crowds to peer at the ghost army several metres below – rank upon rank of standing, crouching and riding figures, each unique with its trimmed moustache or beard, immaculate top-knot, flowing tunic or breeches, and accompanied by the magnificent Karashahr horses from the Turpan region near the desert.

A young tour guide was exulting in the stories of hatred against the emperor. After his death, people smashed some of the figures and stole their weapons, so they would not be available for him in the world beyond. One of his sons held out for four years as his successor, before being overthrown in an uprising which inaugurated the Han Dynasty. Not for the last time, the man who led it and became emperor was born a peasant.

It left a strange aftertaste. I felt awed by the size of the undertaking but for all the craftsmanship, there was something macabre about it. By what power could one human being compel so many others to give their labour – and risk their lives – for his immortality?

Throughout history, Chinese emperors have reserved for themselves a particular word that means 'I'. Even their names became taboo; no one but they could speak such words, and anyone who had previously had the same name had to change it! As elsewhere in the world, the emperor spoke for the people; in him was their ego. And his power came not only from arrogance or refinement or cruelty, but from them. They expected it; and until individuality started to emerge more widely (in Europe first, then in the larger world), they needed it.

I do not 'like' Qin Shihuang; but I can see that in him there developed, long before it did in most people, an experience of being an individual. It was this, I suspect, that he was so desperate to keep alive and which was the source of his power.

Our rooms were opposite the toilets and early in the morning I awoke to the saw-like scraping and rasping that accompanies the process of clearing one's throat in China. I emerged from our room into the stink of ammonia and rancid carpet and quickly closed the door behind me. The door next to ours was open and I heard a thud followed by Lucy's unmistakable laughter. I peered inside; she and Tom were juggling with empty beer bottles while Cameron was reading in bed. 'Don't you guys have a sense of smell?' I asked.

'Oh, yeah, I forgot to shut the door,' said Lucy, still focusing on bottles. 'Take a joss stick if that helps. There's a pack on the window ledge.'

Through Clare we had our tickets for the evening train. It allowed us a last full day to enjoy the city without distraction. While Luke went off with the others in search of adventure, Thu and I headed for the old part of town, a foretaste of the Muslim cultures that lay ahead.

Although most of Xi'an's mosques were destroyed during the Revolution and their ritual prohibited, the greatest of them, twelve hundred years old, somehow survived. Through an elaborate gateway we entered a haven of peace. The architecture and calligraphy were Chinese, as in Buddhist temples; only in its alignment towards Mecca did it reveal its Muslim origins – and in details such as the Arabic inscription fundamental to Islam, 'There is no god but God; and Mohammed is his prophet.' The paint was rundown and some of the finely carved wood splitting with age, but there was a hallowed feeling and it was clean.

Men wearing white caps and baggy clothes were chatting or walking quietly along the paved avenues, past bushes and trees, beneath arches and through prayer chambers, to the main hall into which only worshippers were allowed. Inside was a line of robed haunches, the prostrate heads which belonged to them hidden from view against the carpet.

Cameron was the first to head off to the station, bound for Wuhan and the Yangzi. As ever, he left it until the last moment and was still conversing with all and sundry as he stripped down to his shorts and T-shirt, and we packaged him into a taxi. His going left a gap but without his buzz of energy Lucy became calmer. It was as if red and yellow had blazed so strongly there had been no space for blue. In the sudden quiet we spoke of more inward things and Thu asked how it was for her carrying such a mixture of races.

'It's like living with the United Nations, I can tell you,' said Tom.

'Or a world war, sometimes,' she added with a laugh.

Then Clare spoke. 'You not need travel, I think. Whole world inside you.'

We left in two taxis; they for Chengdu and the sleepless experience of packed bodies and hard seats and we for Lanzhou and the west. Lucy hugged us; Tom bear-hugged us. Clare was leafing through a dictionary. 'These days happy time,' she said quietly. 'Now you all go. You wandering geese, fly with stars. I panda, home in bamboo forest.'

★

I had a moment of misgiving as we entered, though in truth it was more to do with possible gastric regrets than any conscious foreboding of what was about to happen. Thu and Luke seemed unruffled. Then we were inside the warm steaminess of the Muslim soup shop.

Our journey from Xi'an had taken us through air grey with dust and land increasingly eroded. Such houses as we had seen in the wilderness were of mud. From fertile Shaanxi Province we had entered drought-prone Gansu, drawing closer to the deserts of western China and the uplands that lead south to the Tibetan Plateau. At sixteen hundred metres, Lanzhou was cool as we came out into its sprawl of apartment blocks.

Bleak as our first impressions were, the room in the Friendship Hotel was the best deal we had had in China and we met here with more kindness than in almost any other city. We had thought of Lanzhou only as a stopover on the way to Xiahe – or Labrang, as its original Tibetan name was – the site of a once-illustrious monastery, dating back to a time when this region of China was part of Tibet. Events taught us otherwise.

The soup place was barely big enough for its three tables and a space for cooking, into which an elderly man welcomed us to watch as his son made the noodles from a ball of dough. Kneading it first, he stretched it out to the length of his arms, folded it and stretched again, repeating the movements at such speed that all we could see was the magical multiplication of strands in an arc above and below – from two to four to eight to sixteen and beyond, wispy and ethereal.

It was an excellent soup, but a fragment of chilli got caught in my throat and made me choke. Confident of being able to breathe through my nose, I opted for swallowing rather than spitting back into the bowl. It was an error; and suddenly, for the second time in three weeks, I was struggling for the breath of life. Time stopped. I was aware, as from a distance, of the gentle owner and his son looking on in astonishment, and of another client turning his back and staring at the television above the shelf of bowls. And when the crisis was over, although it had been less violent than before, I felt worse because it seemed such a setback. On our way now into remote parts of China, fear dug in – most of all into Luke.

Back in our room, in that clean hotel with toilets you had to look for because you could not locate them by smell, we spoke together about death. 'Of what lies beyond, I don't think I have fear,' I said to Luke. 'It's the process of dying that brings it up. How the body struggles to stay alive!' I told him then of my father's death.

I had been in England, he in Italy at the time of his final heart attack. He died while I was in the bus from the airport and his body was in the morgue when I arrived. Outside, a mechanical digger was excavating a trench, the noise and exhaust fumes as intense as the summer heat. It took a while to persuade anyone to let me in, but I was adamant.

Some years before, after returning from Vietnam, I had had an argument with him about death. For him it was clear that one 'simply snuffs out'; for me, that one lives on in another dimension. I did not then have the vivid concepts I have now about life beyond death but from Eastern thought, Jung's writings and my own dim sensing, I had at least the foothold of belief. It was painful that we could not find common ground – for him, perhaps, even more than for me. My last words at the time, spoken in pique and youthful arrogance, were, 'Well, one day we'll both know, and you'll see who's right.'

The marble-floored morgue was cold, dimly lit and empty but for the rows of beds with bodies covered by sheets. Which was his? I went towards one from which a pair of feet protruded. They were swollen, but I recognised them and when I grasped a big toe, it was still warm. It was at that moment that the tears came in a flow I made no attempt to stop – unleashed not only by grief but an extraordinary feeling of joy. His presence was there as palpably as his body and during those few special moments, I expanded upwards with him.

I took the sheet off his face and saw with shock the anguish in its lines and crevices – no doubt made worse by his philosophy of nihilism; for from such a belief can come neither comfort nor meaning in the face of suffering. It is a lonely road that many tread who hold those views and through what I read on his face I have learnt to respect the courage of it.

Luke was silent. 'How can you know that what you felt was true?'

'How do we know anything? That we're in a room in China, for example?'

'I can see it. I know how I got here, because I did it myself.'

'Do you realise what you've said? *I* see, *I* know, *I* did. What is this I?'

He paused. 'I can hear what you're leading up to. You're going to say it's not just my body. But the fact is this awareness only exists because I'm in my body.'

'Wonderful! Let's look at that sentence. You can even *meditate* on it! "I – am – in – my – body." "My", for example; does it not presuppose the existence of an I, separate from the thing that's owned? Then, "in". We only know of "in" because of "out". Right?'

'But this is playing with words. They can be used to say anything.'

'Only if you lose sight of the context. We're talking about death because we've just been close to it. That's no game. I'm saying, *I* exists independently of the body as well as in it, and that this truth is so fundamental we can't help expressing it in language. I'm also saying that following these thoughts is one way of coming to certainty about life beyond death.'

'All right, you win for now. But my interest is in this life. I want to get on with it and for you to look after yourself. We must phone the travel insurance people again and speak to a doctor. Maybe we have to give up the idea of Tibet.'

It took much of the following day to get through and in the meantime I was doing a crash course in the art of conscious eating. What an ordinary thing is swallowing – and how precious when one realises one's life depends on it!

In Zen Buddhism the attempt is made to still thoughts and feelings to the point where one's full concentration is on what one is doing; hence the focus, as in old monasteries in the West, on simple acts performed over and again each day – walking, sitting, carrying a bowl, cooking rice, eating, chopping wood... Zen masters choose not to speak of God or the spirit; their attention is on *being*, on the '*is*ness' of each moment. One is *in* the action, one *is* the action; then doer and deed fall away and all that remains is... *is*. Until, perhaps, that goes too.

I did not take the art of swallowing quite that far, but I survived the meals and the storm died down. The response from the medical people on the phone was as practical and reassuring as before and our spirits revived. The journey was still on.

When we took the bus to Xiahe early next morning, we assumed that Lanzhou had given us as much teaching as we were due this time round, and that when we returned it would be to rest a night and prepare for the train to Jiayuguan where the Great Wall ends. Again we were wrong, but that particular trauma still lay three nights into the future.

In the press of bodies and sacks, as we climbed slowly towards three thousand metres, Luke insisted I read his copy of *Beijing Review* – an English language, pro-government newspaper. In our cycle of monthly exercises, Thu and I had moved on from positivity to open-mindedness so I accepted the challenge.

Receiving information in this way, the bias or vanity or downright error of the person speaking or writing is given no more importance than the fact of having a wart on one's face. It is not a question of agreeing or disagreeing with what is stated, but simply taking it in. Nor is it intended that one renounce one's powers of judgement at other times. It is an *exercise*, one of many on the thorny road towards overcoming egoism.

As in other issues, several of the articles were in praise of what was being done in Tibet. Attention was drawn to the huge amounts of money and materials being poured into it, the heroism of Chinese volunteers and the advances in education, job training and socialism. 'Doesn't it make you *ill*?' said Luke.

I gave a Chinese shrug and turned to Christopher Houghton Budd's book, *Of Wheat and Gold*.

> So enormous are the surpluses generated by the simple fact of the evolution of individuality that we completely delude ourselves when we speak of an absence of money or of an insufficiency of goods today. These are problems of our own making... One need only calculate the amount of effort expended in producing things which are merely destroyed... to experience how much could be made available to mankind if this wealth were deployed instead in things we used up creatively, rather than threw away in deeds of destruction.

'What does he mean about surpluses generated by individuality?' Luke quizzed.

'Think of all that Qin Shihuang got done during his lifetime,' I replied. 'In the world today there are millions of people with that same force of individuality.'

'Building empires, you mean? Tyrannising other people with their wealth?'

'That's not the only way of using it. Isn't it also the power we use to discipline ourselves? And help one another?'

It was on this note that we reached Xiahe, the air crisp and clean against bare hills. We were light-headed, almost giddy with the altitude and the life in the rutted main street. 'Wow,' says Luke. '*This* I can handle.'

Monks of all ages, in rust-red cloaks and shawls of cerise, mingle with old men in Maoist blue and others in Western clothes. Here and there are furry high boots and sheepskin coats, the women with long plaits reminiscent of Native Americans, faces dark and leathered, wrinkled like dry earth. Young children are walking on the road in a higgledy-piggledy line, holding hands in pairs, cheeks rosy, school satchels on their backs. Behind them, a curly-horned goat pushes open the door to the Bank of China.

Shops spill onto the sidewalks in a festival of colour. We stop and browse, breathing the smells of incense, yak butter, leather and fleece, feeling the silk scarves (or *katags*) used as ritual gifts, gazing at the woolly hats and gloves, the boots and knives, small gongs and bells and hand-held prayer wheels with embossed calligraphy. A stooping couple, heads shaven and in maroon robes, walk by holding hands. Three young monks look through piles of cassettes and CDs in a stall pumping out the beat of a Chinese pop song.

We pass a long covered walkway with cylinders on vertical poles, about two metres high, gaily painted in red, yellow, blue, green and white, the colours of the elements in Tibetan tradition. From time to time an elderly person shuffles along it, mumbling mantras and turning the wheels with their pictures and prayers.

We take pedicabs to an old hotel that was once the residence of *tulkus* (those who have reached enlightenment), past the red walls and glinting gold of the monastery, over the bridge with its lines of prayer flags, and back in time to women beating stalks on the dung-splattered road or breaking the dusty soil with hoes, to mud houses, donkey carts, pigs and long-haired yaks peering in bemusement.

It is four thirty and the wind has a bite. We rest, grateful for being where birds fly free and the river gurgles as it hurries towards town. Mountains on both sides of the valley. No snow as yet. After dinner there is even hot water in the shower.

But none of us slept well – though we did not know it, an effect of altitude. My mind relived the day's impressions, then explored on towards Tibet and the Himalayas. That titanic, east–west body of rock and ice, how different would our planet be without it!

There are maps of the Pacific, which illustrate beautifully the congealed swirl of rock and canyon, from the Himalayas through South-East Asia to New Guinea and the northern tip of Australia. For the first time I was able to picture this – the pathway along which our journey had taken us – not only as the scar of past activity, but a flowline of energy active still today. I grasped that little bit more fully the connectedness of all things and all parts of the earth.

In the high places one is in a different atmosphere, which affects both body and mind. It becomes easier to raise oneself to a larger perspective, from which to look out over the world and one's life. One is closer to the spirit. Perhaps it is out of an intuition of this, that people generally seem to have been more affected by the brutality in Tibet than that in Xinjiang Province or East Timor or Irian Jaya.

Next morning we cycled to the monastery. In the lanes outside, with their crumbling white and terracotta walls, we gave ourselves over to the whims of the maroon-clad novices. They rode on our bikes, scrutinised our guidebook and looked through Luke's lenses, prancing about, chattering, trying out English words and joking, pausing only as two ancient lamas with yellow ceremonial hats balanced on their shoulders walked by. 'We, Tibetan,' said one of the boys, puffing out his chest. The cry was taken up by another. 'China, no good. This, Tibet.'

Across the main courtyard was a solid three-storey building, its earth-red stone walls topped with small stupas of gold. As in the tombs of the Etruscans and the sacred gateways of Japan, the walls tapered off gently from wide foundations to a flat apex, like a cut-off pyramid. The same angle was repeated in the dark blue window frames.

There were twelve people in our tour, among them an English man who seemed knowledgeable and asked detailed questions. From our guide, a middle-aged monk, we learnt that though the main buildings had been protected by the army during the Cultural Revolution, the residential areas and anything of artistic or religious value had been abused. From four thousand monks, its population had shrunk to five hundred (and more recently crept up again to a thousand) in what had once been a kind of university of Buddhism.

Many of the halls were dark and musty, but in one were colourful tableaux made of yak butter depicting round-eyed dragons, azaleas, peacocks, unicorns, a jewelled bodhisattva playing a lute, and meditants whose hand gestures indicated different stages of inner progress. Though protected behind glass and cooled by fans, their smell was rancid. They can be kept for many months, we were told, before being returned to nature as symbols – like sand mandalas – of the impermanence of all creation.

The destruction of the prayer hall (by a fire attributed to faulty wiring) is another such symbol. The new building with its forest of square red pillars was in twilight as the monks are now wary of electricity. The paved floor was covered with prayer mats. All around were bright murals with Buddha images, cluttered shrines, altars and statues, the air thick with incense.

In the open area beyond, monks were rehearsing a ritual dance to the accompaniment of cymbals, drums and huge brash trumpets resting on the ground. Their movements were slow and trance-like, with arms wafting in and out. Small boys in maroon chased each other with sticks. An older monk berated them and they ran off laughing.

On the walls of buildings, over doors and windows, horizontal strips of white-frilled fabric billowed out in rhythmical waves to the passing breeze; on the hilltops beyond fluttered lines of coloured flags, scattering the prayers written on them to the elements.

The dance finished and a strident but full tone sounded through the air, on and on. I looked up to see a figure on one of the roofs, blowing into an arm-length bugle.

The English man was staying at our hotel. He knew Tibet well, but to our surprise his love of the country did not entail disrespect for China. 'It's only a matter of time before it becomes the leading superpower,' he remarked. 'They'll do a better job of it too. They're resourceful, so the environment will be less abused. And I suspect they'll leave us to get on with our own lives.'

Luke was struggling. 'What of their contempt for human rights?'

'Not good; but not as bad as the Western press makes out. It suits powerful nations to point the finger at them and cover up their own meddling in other people's affairs.'

'Isn't that what the Chinese do?'

'Of course. It's politics. People everywhere put their own needs first and pretend it's altruism. But frankly, Westerners are better at it than Eastern people.'

We shared some of the frustrations we had had, and again he brought a different perspective. 'Yes, we all get tired of having to pay more in trains and hotels, but you have to realise the Chinese prices are subsidised by the government and this is reflected in the low level of salaries.' He also said that power cuts and water shortages in hotels are hardly surprising considering the population that has to be serviced and the harshness of the climate in many places. 'It occurred to me once, when I was washing my pack and clothes after a few weeks of roughing it, that I had used as much water as a Tibetan uses in several months.'

We turned to practical details about getting to Tibet. We had heard of people entering from the west, near Kashgar, and hitching rides in trucks to Lhasa, the capital. It was our last glimmer of hope for combining both places and that evening it went out. He said that at the best of times it would need three weeks, with virtually no food along the way. 'At this season you might not even get through. People have died of exposure in the backs of trucks.'

Late September and all at once winter was racing towards us. The only other way of getting into Tibet by land would be the thirty-hour bus marathon from Golmud, in the north. 'They'll fleece you and it's a hellish drive,' he continued. 'But the passes should be open till the end of October.'

'And what of Tibet itself?' I said, as he got up to go. 'Are you as confident about its future under the Chinese as you are for the rest of the world?'

He paused. 'There's nothing I'd like more than an independent Tibet; but I can't see it happening. At least not until the world has got beyond the politics of power.'

It was another night of little sleep. In the silent hours, the image came of Tibet – and other such places – as wounds in the side of humanity. In the archetypal story of Parsifal, the young knight in red armour meets the Grail King Anfortas and is shown the awful suffering of a wound that cannot be healed, except through the asking of a certain question. Parsifal has been brought up not to ask questions and has to undergo years of torment because of his failure to release the king. When at last the opportunity comes to redeem this, the question that initiates the miracle is the simplest one imaginable: 'Uncle, what ails thee?'

It is not the words, of course, that bring the transformation, but the timing and the entire soul disposition out of which they are spoken. 'Humanity, what ails thee?' In how many people does this thought have to come to life for a new age to be born?

An answer formed in my mind: Tibet's pain will diminish to the extent that humankind takes it on and that we recognise in ourselves the affliction, and the weapon which causes it, rather than just seeing it all 'out there'.

Our guide at the monastery had invited us to come back for the early morning prayers. When our alarm made its dreadful beeping at six, the room still dark and freezing, my first response was to head back to sleep. But the knowledge that I was squirming out of something I had resolved to do tapped at me like the clock's ticking and ten minutes later I was up.

The chanting alternated between recitation of mantras and the sub-bass intoning that seemed to call on the power of the depths. The rhythms changed too, to the beating of gongs and wood on hollow wood. It called one to flow out into it, as one does into the waves on the shore. As a Buddhist one trusts where the current will take one. I can respect it and let it lead me a certain way. But only so far.

Like many from the West, I went to the East in my twenties in search of meaning. For all my years at school and university, I was ignorant of the spirit in my own culture. Into the places left empty in the soul I drank the focused simplicity of Zen and the harmonies of Chinese philosophy, the huge time spans of Indian thought and the practicality of martial arts. I strove to empty the mind and delighted in the riddles of Japanese *koans* – to search without searching, for 'gateless gates' and 'soundless sounds'. By comparison Christianity seemed then a maze of dogmas which people could preach, but not explain.

Yet something was lacking. There was often a subtle disdain for thinking; it was dismissed as intellectual and cumbersome, whereas truth was always simple. I could accept this only with a reservation: such insight has to be discovered and *earned* by each person, otherwise it is mere platitude. In advocating the illusory nature of the individual self, many Eastern ways were also denying the very aspect of reality which is *not* impermanent – that world of experiencing we encompass in the tiniest of words, *I*.

I believe now, having researched more widely, that this nihilism does not come from Buddha. His way of teaching was to draw attention to what was *not* real, without allowing speculation as to what was. In this way the pupil has to discover it in actual experience. One is led to the point at which one's normal assumptions appear subjective and transient; but if Buddha had stopped there, he would not have been able to maintain his own identity to preach the overcoming of the self. With what, after all, does one do the overcoming?

The chanting drew to a close. We sat in silence. Some of the monks were wrapped in stillness, others fidgeting or communicating with each other by gestures of face or hand. Then it resumed, led by an elderly monk, in an antiphonal rhythm of single voice and congregation. Waves of sound welled and cascaded as incense mingled with the morning light and dust.

7

The bus ride back to Lanzhou was fine. It was after it that the nightmare began. Justin and Luke were on the seat behind; alone by the window I breathed in the bracing air, the afternoon light yellow and tender beneath a blue sky, high and vast, with wandering wisps of cloud. Dusky hills repeated themselves to the horizon, curves and lines exuding a brooding power as if waiting to burst into new life. Away to the south, invisible yet, the Himalayas.

Afternoon turned to twilight and, as we continued to descend, twilight to darkness. I felt drowsy and attached my waist pouch to the bar on the seat in front.

It was nine o'clock by the time we reached Lanzhou's centre and were asked unexpectedly to get off at a street corner. We gathered our luggage into a pedicart and Luke went with it to the friendly hotel where we had stayed before. Justin and I followed in a motor rickshaw. We had gone only a couple of minutes when I realised something was missing. 'I've forgotten my hat,' I said, still dazed.

'What about your belt?' His words seemed far away. 'Thu, your belt. Do you have it?'

I touched where it should have been and felt instantly nauseous. Justin stopped the driver but it took a while for him to understand, and by the time we got to where it had been, the bus had gone. I was aware of Justin's angry silence and worried about Luke waiting at the hotel, but the driver beckoned us to climb back in and drove off purposefully into the night.

He took us to the terminus, deserted now but for empty buses, eerily lit by lights from a building across the square. We moved from one to another, peering into the ghostly interiors. Ah, dear consciousness, what colour had it been? Justin said blue and white; I was sure it had a red stripe. The driver called us to follow him through a maze of corridors to a second-floor office, outside which was a man, bent double on the floor, right hand manacled to left ankle. He hid his face, and the official inside gesticulated for us to go somewhere else.

On through dark streets to a brick building, up a metal stairway and along a balcony to a bare room with a desk, some chairs and a bed, on which a man in a singlet and police trousers was rubbing sleep from his eyes. Other officials came in as the driver launched into our story.

I was worried about Luke. He must be thinking that we had had an accident. We tried to explain and begged them to phone the hotel for us. They nodded and looked grim. Had they understood? Events were slipping out of control. Justin was still hostile. My mind went faint. It was ten o'clock.

In slow motion one of the officers sat down at the desk and lifted the phone. He spoke into it at length, then turned to our driver, seemingly haranguing him with sharp gestures. The driver left, though we had not paid him. What now? Were we being arrested?

Our hosts gave us hot water to drink, casually asking about Australia – many cars, few bicycles, desert in the centre, salaries of many hundreds of dollars a month, a game called cricket. They chatted on among themselves. Was anything happening? The phone rang, then a young woman walked in. In textbook English she told us her job was to deal with foreigners and that we must make a statement. So the process was only just beginning. What was in the belt? Passport, glasses, traveller's cheques…

The door opened again and in came Luke! The driver had gone to the hotel and given him a lift. 'A good man,' he said; then added gently, 'It'll be all right, Mum.'

We handed in what we had written and the lady said she would phone the next day. 'If we do not find, we give a certificate of lost passport, to use for travelling,' she went on. 'Nothing to worry. Now you go.'

'You're not the first person to whom this has happened,' said Luke, putting his arm round my shoulders. He told us cheerfully how his aunt, Justin's younger sister in Bangkok, had once lost her and her husband's passports on an Indian train. Then she mislaid her new one. The official at the embassy said if she lost the next one, they would not replace it.

'I'm sorry for causing all this trouble,' I said, feeling Justin's reproach. 'I feel awful.'

'Haven't I been patient?' But there was still a darkness about him. It reminded me of how I used to feel next to my mother.

We passed a food market – a frenzy of sizzling and steaming, naked bulbs highlighting the colourful display of meat and vegetables. We ordered the local soup, bubbling on charcoal braziers and adorned with carrot, capsicum, quail eggs and globules of oil; but I could hardly eat. 'You guys look smashed,' said Luke. 'They've given us a great room. You'll see.' On one of the tables was a printed card. *'We wish you a good night sleep. All the staff care for you.'*

Justin was awake before me. 'Does it mean that on some level you want to quit?' he said, as I struggled to take hold of the day. 'Is the journey too much?' It was not yet out of compassion that he asked but in order to find meaning. It is his way of coming to acceptance.

To my surprise I had slept well and, although shaken, felt strong. I had been focusing on a feeling of openness for whatever might eventuate, even our having to stop; but it was not what I was looking for and I said so. Luke suggested I set about getting a new passport and cheques right away. 'Who ever heard of Chinese police helping travellers?'

There was a knock on the door and the floor lady shouted that there was a phone call for me. 'This is the police office.' It was a woman's voice. 'We've found your bag.'

My hat was there too. Only a silk scarf, which I had dyed cherry pink for the kindergarten, was missing. Before signing the receipt, I had to count the cheques, painfully aware that the three thousand dollars they represented would have been about eight years' pay for those who had retrieved them.

'How did you find it?' Justin asked.

'We found the driver this morning. He had locked it up in the bus to keep it safe.'

'Is there anything we can do for you and for him? We'd like to express our thanks.'

'It is our duty,' said the man behind the desk. 'In your country it would be the same.'

Images from the day mingled with the train's lumbering, creaking, shrieking and lurching, as we headed on westward during the night. Mercifully the loudspeaker at our end of the carriage was out of action – thanks to Luke, who by now had the process of unscrewing the cover and disengaging one of the wires down to a fine art. In places there must have been only one track, because we often waited for other trains to pass. I came to understand why it would take at least twenty-four hours to reach Jiayuguan. So what? I hope my scarf is with the bus driver, I thought. I would gladly have given it to him for his wife, had we seen him again.

I relived the anxiety of the night before and the tenseness between Justin and me. With all the differences between people, particularly now when personal consciousness is so strong, what is astonishing is not that couples split up but that they remain united. That is why I see relationship as a kind of initiation for, like all such paths, it leads one beyond one's habitual way of being.

Whether a marriage is launched by romantic love or the wheeling and dealing of older members of the family (as in my parents' case), one has to nourish it – to be willing over and again to begin afresh and listen to each other. Otherwise, like everything living, it grows old and dies; the willingness to forgive hardens into expectations and we encase each other in past mistakes, no longer seeing what is new. Am I to blame Justin for his harshness or respect his struggle to overcome it? Will he still hold me to my carelessness tomorrow?

Words flashed into my mind from the enigmatic dialogue between the Golden King and the Snake in Goethe's fairy tale, *The Green Snake and the White Lily*:

'What is more precious than gold?' asks the king.
'Light.'
'What is more refreshing than light?'
'Conversation.'

Dust is everywhere in Jiayuguan – in nostrils and hair, beneath clothes and fingernails. There was a layer of it on the table where we had our lunch in town but it did not appear to be in the food, which was good and generous. In the afternoon we headed off through it, to the fort built six hundred years ago to mark the end of the Wall of China.

We went first to a renovated extension leading to a bare outcrop of rock to the north. A cold wind was surging across the desert, tearing at the poplars on its edge. Northwards it must stretch, I thought, this waterless ocean, to the steppes and grasslands of Mongolia – and beyond that, the Siberian tundra. How much of our planet is desert! To the west it extends, off and on, to Israel.

In the fort, stark as it was, there was at least the comfort of courtyards, rooms and gateways with dragonish roofs and red-painted supports – and names like Gate of Enlightenment or Conciliation. Unlike the Wall, its lines are straight, in the form of a square. But for the roof details, it could have been built in any part of the world, a creation not of Chinese culture but military planning based on reason.

On the high battlements, we stopped by a yellow and red triangular flag straining in the wind like a wild thing on a leash. Had its jagged movements been vertical, it would have been flame; even its searing sound was of fire. It was as if alive, though its 'life' was entirely outside. Nothing inner, no feeling or organic body, yet in its dancing and screaming I could imagine beings of wind and sound and Dervish dance.

On westwards by bus the next day, through a parched land of rock, slate and sand. Beyond were bare mountains, mauve and grey and worn into gulleys, like lines on the old people's faces. We blew a tyre and while the driver was changing it, I felt myself expand in awe into the silence, until I seemed to vanish and something in me trembled and drew back, struggling for a foothold.

I used to yearn for landscapes like this and realised now they had reflected my inner isolation, which in turn was partly a lack of self-worth going back to childhood. Ironically, what obliged me to face it had been the trauma with Justin. For a long time I had sheltered behind his abilities, content to let him take the praise and blame for how our work eventuated. When the conflict burst – as it had to if we were to grow – it jolted me to my senses. The 'I', which had only timidly participated, was now fully on earth. I no longer felt lonely, nor did I yearn for solitude. And now that I did not crave it, here it was, around me.

It was twilight as we entered again the realm of life, past neat patches of vegetables and crops protected by poplars. Dunhuang, another oasis, with a touch of nostalgia and the smell of snow in the autumn air. We crossed a swollen river. How could there be such abundance? There seemed to be no shortage of water anywhere – though the showers we had longed for at our clean and spacious hotel had tiny holes and the spray hardly wet us at all.

'Shall we have a party for Mum?' Justin joked with Luke in the morning.

I grew up in a culture where birthdays are less important than anniversaries of death, when one is born into the spirit. For many in Vietnam, New Year is the only birthday they know and everyone becomes a year older. I had never had a party for myself.

After breakfast they disappeared mysteriously, saying they thought I looked tired and should rest. They came back with a pink scarf to replace the one I had lost; also a pair of orange long johns. 'I thought I was buying them for myself,' said Justin unromantically. 'But they're too small.'

Luke started complaining of stomach pains. 'Is it surprising, considering what you had for breakfast?' I suggested. 'A pancake with fruit and honey, and milk coffee; then a set meal with eggs, sausages, toast and tea, followed by a bowl of fruit and yoghurt, more coffee and a Coke!' He tended to go berserk each time we came to a place serving Western food. 'Besides, it's no longer T-shirt weather.'

'Yeah, yeah,' he said – and rushed to the bathroom.

We walked through the tree-lined streets in search of warm clothes. The stores were full of local wares and food was plentiful at the market. 'Can you come and speak to the lady who sold the long johns?' said Justin sheepishly. 'I'm sure I paid far too much.'

Vivid are my memories of my eldest sister bargaining in the market when I was a child. The prices were never fixed and each purchase was a social process, the seller starting too high, she too low. We would hear about the storm which had destroyed much of the harvest, and of how the monkeys had done their bit too; not to mention the war. She would let it be known that others also had their misfortunes, and slowly the price would find its equilibrium.

The woman was wearing a red kaftan and scarf, tied up at the back in the way of desert folk. She seemed a bit puzzled seeing me with Justin. 'We don't want it,' I attempted in Chinese. She shook her head, uttering a string of words. A small crowd gathered and I was aware of her neighbours listening in. 'Thirty yuan. Expensive.'

'How much?'

'Ten.'

She looked at me keenly, and I sensed her respect. 'Here, fifteen.' She wrapped them in newspaper and pressed them back into my hand. Watching faces became approving grins.

In the late afternoon, we hired bicycles with a couple of Australian girls staying in the hotel and rode out to the range of sand hills at the edge of town, happy in the freedom of air and light. A man in a jacket and pink shirt greeted us with a *'Ni hao?'* (Hello) and a gold-toothed smile, and rode alongside.

The dunes were fenced off and he came with us to buy tickets. He seemed interested in our teacher cards and Justin warned quietly he might be a security agent; yet he followed us up the steep ridges to the tallest of the 'peaks' and when we took off our shoes, did the same. We gazed over the exquisite curves and ripples, golden in the sunset. Luke and the girls rolled down the slopes, waded up shin-deep in flowing silk, and rolled again. Justin joined them, then I, then our smartly-dressed companion. Agent or not, he had become one of us.

A last blaze of brilliance, then a warm hushed glow, enveloping. Cooler air, the sounds of people heading back to the perimeter – and suddenly it was just us and the evening star. So the celebration began, with dunes for a cake, sunset its colours, stars for candles and light – and for music, a silence that became an element like the air, around us, above, within. Pastel veils flowed imperceptibly into one another and as darkness breathed away the light, the dunes became pyramids of indigo before merging with the dome above. Venus, radiant; and, much closer now – only thirty degrees away – Jupiter. What a journey it had made since we were in Bali four and a half months before, from the opposite side of the evening sky!

Back in town we ate together, the six of us. Our new friend Shi, who said he was in Dunhuang on business, was puzzled by our Western way of paying individually for our food, but as before, followed what we did, his face bubbling with smiles. 'We meet again,' I understood him to say. 'My house far away. Wuhan. Wife and son, six years. You come visit.'

A young Chinese man by the name of Bear, with a ponytail and Mickey Mouse T-shirt, ambled over to our table, introducing himself as an artist-photographer-traveller. As he translated what we told of our backgrounds, Shi looked at each person in turn, grinning unstoppably. Bear said we were the first people from the West Shi had met.

We spent the next day immersed in the superb art of the Mogao caves, a jewel of the Silk Road twenty kilometres from Dunhuang, amidst dunes, cliffs and the autumn leaves of apple and apricot groves. There are almost five hundred in all, created by different families after the example of a monk in the fourth century who had a vision of a thousand Buddhas and dug out the first cave. For ten centuries the tradition continued; then the caves were sealed up to prevent their contents falling into the hands of invaders. It was not until the twentieth century that a Taoist monk rediscovered them and tentatively allowed others into his secret, with the result that many of the artworks and manuscripts are now in museums in the West.

What remains is nevertheless one of China's richest treasures. Its survival during the Cultural Revolution is a result of the intervention of the premier Zhou Enlai, who sent the army to protect twelve places of national heritage. Among the others were the Forbidden City and Temple of Heaven, Labrang Monastery at Xiahe and the Potala Palace in Tibet.

Our only way in was with a guide. The young man assigned to us was about as bored as a person can be without actually falling asleep. The only thing he said with any zest, and with an appropriately lewd grin, was that we could see the Tantric caves with their erotic murals for an extra fifty dollars each – a favour we declined.

The main colours that remain on the statues, frescoes and ceilings are terracotta, ochre, turquoise and olive, black and blue – faded and blemished, but with stunning variety. It is a wonderful interplay of India and China in deep religious devotion. Figure after figure is depicted with the halos often associated with Christian art. The most sublime of them, the Buddha, has a multi-layered aura around the whole body, out of which the halo emerges as a smaller circle, sometimes peaking upwards like a Muslim arch.

As well as scenes from Buddha's life, we saw angels, guardians and demons. In one of the caves was a figure of Maitreya, the future Buddha, carved into rock nearly thirty-five metres high, not in lotus position but on a seat with feet on the ground. In some was the symbol of the cross, small but distinct.

How exciting to experience this tentative meeting of streams! How many more secrets of the human journey are buried within the desert? Since it is a day for unveiling secrets, let me speak of what it is that draws us now farther west into the desert towns of the Tarim Basin, although it is off our route to Tibet.

We have read that, prior to what science knows as the last Ice Age (and which the Old Testament and many other documents refer to as the Flood), there was a continent where the Atlantic Ocean is now, and on it the civilisation of Atlantis. Its culture was regulated by priest-kings, high initiates trained in the various mystery centres. Before the continent sank, over ten thousand years ago, migrations took place west and east under the leaders of these various streams – hence the similarities between cultures in so many parts of the world.

The group that travelled farthest, through Europe and Asia to the Tarim Basin, was led by the highest initiate of all, Manu, described in legends as part-man, part-god. Their journey took them north of the Tienshan or Mountains of Heaven, then south and west into the basin itself, bordered by mountains on three sides and at that time well-watered and fertile. The open side, to the east, is the Turpan Depression – or Oasis of Fire – now the hottest place in China and the lowest on earth after the Dead Sea. It was there we would be heading in the coming days.

When we got back that evening we found Shi and Bear had moved into our hotel. Next morning Shi came to our room with a book in his hands. 'For you,' he said, using words he had rehearsed with Bear. 'Friends. My country.'

It pains me now that we said no. The book was about the caves, but it was bulky and in Chinese and we had to be ruthless to keep our packs from growing daily heavier. He tried to insist at first, but his timid respect for the strange ways of foreigners prevailed and he said he understood our difficulty. 'I buy English,' he managed to communicate. 'Send Australia.'

We have learnt since what we should have known already from our Africa journey, how hard it is to stay in touch with people in distant places. Not only do letters get lost and addresses change, but one writes into a void, not knowing if one's words are still in tune with the other person. Meeting in the flesh, there are a hundred ways of sharing. Now, from a distance of space and time, I feel closest to those we met in China when I look, not out towards their country, but within myself. The English version has not reached us and we do not know if the photographs we sent later to Shi got through.

We all left the same day, we west to Hami, the girls and Shi back east, and Bear south to Golmud and Tibet. Our bus was the first to head off and the others came to see us go. Bear gave Luke what he called an international handshake, as the meeting of palms turned into a mock arm-wrestling; then Shi, to my astonishment, hugged both Justin and Luke with tears in his eyes. He thrust a bagful of fruit into my hand, then turned away to catch the same bus as the girls, to look after them, he said, although it would mean going out of his way.

Desert to the horizon, Luke's stomach still delicate, so much so that when we stopped for lunch at a desolate cluster of restaurants in a treeless, sun-scorched landscape, he slept on in the bus. Nearer to Hami, the occasional scrub or scraggly tree broke through the crust; then on the edge of town, fields again and sprouting things, and piles of yellow melons famous throughout China.

Our hotel by the bus station had concrete floors and grime-stained walls. There was a dank smell in the room, unclean bed linen, no shower, only cold water in the communal basin, the toilets blocked and unbreathable. Luke was exhausted. I could feel his spirit sinking by the minute. The grey surroundings were getting to him and he was making himself worse by obsessively reading the *Beijing Review*.

'Listen to this. "Tibet's peaceful liberation…" Blah blah blah. "Despite obstruction from foreign separatists…" Blah blah. Crap.'

'Leave it, Luke,' said Justin. 'It's not what you need now.'

'I hate this place. The lying and hypocrisy. How come you can be so *reasonable* about it all? Can you imagine what it's like to be *young* here?'

Hami was once a caravanserai on the road running north of the Basin. Its traditional inhabitants, as in many other parts of Xinjiang Province, are Muslim Uygurs, people of swarthy Caucasian appearance such as we met on the boat to Shanghai. Their relationship to Beijing has been volatile. Attempts to achieve autonomy were crushed in '49, as have been the various demonstrations since, in one part of the province or another. Forty years ago, ninety per cent of the province's population were ethnic peoples; now almost half are Han settlers.

With the influx of industry, the old oasis has expanded and disintegrated into a town of dismal architecture and heavily polluted air. We felt the acid in our eyes, along with the desert dust; but were met with friendliness and a good meal, laced with chillies and shy giggles.

Surprisingly we slept well and Luke looked stronger in the morning. Our main problem was the toilets which were now locked. A man from a nearby room tried the door, then spoke to the girl at the desk by the stairs. '*Mei you*,' we heard her reply. No.

'What can it be like to have a job like that?' said Luke.
'Why not ask her?'
'Are you joking? She looks at me as if I'm dirt.'
'Ask for hot water. That's something she *can* give.'

He came back fuming. 'Guess what she said. Mei-bloody-you. I can't stand this place!'

There was a knock and in came the girl with a fresh thermos. For a moment she almost smiled, then turned and left. We were hungry and used the water to make instant noodles. At least that would be safe for stomachs that needed to be in good condition for the night bus. 'Sometimes I wonder if there's any point in being here,' Luke went on more quietly. 'Our presence only makes it worse for local people. What has the West produced for them? Colonialism, capitalism, consumerism. Even Marxism. And yet the Chinese were inventing things long before the rest of the world. Why did they stop? It doesn't make sense.'

'Maybe because they valued the past so much and didn't want it to change,' said Justin. 'Whereas in the West, it's what's new that counts. Things are out of date almost as soon as they're created.'

'And where has it brought us, hey? To the brink of destruction.'

'You're not the only one who feels rage, Luke,' I put in. 'I believe it's in people here too. Even if they long for the wealth of the West, they must feel betrayed. They've lost the old spirituality and there's a hollowness which materialism can't fill.'

'So why are we here, then? What good does it do?'

'Maybe just this,' said Justin again. 'You've been brought up in the world of plenty. You know its benefits but also its dangers and deceptions, and this has woken you up. You've started to think for yourself. And now you know what it is to feel powerless.' He paused. 'Isn't that precisely when something new can begin to grow? Right there in the darkness. The strength to change in some way so that you can be of more use to others?'

Luke was silent.

'Perhaps someone like Shi, who may never leave China, could sense this,' I added. 'Perhaps he sees now that there's more to the West than all the stuff we produce.'

'Haven't we also received from him?' Luke countered.

'Exactly!' It was Justin. 'The pandas and the wandering geese! With each encounter something given, something taken, each of us coming away a tiny bit different. And more awake.'

'But dammit!' Luke shouted out suddenly, his voice cracking. 'Why do I feel so guilty?'

We were silent and I longed to hug him but it was not the moment.

He was quiet for the rest of the afternoon. There were to be more storms ahead; but something stirred in him that day in dismal Hami.

8

A shout of 'Tulufan' roused us from our half-sleep. Landlocked Turpan, as far from Shanghai as from the Persian Gulf and Arctic Ocean. It was still dark. The driver waited patiently while Thu gathered our things together and Luke and I got the packs off the frosty roof. The bus revved garishly and disappeared into the silence. We stretched, breathing in the crisp dryness, Orion and Sirius blazing above and, low in the east, the red slither of a waning moon.

We seemed to be on the edge of town at the end of a wide street, deserted but for the silhouette of a lady stoking an outdoor stove and a man sweeping the pavement in the yellow glow from their shack. Dogs barked; the straw broom swished rhythmically.

Their restaurant consisted of a table which could either be on the pavement or in the single room where their bed was. We chose the open air. The man disappeared with a bucket; the woman, visible now in padded jacket and baggy pants, blew on the fire until it roared, and stirred green leaves in a wok. She rolled out some dough and put small stuffed blobs of it into a steamer, as her husband struggled back with the water.

Officially all of China sets its clocks to the time that suits Beijing. At the new Oasis Hotel a man and woman in uniform were asleep on the sofas in the lobby, though in theory it was seven thirty. We sat and dozed and slowly the world stirred into activity. The sleeping figures became a guard and a receptionist with a gentle smile. Next came a cleaner with the archetypal bucket and mop.

We wandered out into the unhurried bustle of a town in which the Muslim Uygur culture still prevails – women in colourful long skirts, their heads unveiled, most of the men in baggy trousers and shirts. Clusters of grapes hung low above our heads on the shady sidewalks, dappled with dancing images of the new-risen sun. Restaurants and cafés spilled onto the paving, to the whirr of bicycles and the intermittent clatter of trucks. A steady trickle of people was flowing in and out of a small mosque, topped by a dome and sickle moon.

Houses along the back lanes brought to mind oases in the Sahara – simple mud-brick dwellings grouped behind walls, with a communal gate and yard. Open channels ran down the streets, in which children were splashing and women washing pots. Through the mud walked others, with baskets of local spinach against their hips, or piles of round flat bread. The market was coming to life, a rich medley of food, fabric and trinkets, and tea houses where men sucked smoke through bubbling water pipes amidst smells of ginger and aromatic spices.

We came to John's Café, a haunt of backpackers, where Luke gleefully read every English notice on the board and launched into conversations beneath the trees. Words filtered back – China, mei you, smile, ripped off, racist, Tibet… He was beginning to offload. 'It's as if we're in an Arab country,' he exulted.

'Isn't it another face of China?' said Thu.

Our room had curtains and generous windows through which the sun was streaming. There was no hot water but the cold shower was invigorating in the growing heat. Then, how good, simply to lie on our clean white-sheeted beds and sleep!

Dinner was an eventful occasion. Near us was a group of four Chinese men and one of them helped us order. As the meal progressed, the noise from their table grew in volume, reaching a climax from time to time as they raised their fingers and shouted out numbers – and one or the other downed his beer in a gulp. Loosened by alcohol, the friendly man invited us to join them. He said he was a civil servant, his companions a driver for a tour company, a captain and a doctor. The conversation turned, in the normal way, to salaries. The officer's was the highest, at seventy-five dollars a month, the doctor's and his the lowest at half that.

They wanted to know about life – and morality – in capitalist Australia. 'In some ways, it's more socialist than here,' I suggested and gave the instance of my skin graft, which had been paid for by the state. This stunned them, for it went against everything they had heard.

The driver asked what we thought of China. Luke said he thought the people were not very happy. 'How can we be?' came the reply. 'We earn little and sell our things cheaply to the West. But we love our nation.'

'Maybe that's the difference,' Luke went on, though the remarks were addressed to me as head of family, in true Confucian style. 'Here people are encouraged to be nationalistic; in Australia most of us dislike nationalism.'

'It's a tradition. From our five thousand years of history.'

'Isn't it time to change, so people can meet as individuals? Haven't we fought enough over it already?' The doctor said something and I sensed his sympathy, but his friend did not translate. We were told they disagreed.

Our last interchange was about communism. The civil servant and the captain were Party members, the driver was hoping to become one. 'It is our religion,' said the translator. 'Just as in the West there is Christianity.' He made a cross over his heart, adding that it was not easy to become a member; one had to excel in one's work.

The following day we joined a small tour into the desert, our companions two English girls fresh from art courses at university, two young Korean couples studying Chinese in Beijing, a lanky unshaven Irish man called Simon who had recently come up from India and Pakistan (which he loved so much he looked as if he had been born there, despite having suffered from amoebic dysentery in the one, mountain sickness in the other and with a legacy of glandular fever from them both), plus a grumpy driver who saw it as his task to get us to the designated sites and back as fast as possible.

High on a cliff above a river lined with poplars and old mud buildings are what remains of the Bezelik caves. We felt the sadness of a place, once vibrant with Buddhist art and devotion, now desecrated – not by Muslims and Red Guards only, but archaeologists who cut out whole frescoes and took them to the West. Some of the finest were apparently in the Berlin Museum when it was blitzed during the Second World War.

Deserted Gaochang, capital of the Uygur kingdom in the ninth century, was a more uplifting experience. Because of its size, we hired a donkey cart and swayed to its gentle rhythm along the straight rutted streets bordered by ruined walls of mud and stone where once had been government offices, shops, houses, a palace. Our driver alternated between goading the donkeys with grunts and whip, and trying to lure us into buying souvenirs which he produced like a magician from a box: skull caps, daggers, ornaments, melons, postcards. Thu bought a bell and its clear tinkle accompanied our stately tour of the city.

The ruins of Jiaohe, a garrison town on a sheer table mountain bounded by two rivers, are older and more worn-down – the legacy of Genghis Khan, who razed the place in the thirteenth century. The walls are but a maze of fragments and standing lumps, bereft of the culture that was once imprinted on their surfaces.

What spoke most was the searing heat, flat crumbly desert, distant bare mountains, silence, and thoughts of the past. The earth gives and the earth takes back – our creations, as well as our bodies. Science knows it as the principle of entropy, the inevitable falling away of form into chaos. Why do scientists not give equal attention, I wonder, to what the power is that brings the form into being in the first place, whether in nature or through human actions, and upholds it against decay for as long as it does?

Though we found no trace of them that day, the Tarim Basin has seen the confluence of other religious streams besides Buddhism and Islam – such as Manichean Christianity, a sect founded by the Persian, Manes, in the third century. His work was systematically destroyed by the Roman church but his influence on Asia was enormous, carried partly through the arterial flow of the Silk Road.

In contrast to the Roman doctrine of sin and punishment, he saw evil as a challenge to awaken a love strong enough to transform it – and taught of Christ as the cosmic spirit of the sun who had come down to earth to penetrate matter with light and human souls with love. In

1907 manuscripts of his teachings were found near Turpan. Some years later, others were uncovered in Egypt.

They are illustrated by a legend. After the separation of light from darkness in primeval times, there arose a dragon in the depths which threatened to devour all beings who opposed it. So the King of the Paradise of Light created Man and sent him into the darkness to fight it, armed with the five powers of breath, wind, light, water and fire. It was too strong, however, and devoured its opponent; but the love which Man carried for the Creator was taken in too. And so, within the dragon, there grew a longing for the light.

Sun-weathered and thirsty, we came to an oasis watered by one of a thousand underground channels, some as long as forty kilometres and two thousand years old, nourishing the almost rainless Turpan Depression with the snowmelt of the Tianshan range. We went down into a tunnel, through which the cold clear crystal-fresh life-sap was flowing. We scooped it up and drank, bathed our feet and splashed, as the sounds echoed against the rough-hewn rock. Here was a holy place, the holiness of water in wilderness. Nearby were flowers and small trees, full green leaves and the tinkling spray of fountains.

Does it *really* make sense that life, in its variety and vigour, has its origin in minerality? That plants die and their components go back to the earth, I can see and accept. That *life* can arise out of non-life, simply through a greater complexity of molecules, makes sense neither to my mind nor experience. Something else is active, which builds and moulds and sculpts, not from outside only like a sculptor carving rock, but weaving through the substance itself. This dynamic forming energy is known to spiritual science as the *etheric*.

What we see as the plant is the matter it contains, but the patterns within which each cell is placed are created by the flow of its etheric organisation. The substance makes visible what is otherwise invisible. Science is used to the concept of waves of energy revealing their form through the undulations of water. A cork on the sea simply bobs up and down as waves pass 'through'; so too with the water surrounding it. Why is there such reluctance to explore an analogous concept with regard to life? Perhaps it is because the etheric cannot be measured or defined in terms of electro-magnetism. It is the manifestation, closest to the physical world, of the spiritual.

Though our priority now was to head back east to Golmud as soon as we could for the dreaded bus ride to Tibet, we spent another day in Turpan – Thu and I in the quietness of our room, Luke padding round town with his camera and playing pool with Simon, who came with us in the evening to watch a performance of Uygur dancing. It was an informal event, on a stage covered by vine trellises in the open air.

The gutsy flowing music, with its strong rhythm and high metallic tones, came from an orchestra of tambour drums, ukelele, xylophone, accordion and a 'violin' that rests on the knees. The dancing was vigorous and fresh, with what seemed like elements of Greece, Turkey and Central Asia, along with Cossack leg jerks and the otherworldly wistfulness of Gaelic tunes.

Their costumes were outrageously colourful, especially the reds and pinks – men with moustaches, leather boots, breeches and long shirts; women with waistcoats, floor-length dresses and flashing eyes, hair in plaits below the waist. Many of the dances acted out the age-old rituals of festivals and courting – the women graceful and coy, while the men cavorted and jumped. They merged... feminine, masculine.

Simon came to the bus station the next morning and it was time for another goodbye. I looked out of the window as his gaunt shape, sad but smiling, gave way to the scorched wilderness.

> The grey road, the sand,
> endless; a mud house, a red scarf;
> Hey!
> It's snowing on the mountains.

Of Manu, the initiate from Atlantis, we had found of course no trace – and one may ask what we hoped to achieve by coming to the desert out of mere 'belief' in what we had read. I could answer with a further question, one which I wrote about in my journal that evening:

> *Isn't much of what we call knowledge really belief? No one has seen an atom, yet most people speak of atomic theory as if it were a fact. Likewise with the atom bomb tests that have been taking place for over three decades at Lopnur, south of Turpan; I 'know' about them only through what I have heard and read. It becomes, then, a question of what one chooses to accept, based on one's own criteria of judgement.*
>
> *The thought that such events have occurred has affected the way we experienced this desert. It is not a matter of blindly believing, but of living with the information and testing it through one's knowledge and perception. The same is true of what we have read about Manu; it has afforded us a perspective to which we would otherwise have had no access.*
>
> *What makes sense to me then? It is this, that what Manu and his companions brought over from the dying continent of Atlantis is what the Chinese have tried to maintain as their*

extraordinary culture for thousands of years, despite all the changes that have blazed through other parts of the world in the meantime.

Does this not explain why they isolated themselves for so long from the outside, for fear of defilement? And is this not also the source of that mysterious and magical Golden Age in the distant past towards which so many Chinese philosophers have turned their gaze?

9

The sun shone brightly through the windows. I sat up, awake for once before Justin. A mass of ethereal gold fluttered like butterfly wings outside. I looked down to the street. Tall slim poplars on both sides, a carpet of leaves on the ground.

I had imagined a gloomy concrete town, for nothing we had heard or read about Golmud had been inviting. Most travellers knew it as a high-stress terminus for the long ride to Lhasa. Maybe they had not been here in autumn, or taken the time to experience it in its own right. For us there was no option of racing on. We needed to acclimatise to the altitude, I most of all. Our journey here had knocked me badly and the thought of the bus trip ahead with passes over five thousand metres, scared me.

We were all somewhat breathless as we walked the short distance to the China Independent Traveller Service. On the way we met a Dutch man who had just come in from Lhasa. Tickets from that end had cost only twice the local price as opposed to the ten times, which we had been told the officials would charge us here. 'It's all so *arbitrary*,' Luke said angrily. Then we entered CITS.

The staff were moving rooms and the place was a chaos of tables, chairs and shelves. A man was sorting things out in a corner while a woman glided around with a feather duster, slippers flip-flopping. Another was adjusting the swivel chair behind her desk. She had a round face and a high voice. 'Normal price is one thousand and sixty yuan each,' she said in clear and fluent English, 'which includes a three-day tour of Lhasa. With teacher cards, you are entitled to a reduction to nine hundred and fifty.' She looked at us defiantly.

'Almost one hundred and twenty dollars,' said Justin, with an edge in his voice. 'It's too much. We'll go without the tour.'

'That is not possible in the Tibet Autonomous Region. If you wish, you can go away and think about it.' And she gestured us towards the door.

Outside the Dutch man was basking in the sun, by a dried-up fountain clogged with rubbish. Friendly greetings turned into a sharing of pique. I knew it was a way of releasing frustration, but the tone rankled. Why were Justin and Luke so upset, seeing as we had known already what the policy was? As we moved on, the man called after us, 'By the way, you should meet the four people in number nine. They're also going to Lhasa.'

I needed to be alone and headed for the shower, open for only two hours each day. It was filled with steam and sounds of drenching water. A dim light hung naked from the ceiling. Through the mist there loomed four large shower heads, three of them with no more than a trickle. Under the good one stood three figures, who I took to be a mother and two daughters, of about ten and thirteen. The girls were rinsing their hair and foam was floating round their feet. At intervals, one or the other would silently glide to the next shower, then come back again. The mother was caressing her full body with a washer – neck, breasts, abdomen, thighs, shins, heels, then up again, over and over, as in a dream. Water fell, steam swirled.

Room nine was on the ground floor and we were warmly invited in by its three American occupants. 'Peter's not here,' said the only female. 'I'm Amy and this is San – and Luke.'

'Hi, Luke,' said Luke. 'We've heard you're heading for Lhasa. Thought we might compare notes about the dragon woman at CITS.'

They laughed. 'There's no way I'm paying that sort of money,' said San, flicking his dark hair to hang loose down his back. Though he was well built, he had an almost childlike face with long curly eyelashes. 'Peter's following a lead about other ways of getting there.'

He came in then, tall and affable. 'Hi, good to meet you,' he drawled. 'I've got news, guys!' His friends cheered as he sat down on a bed, smiling behind steamed-up glasses. 'There's a man who reckons he can get us there for half the official price. He'll phone in the morning to confirm. If he can't, I vote we go to the station and do a deal with the driver.'

There was silence as the others took in what he had said. 'What about you?' He turned to us. 'Do you want to join us?'

'When do you plan to leave?'

'As soon as possible. Tomorrow.'

In the evening Luke persuaded us to set aside our vegetarian preferences and have a Mongolian hot pot dinner. It was served in a tall metal dish, filled with boiling water, charcoal glowing in an island in the middle. Into it we dipped paper-thin slices of mutton, vegetables, beancurd and noodles and ate them with a special sauce, ending up with the soup. The restaurant was warm and full and its ambience did as much as the food to raise our spirits.

We wandered back past a market place with steaming pots and sizzling noodles, meat grilling on small fires beneath the blanketing hush of night. A young couple invited Luke to join them on a bench and the food seller pressed a kebab into his hand with a cup of tea. There was no electricity and candles and gas flames shone through the smoke like a scene in a Rembrandt painting – a cheek, a hand, poignant, intimate. Reflections of the Tao.

We decided to go back to CITS. The room was in better shape by now, with the same diffident woman and her silent colleague in the corner. 'Is tomorrow's bus Chinese or Japanese?' Justin asked. We had been told the Japanese one gets there in twenty-four hours instead of thirty to thirty-six and was less cramped.

'Chinese. Also the day after. But it is only one year old and just as fast. It will take twenty-eight hours.'

Justin and Luke were uneasy; people had told us to insist. They had also warned us about being given seats above the rear wheels. We went ahead, but on the basis of having front seats, where there was more legroom. While we were filling out the paperwork, there was a phone call and I heard the woman repeat the words for twenty-one, twenty-two and twenty-three. 'Your seats are not in the front,' she said blandly. 'They are in the middle.'

Then the madness began. Luke was on his feet; the lady's singsong voice went up an octave. 'We're paying nine times the local price,' Justin was saying loudly, 'and you give us seats above the wheels. You say China welcomes friends; but you turn us into enemies.'

'Rules are rules. Chinese people pay according to their rule, you according to yours. You earn much money in your country. Why are you so mean?'

'You don't know anything about our country,' Luke shouted, stamping his foot and pointing his finger. I was shocked and pulled at his arm, but he brushed me away. 'You just want to rob us. You rob foreigners all the time.' And he banged on the table. I cringed with embarrassment. The man in the corner got up and moved towards him, shouting in Chinese. I thought he was going to hit him, but he stopped and stood awkwardly by the desk.

'Your son is very rude,' said the woman to Justin. 'And you do not control him. I consider him my little brother, so I don't mind. But you must know I'm only doing my job.'

The other woman, still dusting, chose that moment to come near, beckoning Justin to an empty chair. 'I'm not moving,' he glared. 'I'm a guest here and this is my chair.' She spoke rapidly, then leaned over and opened a drawer. Justin stubbornly stayed in his seat while she took out two large ink blocks and started stamping a pile of paper in front of him. We watched in silence as if mesmerised. Swish, rustle, stamp, over and again.

'Your seats are not over the wheels,' said the woman behind the desk. 'If you want them, you must pay before three. I have work to do. Please leave.'

Sunlight sparkled on the leaves. A small boy wove past, as though pulled by the metal hoop he was wheeling with a stretched-out coat hanger. Smaller ones toddled behind, whooping gleefully. They saw us on the low wall and stopped in their tracks. 'Bye-bye, hello,' said one, timidly waving a hand – and the chant was taken up by them all. Until, like birds, they were gone, following the wheel on the dirt.

'I think you two behaved disgracefully,' I began.

'Dammit,' Luke burst out, near tears. 'Can't you see she treated us like dirt?

'That's how you treated *her*. You wouldn't have done that in Australia. It was only because she was Chinese.'

'I don't understand you. Sometimes you seem to agree how horrible they can be; then when confronted by them, you change your tune.'

We must have looked absurdly sad and serious. The poplars rustled joyously as we walked back to our room, Luke dragging his feet. His bed was a heap of clothes, books, photographs and camera equipment. He sat on the edge, staring at the floor. 'I feel awful. I hate everything. Travelling. China. I hate *myself*. I want to go home.'

'You can,' I said gently. 'If that's really what you want. You can settle down in Adelaide in preparation for next year. We have many friends there who'll help.'

'Or you can come with us to Tibet,' said Justin. 'We're so close now. So what if we're being fleeced? What we experience lives on. Money passes away.' He continued jauntily, 'I'm going back to pay for the tickets. Anyone feel like a quiet and friendly encounter?'

Luke started to clear his things away and I helped him. He lay down and in the silence I stroked his forehead, thinking back to my own turmoil at nineteen as a student in Sydney – the longing to be something, the cold reality of limitations. Becoming conscious is a two-edged affair: one expands into the freedom ahead and mourns the loss of innocence.

'I haven't even taken any photos here.' His voice was blurred.

'Take one for me, of the yellow leaves.' But his breathing told me he was asleep.

We were due at the station by ten. At eight there was a knock on our door and in came three crestfallen Americans. 'Hey, we thought you'd made it,' exclaimed Luke.

'Well we didn't,' said Amy. 'Peter's on the bus with all our gear and we have nothing left but the clothes we're wearing.'

'What's more, we've got his passport,' said American Luke – who volunteered later to be called by his initials, LT, to avoid confusion. 'So God only knows how *he's* getting on.' Even sunny San was down in the dumps.

'But that's great,' Luke said, unabashed. 'It means we'll be on the same bus!'

They told us the rest as we shared the sticky buns and tea that was all we could get for breakfast in the cavernous hall attached to the hotel. At first the driver had seemed willing to do a deal and they got on board and waited. Then another man said they had to go with him to get permits, while Peter stayed with the gear. It became a wild goosechase and by the time they got back, the bus had gone. It had taken them the whole day to get nowhere; and in the evening they checked again into their room, empty now but for three bodies and four beds – on the spare one, LT's white canvas hat and the single toothbrush they had bought to share.

Our seats were in the middle not over the wheels and, cramped as it was, the bus was in good condition. Our friends had the row behind and we shared our warm clothes, sleeping bags and food. About half the passengers were Tibetans, in ragged sheepskin coats and, here and there, exotic tall hats. Many of the women had their hair in plaits, woven with turquoise and amber beads. They wore long skirts with striped aprons, earrings and scarves, their faces weathered but dignified with dark eyes and some with long straight noses.

There were three checkpoints going out of town; then we entered the wilderness, sun-drenched, monotonous, powerful in its starkness. Far ahead, snow on high peaks. We started to climb; slowly, then more steeply, on and on, stopping at a small settlement for lunch. We must have been over four thousand metres and it was bracing cold, the sky unfathomably blue, the light glaring.

I felt elated, my mind clear and sharp, as if in consonance with the environment. I found I could stay with a thought much longer than usual. I could 'move around' it and see it from different angles, or 'climb up' to a 'higher' perspective. It is no surprise the Himalayas have always been a holy place for meditants. On the occasions when Christ spoke on mountains, it was with his disciples alone, in greater depth and scope.

I used to feel closer to the sea – the drama of its air and clouds and waves, bringing movement to the mind and breath to the soul. It was by the waters that Christ often addressed the multitudes, in pictures and parables; by the sea, too, that the Greek civilisation came to flower, in such beauty and grace. Now it was time for me to get to know the mountains.

Two students from Xi'an helped us order food. We ate together and at the end they insisted on paying. 'You are guests in our country,' they said and quietly disappeared as though to avoid the embarrassment of being thanked. This was to be their first visit to Tibet. They said being Chinese is not easy.

Then the hammer fell, the bus crawling relentlessly in first and second gear as it started to snow. In the fug of breath and cigarette smoke, I felt a violent pain at the front of my head and was suddenly sick. 'Just relax.' Justin's voice far away, as in a dream. 'Other people are throwing up too.' I longed for the bus to stop. When it did I wandered out, wondering vaguely if my bones were turning to ice – and chucked up again as soon as I got back to my seat. My head was throbbing like a wound and I was being tossed up and down and around in an ocean of vertigo. Luke stroked my hand. 'Keep it up, Mum. You'll feel better when we're over the pass.'

Once or twice I managed to open my eyes and peer into a landscape of gravel and sand and the occasional stark compound. Night descended, the bleakness closed in like fog. How would it be to live one's whole life in such a place? Justin told me the heating had been turned on and the pipe beneath his feet, running the length of the aisle, was so hot it was melting the soles of his shoes, while I was freezing by a window that would not shut, with snow flakes wafting in. I dozed, but pain and nausea kept sleep away, like guardians at a threshold. At intervals I would come awake with a start, submerged under a universe of white foam, crushing but ever light. I felt a panic that I would never be able to move again – as though in death. 'The dark hour before the dawn,' said Justin.

We stopped at a compound. Interminably. Dawn crept in, apricot pink, and at last we were going down, *down*. From time to time an outburst of chatter from the Tibetans would filter through, followed by a cheer. 'Gazelle,' shouted Luke. 'Marmots... goats... ponies... yaks.' And occasional nomads, bulky with sheepskins, on the scree and grasslands. Light was gaining.

We stopped at an icy fast-flowing river and the Tibetans went down to wash. It was a joyous sight, people in their exuberant clothes and colours scooping up water and letting it pour onto their heads. A festival of purification on the pilgrimage to Lhasa.

Luke raised his arms, exultant. 'We've made it, Mum. Do you realise? We're in *Tibet*.'

Part Three

If the stars should appear one night in a thousand years, how would men believe and adore – and preserve for many generations the remembrance of the city of God which had been shown!

>   Ralph Waldo Emerson
>   *Nature*

Tibet

1

It took twenty-eight hours, as the lady had predicted. And through her fog of pain Thu was as gleeful as the rest of us when we arrived. A minibus was at the station with a young Tibetan called Dorje who was to be our guide. We were suspicious at first, but he seemed genuinely warm and was happy to take us to a hotel in the Tibetan part of town rather than the Holiday Inn as we had presumed.

'Lhasa,' I had said to Luke on the way. 'What does that word mean to you?'

'High place, mountain air, Buddhist chanting, destruction. Potala Palace.'

'And Tibet?'

'I keep hearing of Mt Kailash. Do you reckon we could get there?'

Many are the influences that have come together in the mountain crucible that is now Tibet. As elsewhere, its earliest inhabitants were intimately connected with nature. With our modern intellects which cast a shadow over other ways of thinking, we tend to dismiss such cultures as primitive and pagan. But just as it is normal for a person now to read and write and understand abstract concepts, so was it natural in the times following Atlantis to perceive nature spirits and communicate with the dead. People had a sensitivity that shows itself in their legends; and their worship of deities, though it sometimes degenerated into sorcery, sprang from a deep and genuine devotion. In Tubo – as Tibet was then called – there was a special respect for mountains, which were seen as dwellings for the gods on earth.

Legend has it that Tubo's first king Nyentri Tsenpo came down from above by a 'sky cord'. When his reign ended, he was drawn back up. So it continued with his successors, until the time of the sixth king whose name means 'Slain by Pollution', when the cord was cut. What more eloquent imagery could there be for the gradual descent of the human spirit into earth existence, and of our being cut off from its source as we became enmeshed in matter?

From India came not only Buddhism but Tantric Hinduism – whose followers seek to enable the energy of certain deities to flow through them. With its exotic pantheon of gods and spirits, fearsome and benign, it blended readily with indigenous practices, and when combined with Buddhism, developed into a series of yogic techniques, sometimes sexual, for accelerating one's path towards enlightenment. We came to recognise its influence in the exuberant paintings of Tibetan shrines in which saints and meditants are encompassed by an environment of brightly coloured, swirling energies.

And then there were the Mongols who wreaked their thirteenth-century mayhem throughout Asia. Story has it that when they returned from Tibet, they brought back to Godan Khan, grandson of Genghis, accounts of the magical powers of certain lamas and this ushered in an alliance between the two countries, which continued on and off for several centuries. Tibet's religion became Mongolia's, while its affairs of state dwindled into subservience.

Spaced out with tiredness and thin air, we checked into the Banak Shol – an old building with the characteristic windows we had seen in Xiahe, thick frames painted black, the partitions red and blue with touches of yellow. Our room looked over a yard in which thickly clad women were scrubbing sheets in a trough, chatting and singing as they worked. Judging from the people on the bus and our first glimpses of their capital, spitting seemed not to be the pastime it was elsewhere in China – though the toilets were as gruesome as ever.

We wandered through streets awash with life in fantastic variations – women with hair in a lattice work of braids, babies on their backs wrapped in wool; men in fur boots and rugged smocks; weather-beaten faces which, like parched lands watered by rain, would dissolve into a giggle, a laugh, a rotten-tooth smile; the foetid smells of a poor city; dogs and occasional cows, donkey carts laden with yak dung, bicycles, tricycles, street vendors; the swish of feet and cloth on paving, and blasts of minibuses and jeeps. On a sidewalk near the hotel two boys in grubby ragged tunics were dragging the corpse of a dog. They heaved it a few metres, then gave up and ran away. In the sun it was hot but the air was cool.

Old buildings lined the streets up to four storeys high, gaily painted, with flowers at the windows. We glimpsed rooms cluttered with statues, wall hangings, photographs, altars. 'Is this *China*?' exclaimed Luke. 'Why did they take this place? What do they *want* it for?'

Lhasa is really two separate towns – the old one, which is gradually being restructured, and a new one alongside it. As in Xinjiang, one of the most effective methods for welding Tibet onto China has been to flood it with settlers. Although it is considered a harsh place to live, it has reached the stage where there are more Hans than Tibetans in Tibet.

Taking it slowly, we ventured into the Chinese part in search of a bank. The change was stunning – wide, almost empty streets, grey shop fronts. The bank was large and luxurious – air-conditioned, carpeted, adorned with plants and uniformed staff, little different from its counterparts in Singapore or Sydney.

Dorje was happy for Peter to be included in our tour despite his unconventional method of getting to Lhasa, which had involved being buried beneath other passengers at each checkpoint and glued to the driver at each stop in case he drove off without him. So the group of seven – the four Americans and the family of three – became more closely bonded, none of us even dreaming of the journey we would undertake together less than a week later.

We began at the monument that dominates the city. Once the seat of government and residence of the Dalai Lama, a fortress and prison as well as a palace, the Potala is a cliff wall of white and earth-red brick topped by gold, with row upon row of windows, each with a canopy of wave-like cotton and a dark frame. There are said to be a thousand rooms, only a few of which are open to the public. They span what are actually two palaces – the Red one which was the residence and the White one in which are most of the chapels and rooms of state. Though many of its treasures have been stolen, Zhou Enlai's intervention at least saved the building and its fixtures.

We entered the maze of dark rooms, halls and corridors, shafted through here and there by sudden sunlight. We were almost the only visitors. My first response was of astonishment that so much remains – prayer halls, thrones, shrines, tombs of high lamas, statues, frescoes, wall hangings, jewels, coverings of silver and gold, carved doors with huge brass handles adorned with scarves; and the most magnificent candles in the world, goblets as big as car tyres filled with yak oil and forested with wicks, unendingly flaming. We breathed in the smell of stale fat, the mustiness of fraying fabric and soot-stained ceilings, and the clutter of sacred relics.

Then, as our senses adjusted to the twilight, I became aware of the eerie absence of the man-god at its centre. The thrones were deserted, the lavish robes unworn, the private rooms empty but for memories, bits of furniture, fabric and Buddhist art.

There were still monks but far fewer than before, their activities monitored by videos, microphones and awkward-looking Chinese 'tourists'. Dorje knew where they were and our conversations and movements varied with our proximity to them. Almost all the monks we met were old – sitting in candle-lit chapels or dusting relics and cleaning the floor. One was polishing with his bare feet on rags. He swayed towards me, as though on skis, and put his hand against the bristles of my beard. 'Hmm,' he articulated, deep in the larynx. I lifted a trouser leg to show the hairs there too and he launched into a pirouette on his pieces of cloth.

In one of the rooms a boy, his voice not yet broken, was reading scriptures from strips of paper to an elderly monk who sat cross-legged on the floor making candle wicks. They were unperturbed by our presence though the boy, as any boy would, from time to time glanced across the flickering dust at the risk of losing his lines. The old man got up and gave Thu one of his wicks to put into the drum-like candle. A smile, a grunt, but no word spoken.

We went out to the roof terrace and looked over the city and the dry valley bordered by barren mountains. Gleaming on the golden roof lines and towers were slender stupas, like a series of tapering bells and balls above one another, representing the ascent of consciousness towards enlightenment. Elsewhere were the intricately decorated *finials* – truncated squat columns of beaten gold, topped by a small spire and with 'arms' pointing in eight directions.

We emerged at lunchtime, saturated. In the shelter of our room, I struggled to sort through my emotions by writing.

I cannot accept the justification of history given for the Chinese occupation. By that reasoning, the citizens of Rome have a right to most of Europe, North Africa and the Middle East. But I can see that Tibet pays the price for burying itself away from the world in the attempt to hold the past unchanged; much as China has done. The Potala is more than a museum or a debilitated monastery. It is the mausoleum of a culture – one that is rooted in the ancient soil of spiritual hierarchy, leading up to the priest-king.

At this time when all past secrets are being released, and when the challenge facing each individual is to become one's own priest and king, how could Tibet have remained locked away behind the fortress of the Himalayas? If Mao's army had not wreaked chaos, some other force surely would have. For rather than different peoples clinging to their inheritance, is it not a task now to offer up what we have received into the great world chalice and ultimately to find each culture within oneself? Does this not also free those who have guarded the old ways for so long? Not in Tibet only, but China too.

The group of seven had dinner together that evening. We were all planning to go on to Nepal after Tibet; the question was how and when and whether any of us wanted to make the journey together. Thu, Luke and I were for taking our time. 'Whatever happens is okay,' said San in his whimsical way. Amy and Peter felt more rushed as they hoped to get to Pakistan before the Karakoram Highway closed for winter. LT was impatient for a different reason. 'I'm not getting anywhere,' he said, adjusting the glasses on his high forehead. 'I'm losing touch with my work.' His profession was computers and he seemed older than his twenty-four years.

'Isn't it something to have gotten here?' asked San, astonished. 'What made you come?'

'I planned a short break in China, then someone suggested it would be a shame not to visit Tibet. Chance, I guess. There's no other way of looking at it.'

'Isn't there? Couldn't it be out of a kind of... wisdom?' said Peter in his slow drawl. 'Maybe things work differently over here than at home.'

'Isn't there wisdom in the West as well?' It was Thu.

'There's a whole lot of knowledge. I wouldn't call it wise. I guess we're so preoccupied with making ourselves comfortable, we've lost the spirit.'

'I wonder.' It was Luke's turn. 'Think of the care many people have for the environment – risking their jobs to protect some life form or other which is being exterminated. That's a lot more spiritual than going to a church or temple because it's the thing to do.'

'Tibetans have had that awareness for centuries,' Amy put in. 'Compassion for all sentient beings.'

'Even so, there's something different.' He paused. 'Maybe it's because in a modern society we have to fight through to these ideas ourselves. They're not given on a plate.'

We made no decisions about travelling together. What we did do was start to get to know each other. In a sense, what transpired came out of that.

The Jokhang Temple is the centre of religious life in Lhasa – a destination for pilgrims and a focus for many past demonstrations against the Chinese. In an attempt to strip it of its power, the authorities have destroyed a number of the buildings nearby, replacing them with paving and government stores. We arrived before sunrise, the square already busy with the ghostly shapes of worshippers, donkeys and carts. On its roof, against the yellow sky, was the silhouette of an eight-spoked wheel representing Buddha's wisdom, with a kneeling deer on either side. Rising from below, the smoke and sweet smell of burning juniper.

From the forecourt came the rhythmical swoosh of fabric against stone, the hum of prayers and creaking of joints, as body after body went through the ritual of prostration. Over and again they would stand, palms together above their heads, their foreheads, their hearts; then kneel and slide forward, face down, arms stretched in front. Most used wads of cloth to protect their hands. Some had thin mattresses.

A mass of people was gathering outside the entrance, though it would not open for a further one and a half hours. We merged with the river of pilgrims flowing clockwise along the narrow market street bordering the temple. Most walked, quite fast. A few took the harder way of encircling it with prostrations – among them a frail lady with a thousand wrinkles and a piece of wood to mark where her outstretched fingers had reached each time.

The sun rose and the empty stalls came to life – with faggots, trinkets, coins, candlesticks, prayer wheels, shoes, clothes, knives, yak meat, postcards, fruit. Conspicuous in the crowd of gaunt figures were the tall warrior-like Khampa men from eastern Tibet, their long hair braided with red tassels. Monks sat chanting next to gleeming alms bowls.

Luke wanted to stay with the others; Thu and I opted for breakfast. It was to be a decisive step towards the journey that was now only five days ahead of us.

Jacques was sitting alone as we came into the small restaurant, nursing his head with both hands. I approached him largely out of curiosity as to his background. With his jacket of coarse black cloth, cropped hair, tanned face and long nose, he could have been a local. 'France,' he replied. 'In this life at any rate.' He looked as if he had a hangover.

'But you've been here before?'

'Several times. I'm more at home here than at home.'

'You don't look too happy, if I might say so.'

'Sinus trouble. It's never been so bad. It'll pass.'

His aim was to visit Mt Kailash. I had first heard of it in Australia, but as a place I was unlikely ever to reach. Listening to the English man in Xiahe had brought it closer; reading the *Lonely Planet* guidebook, closer again. Even so, it seemed as remote as the Garden of Eden. Indeed, there are other similarities between the two places. Out of both, according to legend, four rivers have their source, representing the flow of Life into the earth. In both too, there is something super-earthly; but whereas the Garden is to be found only in the etheric world, the Mountain is here in rock and ice. And through Jacques's slow emphatic sentences, it was growing not only into form and colour but the realm of the possible.

He was hoping to get a ride in an army jeep. 'I have a friend,' he said with a smile. 'That's how things happen in this part of the world.'

'Might there be space for three more bodies?'

'It's unlikely. But I can ask.'

What mattered more was that the *idea* had taken root, in Thu as well as me.

We went back to the Jokhang. The doors were open and hands beckoned us in, though a crowd was still waiting outside. The courtyard was filled with people at every stage of supplication, many wearing clothes of the same maroon-brown as the monks. A short man with a cowboy hat, tattered greatcoat and an expression of chiselled stone, was ladling out water from a barrel into rows of cupped hands. Sun and dark shadows – and the homely smell of juniper, horses and sweat. At the far end was a mass of candles, forming a cascade of warmth and flickering light the width of the yard. People spooned in oil from the pots they were holding, mumbling and humming and being blessed by the monks.

Luke told us later he and the others had waited in the queue for two and a half hours before reaching the main hall. 'Wonderful!' was Thu's response. 'You see how much patience you've learnt from being in China.' Our own pathway was somewhat shorter; one of the monks gestured us straight to the entrance.

Inside, in the foetid warmth of bodies and candles, the human river wound on – through shrines and chapels, past tall red pillars and hanging drapes, to the rustling of prayers and the smell of the yak in the oil and clothes of the nomads. We moved in and out of the trance-like flow of grandparents, parents, children, babies, weaving, shuffling, caressing, kissing, even weeping their way among the golden Buddhas, each with its own serenity and grace. From time to time, a monk would welcome us into an alcove and try out his English. In some of the rooms pilgrims were crawling beneath tables and shelves stacked high with dust-laden manuscripts, kissing everything they came to.

A man with long grey hair grinned at us, bedraggled coat above fleecy boots, his oil in a soot-black cooking pot. *'Dali Lama? Dali Lama?'*

But we had no photos to give.

Jacques was in the hotel courtyard trying out his tent. He had seen his friend and there was no space for us in the jeep; but he was still hopeful for himself. On the noticeboard was a note from a German couple asking if anyone wanted to join them in renting a truck to go to Mt Kailash. It turned out their room was across the corridor from ours – and it was this simple circumstance which brought us into contact with Mr Gyanseng.

My first impression was mixed. I liked his smile but did not trust his eyes. 'You know these people?' he asked, pointing to their door. 'We make appointment, they not come. I have good truck. Good price too.'

'How much?' I asked casually. 'Kailash, then Everest and on to the Nepalese border?'

He made some calculations. 'Go Kailash, also go Lake Manasarova. Nineteen days. Twenty thousand yuan, including driver and guide.'

'Two and a half thousand dollars, hey? How many people can the truck hold?'

'Maybe twelve.' He gave his card. 'I come back nine o'clock.' Then he added over his shoulder, 'Maybe German man not want, I think you go.'

San was enthusiastic, Peter quietly interested, Amy non-committal and LT somewhat shocked, but they agreed to come at nine. That's when the third step took place, all in a single day. Gyanseng did not turn up, nor did the German lady, but her partner Klaus did.

He was a big man and the mountain boots he was wearing were of high quality. 'I've been preparing for years,' he said, squatting over a map on the floor. 'Though I haven't been there, I know Kailash like my own hand. Some Tibetans do the *kora* in one day. Foreigners usually take three. The highest pass is five thousand six hundred metres.'

'Kora?' said LT timidly.

Klaus seemed startled. 'It's the sacred circuit round the mountain. You're not allowed to climb it. No one is. That's Tibetan law, not Chinese. Where are you guys from?'

We must have seemed a motley crew; but in response to our questions he got into his stride again and gave us the information we needed to hear. It was likely to be very cold and we should aim to be self-sufficient as there was little food in the area. Tents would be a good idea; there were few settlements on the way. During the kora itself one could probably sleep at small monasteries, or *gompas*, but it would simply be a roof, some walls and maybe a mattress of sorts. We also needed to take seriously the danger of altitude sickness.

He said there was no way of predicting who would be affected. Fitness would not protect one, though one needed it to do the circuit. We would have to drink much more than normal, because rarefied air is dry and one loses moisture in breathing out. He told us tales of travellers whose lungs filled with liquid or who fell asleep and did not wake up. He was like a sergeant-major with a gaggle of recruits; but it was a comfort to think he might be coming and the preparation he had done stirred us.

No commitments were made but I borrowed his detailed maps. The hardest part would be the second day of the kora, during which one climbs nearly a thousand metres to the high pass and then has a descent of many hours before the next gompa. Were we up to it?

There was another question too. Why was I so keen? Was it just a matter of wanting to prove myself? I know ambition well, for I was brought up with it through years at boarding school. It drives one to outshine others, to *succeed*. It is like having petrol in one's blood. When I realised some years ago the extent to which it worked in me, I was thrown into chaos and lost trust in my motives for everything I was doing. Since then I have untied a few knots and illumined some of the dark places. I have less power; but what I have is more genuine.

In legends from the past, mankind is pictured battling outwardly with demons and monsters. Today the joust is within and the courage one needs is that of being true to who one is and where one's inner direction is leading. I told Luke in Hong Kong we would talk further about such things while in China. Whether or not Tibet is China depends on one's perspective, but the time seemed right to honour my commitment. It was also a way of clarifying my mind.

'So are you telling me it's a question of destiny whether we go to Kailash or not?' he muttered in the dark. 'That it's all pre-planned?'

'No, I'm talking about motives – and what lies beyond them. By destiny I mean the very foundation of one's will – beyond ambition, greed, fear, whatever, even altruism. Something like the power that keeps the earth circling through space. We can live our lives paying no attention to it, but that doesn't mean it's not there.'

'Come on Dad, you're rambling. You have to be more specific.'

'Okay. We're here in Lhasa. Out of all the possibilities. Agreed? A result both of our own planning *and* outer circumstances. The same with the other guys. Now, into this unique situation a new opportunity presents itself. And the important thing is that we recognise it. It gels! It wouldn't necessarily do so in other people. But we're also free to act on it or not.'

'You're saying events take place and we respond. Isn't that obvious?'

'But I'm also saying that in some way, beyond our consciousness, we participate in bringing about the events in the first place. And that there is always a wisdom in this, even if we can only see it afterwards.'

He was silent a long time and I thought he had fallen asleep. 'So where is your destiny heading?' he asked.

'I don't know. I have ideas, of course, and intentions. But like most people I'm partially blind. To see the working of destiny, as it is happening, one has to bring consciousness right into one's will, and that I can't do.' I paused. 'Not the will of "I want for me"; the much deeper one of "Not my will, but Thine be done".'

Mr Gyanseng came round at eight the next morning. Klaus and his partner were not in their room, so we walked with him, past the dog corpse which now oozed and stank, to the friendly restaurant where we knew the other four would be, amidst their fried eggs, *momos* (small meat or vegetable pastries), Tibetan coffee and flat bread. They too found him shifty, but seeing him a second time I decided it might just be his nervous mannerisms. He seemed to know what the trip would involve and said he would take care of permits.

He also seemed unconcerned by the fact that foreigners are not allowed to travel in trucks in Tibet. 'No problem,' he declared in the universal way of Asia. 'The driver knows how to manage the checkpoints. Now, how many go? Five, six, seven?' But we were not ready yet to make a decision.

Dorje told us his family were refugees in India and that he had only recently come back. On our way to the Jewel Park or Norbulingka, which includes the building the Dalai Lama designed as a summer residence, he said that of the sixteen hundred monasteries in Tibet before the Cultural Revolution only about ten had survived – and those severely weakened. Thousands of monks had been massacred or sent to camps and most of the wealth stolen.

Though the Norbulingka is held up as an example of the Dalai Lama's luxurious lifestyle, it is essentially a simple structure, a two-storey house rather than a palace. The lavishness is in the hangings, draperies and wall paintings that represent Tibetan Buddhism, many of them mandalas on the *bardos*, or levels of existence, between heaven and hell. He only used it for two years, for by '59 the Chinese were taking full control of the country they had 'liberated' nine years before, and he fled to India as they were about to arrest him.

It was a strange feeling, going through the home of someone who is still alive without his invitation. We were allowed almost everywhere, including his bedroom with its stocky Russian radio and bathroom with its solid British toilet. Clusters of pilgrims wafted by, led on by their fervour, pressing their foreheads and palms against the door handles and floors and anything else that might connect them with the absent owner.

In the museum nearby were photographs of archaeological finds with captions in Chinese and the Sanskrit-based script of the Tibetans. Dorje said he was not allowed to talk about them, but the message was clear enough – Tibet's cultural union with China since the beginnings of history. In another section was a parchment which he quietly translated.

It was about Princess Wencheng, daughter of the Tang emperor Taizong, who was married to the Tibetan king Songtsen Gampo in the seventh century. The alliance between the two rulers is a cornerstone of the Chinese claims. There was reference to gifts in both directions, in the mood that prevails between an 'uncle' (China) and his 'nephew' (Tibet).

What was not mentioned was that the marriage was arranged by the emperor because Tibet's power was undermining his empire, nor that a century later Gansu and Sichuan provinces were part of Tibet and the capital of Chang'an under threat. In the ninth century a treaty was drawn up, guaranteeing for all time the integrity of the two kingdoms and declaring: 'Tibetans shall be happy in Tibet and Chinese shall be happy in China.'

Ironically it was through Wencheng (as well as his first wife, a Nepalese princess) that Songtsen Gampo became a Buddhist and that the religion took root in his country. Through those whom it vanquished, Tibet received a new spiritual impulse. Now the tables are turned. What message will find its way back into the hearts and minds of the current conquerors?

That afternoon we reached the low point of our Kailash planning. It was on the roof overlooking the yard in which people were butchering a sheep, the blood in one bucket, organs in another, everything in piles, nothing wasted. Klaus announced strangely that something had happened, and he and his partner had to go to Kathmandu. Then Amy said she was out of it because of her wish to visit Pakistan. She seemed distant and irritable. San was still keen, LT still unsure. Peter did not show up. 'He has a headache,' said LT. 'I'll go and see.'

It was fortunate he did. Peter came back with him and spoke positively. Our spirits started to revive. 'What about Pakistan?' I asked.

'This is more important.' He glanced at Amy. 'What about you, LT?'

'I don't trust Gyanseng. He wants money in advance, but we're not going to see the truck until we get to Shigatse. What if it's a heap of junk?'

Had Thu and I met Tashi earlier we might have decided to stay longer in Lhasa and not go to Kailash. We had been given her name by a friend who had been at school with her in Germany. Her family had fled Tibet while she was a small child and spent three years in India where she learnt English, before being accepted as refugees into Europe. Our friend had not known her address, only that she was studying at a college in Lhasa. During the first four days we drew blanks every time we tried to track her down. It was on the afternoon of the fifth that we finally found her. That morning we had made our decision to hire the truck.

When it came to the crunch, not only did LT say yes but Amy too. She and Peter had talked things through and she looked a lot happier. 'I know two girls who'd like to join us,' she added breezily. And there was still the possibility of Jacques whose lift was in a permanent state of being about to happen. We paid a deposit and surrendered our passports. 'This is pushing trust to the limit,' mouthed LT, pale again. 'How do we know we'll get them back?'

'No problem,' replied Gyanseng with an easy smile. 'You trust.'

After he had gone we organised ourselves into groups – Peter and Luke to buy tents, cookers, blankets and other bits and pieces; Amy, Thu and San to organise food; LT and I to write out a contract. We moved into our roles as if we had simply been waiting to begin.

A few hours later we found Tashi's college and the flat in which she was living. We felt at home with her straight away – small, but full of vitality, cheerful and intense at the same time. She spoke with concern about the number of young people who could find no work and who turned to violence or self-abuse as a way out, and had hopes of starting a centre for vocational training. Though she chose her words carefully, her pain at what was happening was clear. 'They have taken many things: minerals, timber, works of art. Yet they feel in exile. They long to go home. Isn't that... silly?' And she laughed.

Much of her free time was spent helping a couple of primary schools. 'Come tomorrow morning,' she said brightly when we told her we were teachers. 'I'll take you there.'

We cycled, the four of us, along a dirt path next to a stinking canal to find the first of the schools deserted except for a solitary watchman. He told Tashi the staff had been called away to a political meeting and the children sent home. She said it happened all too often.

We walked through the playground of scorched gravel between two lines of classrooms. Inside it was equally bare – shabby desks on concrete floors, barred windows, empty walls. In the staff room was some calligraphy in Chinese and Tibetan, framed with geometric patterns. 'It is through the teacher that a child develops,' she translated, then added with a laugh, 'Not everything that comes from China is bad.'

We went on through dusty alleys to the walled area below the Potala. 'This is part of the old city,' she said as we got off our bikes, 'a very special place for us.' She paused. 'The whole area's going to be knocked down in a few months and replaced with open paving. There's talk of a shopping complex and a hotel.'

'Damn!' said Luke. 'Can't you stop it?'

'What do you think? I feel more sad for the people who've lived here all their lives.'

Children in bulky rags gazed at us, snot above their mouths, eyes bright. A cloaked woman sat on a stone, cleaning a pot. She shooed away a mangy dog scuffling for offal. We walked through a gate and into a well-kept yard bordered by neat buildings with traditional windows, a clump of trees in the middle, children playing with a ball at one end. Unlike the other one, this school had had support from overseas – until the government had abruptly told the sponsors their help was no longer needed.

She introduced us to one of the teachers, a middle-aged lady with a clear face wearing slacks and a cardigan. In a further section, by a cliff leading up to the palace, were about sixty children kneeling or squatting on the gravel with their small chairs as tables, doing exams. They were tidily dressed, without uniforms. On each chair was a bottle of ink and a number of fingers and thumbs were blotched blue.

The classrooms had curtains and fresh paint. They were full and orderly, a buzz of bright eyes against colourful pictures and ornate Tibetan calligraphy. 'We use our own language in the first two grades,' said our guide. 'Then we have to teach in Mandarin.'

One of the rooms was locked, but she had a key. Empty desks, bare blackboard – and in front of it, three green apples, a pendant of Buddha and two flames in goblets of oil. 'For the children doing the exams,' she explained.

'Why was the door locked?'

'Because it is considered religious ritual and that is forbidden.'

Amidst sugary milk tea and cakes, we showed our much-thumbed pamphlets from the school in Australia and Tashi spoke at length to the teachers about each of the pictures – children in class or playing music, their artwork and writing, festivals, plays, outdoor activities. 'How come you know so much about it?' Luke asked.

'It makes sense. Colour is natural to us, so are singing and movement and stories. If we lose imagination, we lose our culture. Isn't that what's happened in China?'

That evening we had a thank you dinner for Dorje. Next to Amy were the two travellers she had spoken of earlier – Cara from Italy, Tutu from New Zealand. 'And then there were nine,' said San, raising his glass in welcome.

'There may be a tenth,' said Amy, happier than I had seen her. 'You'll meet Ruth later. She approached me today, saying her Indian guru had given her the task of going to

Kailash.'

The door opened and in walked Jacques. 'Careful,' said Peter with a twinkle. 'This is a table of destiny. Those who sit at it may find themselves on a truck heading west.'

'I'll take the risk. Are you going as a guide, Dorje?'

'Why not?' chanted San, glass in the air again.

'I can't. But there's someone who may come in my place.'

A young woman appeared, thin and withdrawn, and sat down next to Amy who triumphantly announced that Ruth had decided to join us.

'See what I mean, Jacques?' said Peter. 'How can you stay away?'

'We'll see. I still have thirty-six hours to chase up the jeep. Tell me, Dorje, who do you have in mind?'

'We'll see,' came the reply. 'I still have thirty-six hours.'

LT and I were up late, finishing the contract. Delays or extra expenses for any reason other than our own change of mind, sickness or incompetence, were to be the owner's responsibility. This included hassles from police. Payment was to be in four instalments. Money for driver and guide were included, so was the minibus to Shigatse.

We also spelt out the itinerary – through Shigatse and Gyantse, both old centres of culture, and on via Saga, Payang and Darchen to Mt Kailash. The journey towards the Nepalese border would include Lake Manasarovar and Mt Everest, via Tingri and Rongbuk Monastery. Nineteen days in all, with an option to extend at our expense.

'Feeling better?' I asked.

'It's insane,' said LT. 'But it's okay.'

Jacques left it until the last evening to announce that he was coming with us. Perhaps he was as glad as we were, though it was not his way to show it. He had a distaste for groups and had already shared his views about travellers who are insensitive to Tibetan customs.

'And our guide?' said LT, as Gyanseng handed back our passports and signed the contract, and we paid our first instalment. He pointed into the courtyard. 'You mean Dorje?'

'No. The young man with him. His brother.'

Afterwards we went to say goodbye to Tashi. I asked her whether she had a faith that kept her going. 'Anyone whose eyes are open is alone,' she replied. 'But there are many who care and work in their own ways. I fear though for what will happen when the Dalai Lama is no longer with us.' She paused. 'I seek help from Tara, the Being of Compassion, known in China as Guanyin. I hold her image in meditation and ask for strength.'

Luke asks what she thinks about our going to Kailash. 'Ah, Kang Rinpoche,' she muses. 'Jewel of the Snows. You are more fortunate than I am. Many believe it is up to the mountain itself who can go there.'

'Not the Chinese army, then?' he says, with a smile.

'No. They simply add to the obstacles. I suppose it's a test of one's will. You may have read Lama Govinda's *Way of the White Clouds*. He says those who have given up their comforts and security are rewarded by bliss when they get there.' She laughs. 'So if you make it, I'll be happy for you. It's a mark of favour.'

It was late by the time we had finished our repacking. Everything finds its way out of one's bag when one is in the same room for more than a couple of days, and we had bought some extra clothes such as woollen long johns, gloves, scarves and hats. I was conscious of how amateur our equipment was. Klaus would have been disgusted. More important would be the response of the wind and cold at Kailash.

We were calm though, and as we lay in bed I spoke a further section of the Prayer of Surrender I had said for Luke in Shanghai.

> This is what we have to learn in our time,
> to live out of pure trust, without any security in our
>   own existence;
> trust in the ever-present help of the spiritual world.
> Truly nothing else will do if our courage is not to fail
>   us.

'How can you be sure there are spiritual beings?' Luke was as awake as I was.

'It makes sense to me. We don't only trust what we can see, you know. Think of the stars. You can't see them through the ceiling, but you wouldn't doubt they're there. Trust in the spiritual world is similar. There are other ways of "seeing" than through the eyes.'

'Such as?'

'You know the word "idea" means "what is seen" in Greek. We even say, when we understand something, "Ah, I see!" In such moments we *do* see – though not with the eyes.'

'Are you saying ideas are spiritual beings, then?'

'Not exactly, but that thinking itself can become a first step towards looking into the invisible. Besides, think of the power generated by an idea. Where does it come from? Even our humble one of going to Kailash.'

His words came slowly. 'Why does it matter anyway?'

'Why does it matter what a cloud is, or a star? Isn't it a question of exploring who we are – and what this universe is of which we're a part? Of becoming whole?'

I got no reply but the deep regular breathing that betokens sleep.

2

From Luke's Diary
Day Three

I feel so happy.

It's as if I left behind a huge black bundle when we crossed into Tibet. Mum and Dad look lighter, too. Sometimes, doing something as mundane as walking along the dingy corridor to our room in Lhasa, I would feel my face becoming a smile. And in the crazy streets I came to recognise what smiling does. Each time one of those wrinkled faces broke into one, I'd feel a kind of warmth. I may be over the moon just now, but in those moments, we *met*.

And now we're here in this wild truck, chewing dust and being lashed by air. I feel like pinching myself to make sure it's really happening. But I know it is. The tangle of legs and bodies beneath sleeping bags; the jarring of hip bones and shoulders as we go over a rut; the cold; the mad flapping of the tarpaulin at the tailgate and sides – that's real, even if the dawn light is still too dim for us to see clearly. Ten in the back, including Norbu, Dorje's brother; two more up front next to the driver, Quzha – pronounced *Chewza*. I love it.

Of course, the journey really began two days ago when we left Lhasa – but then we were in the minibus old Gyanseng, that shrewd owl, finally organised for us. It was sad, saying goodbye to the city – not only the buildings and artwork and the whole bustle of life, but people I got close to like Dorje and Tashi, and even some of the grubby snot-nosed kids in the streets. They'd greet me each time with bright eyes and a grin and somehow we'd talk together, about kangaroos or dead dogs, China, Vietnam, Australia, cigarettes, money, life…

But for once the three of us weren't alone as we moved on. These guys treat me as an equal, that's what I appreciate, though they're in their mid-twenties or early thirties – except for Jacques who must be about Mum and Dad's age and Norbu who's close to mine. As we finally drew out of town, with everyone squashed in and a mountain of gear, a jeep swung in front forcing us to stop. Police? It was Dorje. 'Look after my kid brother,' he said, putting his arm across Norbu's wiry shoulders.

Norbu's brown face flashed into a grin beneath the khaki baseball cap he wears all the time. I like his face; it's honest and open. Peter started speaking into a cassette. 'We're on our way. It's starting. Can you hear the engine?... Hey, guys, say hello to my folks.'

We passed through countryside dry and wild – brown wrinkled hills and occasional nomad tents, shepherds, yaks, sheep, goats, even some cows. Then there were lakes like blue marble and winding streams as we climbed through narrow valleys to the pass. Beyond, we dropped down to expansive flat land along a turquoise river.

'Yarlung Tsangpo,' said Norbu. 'Indians call it Brahmaputra River.'

I recognised the name. It's one of the four that has its source near Kailash and the one which flows east for nearly fifteen hundred kilometres, way past Lhasa, before sweeping south into India.

'We see it again many times,' he went on. 'Good friend.'

Gyanseng was waiting at the strangely named Fruit Hotel in Shigatse, Tibet's second biggest city. At nearly four thousand metres, the temperature was just right as we walked the few steps to the monastery of the Panchen Lamas. On an island in the street outside we passed pilgrims prostrating, while trucks blasted by in front of them. The size of the place was phenomenal – a wide central avenue leading to rows of flat buildings rising one above the other towards the` huge rockface behind. From the highest level at the back flashed the golden stupas of temples and the Lama's palace.

We meandered up through a maze of crumbling alleys, with more dogs than people and the stink of faeces. Dogs, Norbu told us, are what monks who don't make it to heaven tend to come back as. I wasn't convinced he believed it however; and they looked pretty mangy. It was weird moving on from there to the renovated temples – the contrast of decay and brand new shine.

From what I understand, the Panchen Lamas are held in almost as much esteem as the line of Dalai Lamas. The last one was effectively a prisoner of the Chinese and for many years was regarded as their stooge. Yet there were moments when he showed real courage. During the sixties he wrote a protest to Mao and denounced the invaders at a gathering in Lhasa. His reward was fourteen years in prison; but he survived and came back to Shigatse – and before his death in '89, allegedly from a heart attack, denounced them again. Now the new Panchen Lama, still a boy, has been whisked off to China like his forebear...

We wandered on past high walls and huge doorways with their frilly canopies. Peter and I peeped into a dingy courtyard and a monk beckoned us up some steps into a tiny kitchen, dark with soot. A fire was blazing and he gave us salty rich tea with rancid butter. Yuk! Maybe by the time we've done the kora, it will taste different. A novice of about seventeen came in and took out a package wrapped in yellow and orange silk behind some pots. 'Dali Lama,' he said proudly. 'Dollar.' He put one of the photos into Peter's hand. 'You.'

'You,' replied Peter, cool as cabbage, and placed it firmly back.

I showed them pictures of monks in Xiahe from the album I carry. They started chatting excitedly, and others came to join them, pointing at one face or another in the dim light as if recognising family or friends. I gave them one to keep of Labrang Monastery and they touched it to their foreheads.

In another room, cluttered and musty, were monks and boys printing prayers. They were sitting on the floor in pairs, working rhythmically and with phenomenal speed – dabbing ink on the wood block, laying the stretched-out sheet, a sweep with a roller, and lifting the paper wet with print. Between the red pillars were piles of pages already finished; along the walls, ceiling-high shelves for storing the blocks. One of the boys began to sing – his voice unbroken, full, soaring high.

In an alley outside we passed some young novices playing marbles on a doorstep. As we watched, one of the shorn heads looked up, scowled and said something abusive. It didn't hurt as it would have done in Han China. What is it about Tibet that makes me more tolerant?

Most of Shigatse now consists of grey blocks. The old town is being smothered and as we followed the main street from the monastery, we came inevitably to the new section. We walked past long walls of truck depots and warehouses, which seemed to double as public urinals, judging by the smell. But the food in the Chinese restaurant we found was good and the people courteous and eager to please. I wonder how they feel, living here.

Then, afterwards, who should we meet but Klaus and his girlfriend! 'I thought you had urgent business in Kathmandu,' said Peter genially. Klaus muttered something about it having been delayed, but that they were on their way now. I guess he didn't approve of us. The strange thing is, if it hadn't been for him we probably wouldn't be here now.

Day two was devoted to Gyantse and that was great, though the road was a shocker, rutted and pot-holed, and the ground on either side so dry there was almost nothing growing. Far more remains of the old town in Gyantse than in Shigatse. It's away from the so-called Friendship Highway connecting Lhasa with Kathmandu. Maybe that's the secret of its survival.

Most special for me was its sacred tower or Kumbum – square on the lower levels, round above and topped with a mighty gold stupa. From high up peered enormous red, blue and white eyes, enigmatically slanting upwards. I thought I could make out nine storeys, but gave up trying to count as we wandered through the spiral of stairways, corridors and chapels leading off every which way and thronged with pilgrims. In that crazy tower is compressed, no doubt, the whole history of Tibetan beliefs, fears and aspirations. I let the colours and images wash through me in a half-dream, without needing to know their meaning.

We emerged onto a flat roof circling the building. There was no parapet and as we walked round, we gazed like birds over the square mud roofs of the old town, the red and gold of the monastery, the ruined fort on the mountain behind, and the valley, dusty, yellow and brown. We sat. We were not alone. Women, with their colourful clothes and fantastic braids, walked briskly by, little children running to keep up.

A group of men were flattening out cement with stones attached to long handles. They chanted and stamped rhythmically as they struck – stone and feet on concrete, the tempo as insistent as the beating of a heart, continuing even when the singing stopped; then a single throaty voice, and the chorus would resume, surging like a wave. On and on.

Halfway back, the driver took us to a village off the road, along a sandy trail, past dunes. It was like an oasis in the desert, crumbling alleys of sun-baked earth and stone, at its centre a simple monastery. In the dim empty interior two women from the bus slowly spooned out yak butter into a vat of candle wicks, then rested their heads tenderly on the pedestal of the single statue. In total silence.

We climbed a ladder to the roof. The sun was losing its strength; it would be icy cold in a few hours. Looking over the barren landscape, I experienced that strangely sweet sadness that sometimes comes at twilight. How can they grow anything in this soil? We looked down onto a patchwork of flat roofs lined with drying yak dung. A man was stacking faggots, his wife untangling a fleece. A ragged child saw us, froze for a moment, then shouted to its companion. They laughed and waved twigs in the air as I looked through my telephoto. A breeze stirred and the little bells at the corners trembled. *Tink-a-ling, tink-a-ling...*

As we gathered by the bus, one of the passengers managed to tell us there had been even less rain than normal this year. I watched the gaunt faces around us, people of Mum and Dad's age maybe, and the dirt-ingrained kids. And suddenly it hit me – this is for *real*. If the rains don't come, then hunger will. I can get into this bus, I can fly to Australia; but these people are stuck here. Like a small ship sailing towards a storm.

Back in Shigatse we met Quzha for the first time, a short man who beamed quietly as he showed us the truck that was to be our home for the next seventeen days. It looked as new as old Gyanseng had promised – blue, sturdy and well-maintained. It even had number plates and one of those red triangles with an exclamation mark in case of a breakdown. Some use that will be in the desert! Quzha was keen for us to get going at six in the morning, but said we should not load up until then because of thieves.

In the evening there was a power cut, which didn't help the process of sorting out our things. When Gyanseng breezed into our room with a good strong torch in his hand, Dad suggested he donate it to us for the journey – which he did. He was a lot nicer to be with than in Lhasa. Dad shone the beam round the room. It looked like a warehouse with its piles of boxes and bags, our breath already visible in the cold.

I slipped into the girls' room. Most of the group was there, celebrating with biscuits and some Vermouth Cara and Tutu had bought in town. The knot in my stomach started to dissolve and only then did I realise I was feeling anxious. Perhaps the others were too. Tutu was playing some Queen on a Walkman. She sang along with it and I joined her. 'The show must go on...' the words the lead singer Freddie Mercury composed when he knew he was dying of Aids.

Dad looked awful in the torchlight as we staggered around, carting all the stuff into the truck before dawn. He tried to join in then dropped onto his bed, saying he needed to throw up. Amy was in a bad state too and we voted for the two of them to sit in the front. The engine started beautifully and we clambered in. Mum found it too high and had to be pushed from behind which made her ooh and aah and scream.

Apart from the packs we're using as back rests, our gear is stacked at the front end by the three fifty-gallon fuel drums and two spare tyres – water containers, boxes and gunny bags of food, utensils and other bits and pieces (like gauze masks against the dust). Oh yes, and forty bars of Chinese chocolate, not the best in the world but it's going to taste like it in a few days. Then there's Norbu and Quzha's fifty-kilo sack of roasted barley flour, plus half a sheep carcass. The floor is lined with army blankets, supplemented for some lucky people by Quzha and Norbu's bedding – two heavy quilts each stitched together as sleeping bags.

Jacques starts rolling up the tarp and Norbu helps him. Dust swirls in and freezing air, but the sky is a luminous pink with gold in the clouds. Forget the dust and cold; we leave the back open from now on. I look around. Mum's all but disappeared beneath sleeping bags by the food sacks. All I can see is her forehead and tightly closed eyes. San and Cara are buried in a corner next to a tyre. Ruth's propped up against a white bag, muffled in mask and hood. Peter stands up suddenly, swaying on his feet, one hand holding onto a bar, the other fumbling inside his trousers. 'What *are* you doing?' asks Tutu who's next to him.

'Looking for my penis.' Even Ruth is rocking, which I take to mean laughter, though it could be one of her yoga exercises. 'It seems to have got lost.' And he continues to wriggle.

'Oh,' says Tutu, adjusting her dark glasses. 'Well, let me know if I can help.'

Norbu sits upright by the tailgate smoking, his back to the road, dust on his army coat and cap; opposite him, Jacques, nodding to the truck's lurching, his face bandaged in a scarf up to the eyes. I'm between him and LT who keeps wiping his glasses, but is more relaxed and cheerful than I've yet seen him. 'Got it,' says Peter with satisfaction, then sits down and starts singing. 'Oh, my penis, it has gone astray. If you see it, please, please tell it… I'm on my way.'

Quzha seems a nice guy, quiet but dependable. He's happy to stop each time one of us clambers over the gear and thumps on the cab roof; but he's concerned we won't make it to Saga tonight if we don't get to the ferry across the Brahmaputra before it shuts down for lunch. So we keep rumbling on – through a vast biblical landscape of sand and stone and tufty grass, bordered by bare mountains. The unending line of telegraph poles, the rutted track, the occasional truck or nomad tent, a few yaks and sheep... and at the top of each pass, the tall *chortens*, or cairns, with their faded fluttering prayer flags, white, blue, yellow, green and red.

For most Tibetans Mt Kailash is the navel of the world, the umbilical cord connecting heaven and earth. It's quite a thought. It's also what the Greeks used to say about Delphi and the Aborigines about Uluru in the centre of Australia. Maybe there are many such places around the planet. But I know this one's going to be extra special. It's so high up for a start, and isolated. Then there's its shape, like a white pyramid, or stupa.

Four religions hold it sacred. For Hindus it's the throne of Shiva and the rivers that gush from it are his hair; they even trace the Ganges to its underground roots. There he sits, they say, in perpetual meditation; and they see it as a lingam, or phallic symbol, representing the power of creation. Then come the Jains, also from India, who claim their founding saint achieved liberation on its summit. For the Bonpo of Tibet every high place is holy and Kailash, the father mountain, the holiest of all. And finally the Buddhists. According to Norbu, some even connect Buddha with the mountain. He spoke too of Demchog as its guardian – a pretty awesome being with four faces, a blue body and twelve arms!

And for myself? I don't know; but it's going to be a challenge. I've been on enough school camps to know I'm up to it physically. But there's an anxiety about the altitude. What if I can't breathe properly? That's a scary thing. It's going to be incredibly cold too. I wish we had some decent equipment. And I'm not at all sure we've got enough food.

We reach the river just in time and drive straight onto the rough swaying planks of the ferry. There are bicycles and a number of locals, but ours is the only truck. A man in sun hat and dark glasses is carrying a side of mutton slung over his handlebars. Ragged coloured flags flap at either side of the water as we are drawn by cable silently across. Just a few whitewashed buildings, big enough for one room, maybe two.

We pause to brew up some noodles. In the shade of walls, the air is cold; in the sun, blazing hot with all the gear we're wearing. Dad still looks ill. He's afraid it's giardia, the 'big belly' affliction (from gas in the intestines) he contracted when first in Vietnam. He says he'll starve it out and, true to form, sees it as a spiritual challenge. 'Think of all the bacteria in our guts we have to neutralise just to stay alive,' I hear him telling LT. 'The moment we're weak they start to multiply, hey? So what's the power by which we keep them at bay? That's what I need now.' LT wipes his glasses.

As we climb away from the river the road becomes really bad, the undulations so deep we're going at walking pace. Then I see why – huge earth-moving machines in clouds of dust, army trucks, soldiers in neat green uniforms. Quzha veers onto the sand and we make a wide detour at the risk of getting stuck. 'Better this way,' says Norbu. 'Keep clear of them.'

When we stop again, it's at a lake of turquoise. There's a vestige of ice at the edge as we come down to wash and stretch. From all around, absolute silence. 'Fantastic,' I say when Mum asks how I feel. 'I love this. Every minute of it.'

We come over a low hill and the truck lurches to a stop. In front is a tumbling flowing river of black, white and brown wool. Dark gentle eyes and curly horns peer up at us, dotted amongst them the solitary figures of shepherds in sheepskins, leather pouches over their shoulders and sticks in their hands. We wade through the woolly foam, breathing the resinous rancid smell. Amidst gentle and bewildered 'baa baas', I see a boy, only just higher than his four-legged companions, bare-bottomed but with warm boots and clad in wool, hanging on to his father's coat. Quzha starts the truck behind us and the small face twists round to stare wide-eyed, his cheeks bright red and scaling, gunge congealed beneath the nose.

It becomes clear we have no hope of reaching Saga and end up at dusk in a small settlement of sad-looking buildings with no electricity. Dad, Mum and Amy head for bed and Ruth disappears to do her own cooking, while the rest of us go out to the store cum restaurant and eat noodle stew or *thukpa* and, for those who dare, yak meat.

We're whacked and there's nothing to do but sleep. The toilet is foul, so I wander out into the fiendish cold. Dogs roam and snarl. I throw some stones to chase them away and snatch a few minutes with the incredible jewel-like stars before turning in.

Day Four

It's freezing and still dark at seven when Norbu wakes us up; and it's nearly eight by the time we've all got ourselves together. Meanwhile Quzha's outside defrosting the gearbox and engine with a fearsome flame thrower. 'I'd keep out of the way if I were you,' says Dad, who looks better. 'It's a petrol truck.' Quzha seems unruffled and even offers to boil our water (for, guess what, instant noodle soup and tea).

It's all of nine o'clock when we finally clamber into the icy truck, to find that Norbu has hung up the hunk of mutton on a bar above our heads. I wish I could have taken a photo of Amy's face. She, Ruth and San are diehard vegetarians and thanks to their influence there's no meat in the food we have with us. In fact there's a distinct lack of variety and quantity of anything. LT and I are getting worried about it, but so far, daunted by the powerful females, have kept our woes to ourselves. Anyway we're all feeling refreshed by the long sleep. Travelling at this time of the year has the advantage that you don't have to share your bed with lice as apparently tends to happen in the summer.

The dust and bumps are as plentiful as yesterday, but there's a good spirit. Desolate landscape. Why is it beautiful? The play of light, I guess, the colours, the majestic sweep of rocks and dunes, the hugeness. Each time we stop, I feel myself expand and often there's a 'Wow!' or an 'Ah!' or a 'Man!' from at least one of us; and an unfailing 'Awesome!' from Peter.

Above us a waning moon; we're near crumbly mountains. Which came first, the rock that's worn into sand or the sand compressed into rock? Many of the sedimentary layers are at crazy angles – diagonal, vertical, even twisted and curved. Peter's a science teacher, like Dad, and can hardly contain his excitement. 'You know, a *real* geologist would be able to read the past, like a book,' he says. 'I can tell you this much. There's been some *awesome* activity here.'

I like Peter. Talking with him, I try to understand how this great wilderness connects with the lands around it – the Kunlun Mountains and deserts of Xinjiang to the north; the Himalayas and India to the south. From its west, near Kailash, arise the Brahmaputra River, the Ganges, the Indus, the Sutlej; from its more fertile east, the Salween, the Mekong, the Yangzi. What an image! China, India, Vietnam, Myanmar, Pakistan, all made fertile with water from Tibet, pouring at last into the Indian Ocean, the Pacific, the China Sea. Yet the land from which it flows is so barren.

Norbu tells us there are flowers and grasses in the summer; also that in the old days the plains were filled with wildlife – gazelle, deer, wild ass, yak, marmots and hundreds of kinds of birds. LT says he's read of it in the accounts of early travellers, who also spoke of snow leopards and bears in the mountains. When the Chinese invited the Dalai Lama to send a delegation from India to see all the good things that were happening in his absence, the team came back aghast, not only at the destruction of culture but wildlife.

I know the Europeans in America and Australia did the same; but this is *now*. Haven't we learnt anything? There are stories of soldiers machine-gunning wild animals and they've cut down much of the timber that used to grow in the east of the country. Anger rises in me and I realise how wonderful it has been during these days, to be without it. 'Maybe it's not so bad,' says LT kindly. And then we get to Saga.

Quzha parks on the main road and leaves us to walk down the slope and across the filthy stream to the dusty gravel of the 'street'. On either side are shacks and box-like houses, some with a display of goods for sale. The meagre population seems to be pretty equal in Hans and Tibetans, judging by the people sauntering outside. At the far end, Norbu points to a 'People's Hall', the normal square block with a banner of Chinese writing in front.

We locate a restaurant which serves fried rice and eat in the small garden at the back where there are even vegetables growing, and bushes and herbs. As we're leaving, the owner runs out and starts screaming at us for stealing a bowl.

Then her son appears and says he's found it in the yard. Am I still biased against the Hans?

'It's better than it was in '25,' says LT mysteriously. 'I've read that Saga was a sad place of dirty tents, grubby shacks and ruins. Look at it now; we can even buy apples and pears and bananas. And candy.' A cold wind is blowing.

There follows a sleepy lull in the truck. Jacques, still at the rear, puffs on a home-rolled cigarette. I can see it annoys some of the others, but so far it's been tolerated because Norbu and Quzha smoke too. He keeps aloof, Jacques. He can seem quite contemptuous of our ignorance, but he's also given me some good tips about photography, in a fatherly kind of way.

A tyre has worked loose and Ruth has made her home on it, her back stiff as a board, head high, shrouded in a hood. Her eyes are half open and suddenly she's rolling them around, so that at moments only the whites are showing. I kick Tutu whose feet are pressed against mine and see her shaking with giggles as she follows my glance. Ruth's a weird one. She'll stay wrapped in silence for ages then, out of the blue, she's participating in some game we're playing, laughing at the most unlikely moments.

That afternoon we have our first glimpse of the Himalayas, a wavy line of bright white far away to the south. 'Machhapuchhare,' says Amy knowledgeably as we stand and gaze. 'Part of the Annapurna range in Nepal.' The sun's straight ahead of us, the wind biting hard.

We pass a tiny settlement and Peter shouts out, 'Guest house, Norbu.'

'Too dirty,' he replies, his face layered with dust. 'We go on.'

On to nowhere. Gravel and sand, then a trickling stream. The light is fading and the wind screams through gaps in the tarp. Quzha turns off the road and stops by the water. 'We camp here,' says Norbu cheerfully; but nobody budges.

'Isn't there another option?' Peter again. 'I don't reckon our tents are up to this.'

We clamber out. There's no protection except the truck, and it's stony underfoot. Then we spot, half a mile away, three dark tents, sprawled out like giant spiders. Quzha drives to a respectful distance from them and tells us to wait while he and Norbu walk on. They come back smiling and by the time we've lugged our gear over, a spare tent of white cloth and yak hide is being raised before our eyes. We all muck in and it's up in twenty minutes, easily big enough for the whole group.

It's held up by diagonal poles outside at either end, and running along its roof line is a gap for the smoke. There's no mat and the sides don't touch the ground; the front flaps are pegged down in such a way that the wind is broken, not sealed out. But we have a stove in the middle – a soot-black tin with a ring on the top for a pot. A man carries in a sack of yak dung, feeds some in and lights it with paraffin. We spread ourselves around it as a large kettle is brought to the boil and our cooking begins.

Two women in rug-like clothes, the colours of our tent, come in to have a look. Matted hair sprouts out beneath their scarves, faces and hands as tough as leather, but their eyes are bright. They stand motionless, a boy of about eight by their side, then nod their approval and turn. The boy becomes our fire keeper, solemnly showing us how to break up the dry dung. He stares into the flames, then peeps at the things scattered around – packs, sleeping bags, cameras. Not a word spoken. San takes out his juggling balls and the boy's face is drawn to them as though pulled by a string. Then his father enters and he darts out through the flaps.

After our dinner, amazingly, the wind dies down, but the ground's freezing outside. I chat with Tutu and LT for a while, but my mind seems to spiral upwards with the smoke into the dark flickering folds of the roof, and the vast night beyond. How must their lives be, these nomad people? Hardship is part of their nature, chiselled into skin and smile. How alone too – eight adults and four children. I'm aware of Jacques sitting by a candle, shuffling around with a cigarette which contains more than tobacco from the smell of it. Dogs bark endlessly. Then quiet. Would I be me if I'd been born into one of these families?

Day Five

We load up before sunrise. Norbu suggests a sum of money for us to give and everyone seems pleased. When a price is fixed beforehand, money is just a way of getting something; this way it becomes a gift. It feels good. What they've given is a gift too. Norbu's an excellent guy, at home with so many different sorts of people. Quzha as well, though it's harder to get to know him. In fact I like the whole group. Even the vegetarian fundamentalists.

'That's where the white yetis live,' says Norbu, as we glimpse more snow peaks later in the morning. I feel strangely excited. His words bring up feelings from childhood, of courage and friendship and snow, from the story of *Tintin in Tibet* by Hergé.

'They aren't real, are they?' asks LT.

'Sure they are. They're giant yaks who guard the mountains. I saw some as a boy.'

I don't need any more details. I'm happy with the image of Tintin being rescued by the fluffy silent creature on an icy slope. That's how I was first drawn to the name, Tibet.

We stop by a stream and set about boiling the inevitable noodles for lunch. Peter tries out one of the paraffin cookers we bought in Lhasa and it's an abysmal failure. The flame is too weak in the wind and the water only gets to lukewarm. So, apart from Jacques and Ruth's more professional stoves, we seem to be dependent on Quzha's flame thrower.

'Hey, Luke.' It's Norbu. 'You want meat?' He must have picked up my growing resentment. I beckon to LT and we go together to where he's making *tsampa* out of flour and butter tea in his orange-stained bowl. He kneads it into a dough and gives me a generous lump. It tastes smoky, salty, weird. Quzha carves small slices off the frozen carcass and they eat them raw with chilli sauce. He sees our hesitation and roasts a few pieces on his flame. 'Man, that's food,' says LT ecstatically and I heartily agree, while Jacques, who's nearby, asks for the raw deal with the chilli. 'Delicious,' he maintains, but I notice he disappears behind rocks shortly after, and has to stop the truck later to run out again.

We're getting tired and the mood in the back is more inward than normal. LT's reading the huge tome of Paul Johnson's *Modern Times*, about the twentieth century. 'Does anyone know how many wars there have been since '45?' he asks in his mildly quizzical way. Names of countries come back at him, first slowly, then in rapid bursts. We start to count and get as far as ninety-two. 'It's as if there's been a world war without anyone realising it,' Cara exclaims.

Dad says it's like the difference between a bush fire and a peat fire. Peat fires are in some ways more dangerous, because they smoulder underground and no one can predict when they're going to burst out again.

'So how do you stop a peat fire?' asks San.

No one answers. Strangely the image that comes to me is of the brooding darkness that was swamping me in China. I see it more like black oil than flame, but what it shares with a peat fire is the unpredictability of where and when and with what intensity it will erupt again.

That night is the coldest ever. Since there's no wind and the sky is clear, we elect to camp and see if our tents are any better than the stoves. We stop at a beautiful place by a river, where there's even a rockface for protection. But no sooner does the sun set than the cold descends like paralysis. The stream is already half iced over and my breath is a fog in front of me as I struggle with pegs and guy ropes and poles.

Ruth volunteers to be the chef and launches into an elaborate menu which requires several stoves and it's pitch dark by the time the food is ready. Rice with a sauce of onions, garlic, ginger, carrots, marmalade and soya sauce, topped with coconut and mango chutney. I have to hand it to her; it's a long way better than noodles and I guess she scores a few points with all of us. How does she fit all these jars and bottles and tubes into her pack?

We eat around a yak dung fire which seems to have no heat. From afar, it must seem as if we're doing some kind of ritual dance as we jump up and down and around to keep warm. My fingertips are ice cubes.

Quzha and Norbu insist that Mum and Dad use their tent, saying they prefer the truck. That leaves Jacques's tent and the two Chinese ones for the rest of us. I'm with LT and San. Being the tallest, San's in the middle, but his feet must be sticking out, because even I have to struggle to squeeze in. My right arm and leg seem to be welded to the frozen world outside. Through the night rasping coughs echo across the camp. When I shift my position, I hear the crackle of ice above me and drops of frozen condensation shower my face.

Quzha said we'll reach Kailash tomorrow. We're now at about four thousand three hundred metres. What's it going to be like at five thousand six?

Day Six

Everyone's pretty grey in the morning; and Dad, Amy and Ruth cough as if their lungs are splitting. It takes ages to get something warm into our bellies and stow all the gear. Quzha needs a good half-hour with the flame thrower before he can get the engine to turn over and it's ten o'clock by the time we're off.

Tutu and I take a turn in 'first class' at the front. Wow, what a view! A long, long, gradual ascent up a valley that must have been chiselled by glaciers – immense, majestic. She's been teaching in the Philippines for five years and been on the road now for six months. Behind her joviality is a sad childhood, as she begins to tell – divorced parents, a bitter separation, mother remarried, conflict with the stepfather, no contact with her dad. She left home when she was thirteen but managed to finish school and train as a teacher. 'Aren't you scared, travelling so long by yourself?' I ask. 'I wish I could be that independent.'

'If you get on with your parents, don't hurry,' she says, pinching my nose playfully. 'You'll have to cope soon enough.'

We talk about food. What she wants most is lasagne with a good Italian cheese sauce. I wouldn't say no to a steak and chips. We vie with each other in the dishes of our imagination. Then we share her Walkman, listening on one earphone each. We burst into song and I hear Quzha laugh out loud. He tells us he has a wife and two young kids in Shigatse, that he's happy with his lot and thinks trucks are the only things worth driving. He loves the country, the mountains. Who wouldn't?

We come to the main channel of the Brahmaputra and he gets out to have a look, indicating that many trucks get stuck in the summer when it rains. Even now, there are some tense moments as we splash and lurch our way across. There's a cheer from the back and I feel a sudden tingling as I see the gladness on his face. He's into the adventure as much as we are.

We stop there for lunch and as LT and I get stuck into our daily whinge about noodles, Mum produces a packet of dried yak meat which she bought in Saga. I feel nourished by the surprise of it as well as the food itself. It makes up for the fact that she was in the food group but let the more outspoken people have their way.

A tall woman in a brown robe and shawl appears, as if from the ground, and stands gazing. Near her are two boys and a little girl with an old blue anorak down to her knees, bare shins and fluffy skin boots. I offer her a carrot and she chews in puzzlement, looking out beneath wild hair and a tiny plait in the front. When we pack up, the mother gestures for the plastic bag I'm carrying and a used can of Fanta, even some crumpled paper. I add a film canister and she pushes them into the pouch between her coat flap and belt.

On flat ground at the top of a rise, fluttering with prayer flags and peppered with small piles of stones where uncounted pilgrims have prostrated in ecstasy and prayer, we have our first glimpse of Mt Kailash. On the horizon, beyond the expanse of ochre-brown gravel and low hills, the white tip of a pyramid. Another snow peak to the left and past that, a pale blue gleam of water, Lake Manasarovar. To our right, to the north, empty wilderness. Holy or not, it is a place in which to stand tall. And the thought comes:

If my mood were still dark as it was in China, how much of this would I see? What I see depends on me.

Norbu and Quzha gather stones to build a chorten and others follow suit; then we pile back in. The sun is warm and spirits are high. I kneel on one of the petrol drums and look out through the front, as the trail takes us closer to the mirror-like lake with snow peaks on its far side. We pass a turn-off at its western end and come to a smaller lake, Rakshas Tal – for some reason considered dark and 'feminine', whereas Manasarovar is 'male' and bright. Lake of the Moon and Lake of the Sun. People say that when there's a flow between them, it's a good sign. The channel has been dry for years, but according to Norbu recently there's been water.

We lurch over some deep ruts and I climb back down. LT catches my eye and points to the ceiling. The hunk of mutton has slid along the bar and is dangling just above Amy's head. She sees it; and I get ready for the shriek. But it doesn't come. All she does is stare.

The single government guest house in Darchen, the settlement nearest to Kailash, is not the world's most welcoming place. We enter the gate of the dusty compound bordered by a line of single-storey buildings on three sides, and are greeted with the news that we have to pay extra for the same unswept rooms and dirty bed clothes. For a few moments I'm back in China. We fight back with some intensive bargaining and the price is halved, but Norbu and Quzha have to pay the same – with one yuan discount – because they're with us! Once all that's out of the way the manager and his ladies become more human. What is it about the government that even its Tibetan employees become surly?

Dad's in a bad way. With the daily dust and last night's cold, his lungs sound awful and he's anxious about another blockage. He says he won't be up to the three-day walk – or kora – around the mountain tomorrow, but that maybe he can catch us up on the way. With that, he agrees to take one of my cough-inhibitor pills and a bronchio-dilator tablet from LT and buries himself beneath quilts on a bed.

Darchen is about four and a half thousand metres up and many of us are breathless. LT and I browse through the dingy store and find some pre-cooked meals of fish and duck in polystyrene trays, with a cord attached which triggers a device to warm the stuff up. God knows what chemical processes are involved but we buy two anyway. It tastes truly vile but we manage to get some of it down without chucking up. Are we okay for tomorrow?

Day Seven

We wake to a beautiful morning, perfect but for the occasional gusts of wind. Everyone elects to have a day of rest. Dad, as always, has had a quick recovery though he's still coughing. Most of us didn't sleep well and we lounge around and read or write or talk, on the decrepit armchairs against whitewashed walls. Our washing hangs stiff with ice on strings attached to the flat roofs. The frilled canopies above the doors are heavy with dirt.

Peter, Cara and San go off to explore the hills behind the guest house – above which hovers the startlingly white peak, like a magician's hat. LT and Mum shampoo their hair, cup by cup, with hot water from the thermoses we have to beg from the ladies. Even cold water is scarce as the staff have to carry it from the stream outside. I manage to have a wash, or a sponge at least. A real event.

The day draws on and anxiety begins to move, deep down. Cara joins the brigade of coughers and Amy, who's hardly eaten since Lhasa, reckons she has amoebic dysentery. Tutu withdraws with a hammering headache and LT with nausea; but at least Norbu's agreed to come with us. So will Jacques, though he had said he'd go his own way once we got here.

I'm worried about food. As anyone could have predicted, it's running out. There's enough for us each to carry four cooked potatoes, four carrots, six packets of noodles, two bars of chocolate, some dried fruit and nuts, biscuits, sweets; but little remains for the rest of the journey. We decide to take Jacques's tent in case of emergency, also his cooker and a thermos. He still has extra food of his own, such as *churra*, the powerful local cheese which is solid as granite; and he's generous in sharing. Ruth's as aloof as ever. She doesn't participate in the sorting out of supplies but helps herself from the truck, saying she wants to do her own thing. People start muttering. Surely there's enough space out there for each one to be alone. And there's only one path!

I start packing in the candlelight, keeping to as little as possible; but with a wine skin of boiled water, a communal saucepan and my camera and films, it still weighs a ton. It becomes clear Tutu won't be coming and I feel sad for her, having travelled so far. LT's tight and pale, and tells Peter and me in our room that he's not sure either. 'What am I doing here anyway?' he says, burrowing under his quilt.

3

LT did come. To begin with at least. He was with Luke and Justin, who were way ahead within twenty minutes as the path headed west, Kailash itself hidden by mountains. Though the sun had risen, we were in shade and it was freezing. Everyone overtook me; but my heart was light and a new energy seemed to be flooding through me.

The path had begun behind the guest house, at a broken *mani wall* – a mound of rock fragments, chiselled flat and inscribed with mantras. Small chortens marked its course as it meandered past gullies and slopes, climbing gradually between clumps of brown scrubby grass. They became like friends, those piles of stones, reassuring me that all was well and this was the way. The sun shone through and almost immediately it was too hot. By the time I had stripped off an outer layer I was far behind.

The others were waiting by a great teepee of stones with a red banner flapping in the wind and strings of cheerful prayer flags, where the white tip of Kailash appears for the first time. It was on a small rise with a panorama in all directions, behind us the plain leading to the snow-capped Gurla Mandhata range on the far side of Lake Manasarova. The sun was strong, the sky an undisturbed ocean of blue. Silence and space; and the crackling of cloth.

'I'm going back.' His voice was taut, like stretched wire.

'But why, LT?' people were asking. 'We've only been going an hour.'

'I can't breathe. I won't make it.' His face was white. I was shocked. He was young and though thin and bony, seemed strong. If he had to give up, what chance would I have? Justin and Peter offered to take turns with his pack and I suggested he walk with me and not worry about keeping up; but he was in no mood for bargaining. 'You don't understand. It'll be worse higher up. I'm not going to risk it.'

We prevailed on him at least to rest then watched him descend, alone.

'See you in two days,' Luke called. 'Say hello to Tutu.' The effort seemed to exhaust him and he sank down onto his pack. 'I'm struggling too, Mum. I keep missing a breath. It scares me.'

The path continued up and down, over rich honey-brown scree to a wide flat valley. Luke stayed with me for a while but he was anxious about going too slowly. 'It's a question of finding your rhythm,' I told him, still struggling with my own. 'After that you can keep going for ever. As your heart does.'

He started to pull ahead, then stopped. 'You know what saddens me about LT? It's that he'll feel he's failed.' And he walked on.

A solid red-stone gateway, topped by a stupa. An entrance from nowhere to nowhere. Another beginning. Near it, more mani stones in random heaps, their carved letters and forms incredibly fine. I was alone again, though not the last now. Jacques was puffing hard at the chorten and Norbu had stayed back to walk with him. I ventured beneath the arch.

The ground was strewn with objects of all colours and descriptions – shirts, trousers, shoes, bits of cloth, earrings, handbags, photos, clumps of hair... The symbolic shedding of one's old self, as one embarks on the process of purification which the kora represents. The whole circuit is about fifty kilometres long; some pilgrims prostrate body-length every metre of the way to enhance its effect! *What am I throwing off?* Nothing material, but my mind goes back to its old way of clinging to resentment. *Can I let the past go, once and for all?*

On the far side were yaks. They must belong to pilgrims, I thought. I had heard stories of them bringing their families and livestock since the journey can take years, especially if they visit other shrines too. Then I saw the men in padded jackets buttoned down one side, loading up camp gear while brightly anoracked tourists wandered about with ski sticks.

A woman approached me, her face hidden by fur. 'Where are you from?' She was German by the sound of her accent and looked about my age.

'Vietnam.' I presumed that was what she wanted to know. I was too breathless to talk.

'Is that so? I have two Vietnamese foster sons and they wouldn't dream of going camping. They're grown up now. I've just been there to one of their weddings.'

The path drew close to the rustling Lha Chu which courses along the western edge of the mountain. The wind was rising, slapping my face, insinuating its way through layers of scarves, hats and clothes. My companions were dots of blue, yellow and purple far ahead.

I caught up at midday, at a rickety bridge festooned with flags. 'That's Chuku Gompa,' said Justin, pointing to a building the colour of the rock, on a ledge high above. He looked well and happy. 'Some of the others have gone up to see it.' I chose to save such strength as I had and, with Ruth and Luke, we sheltered amongst rocks by the river to eat.

Ruth spread out her clothes, sat on them cross-legged and went into a trance. I drank as much as I could but had little need of food – just dried fruit and biscuits. The river gurgled and whooshed. The wind raced. Ahead of us, dark shadow shredded the light as the valley narrowed to a canyon. Its walls loomed, red-brown, monumental.

No one spoke. We were alone with the silence, Kailash a glistening cone. Watching?

It disappeared as we went on. My mind was as clear as the sky, but my brain wrapped in wool and my pack heavy. The rhythm carried me, one foot, then the other, over and again. Hypnotic. Only Jacques and Norbu were still behind; but we had seen them at the bridge and knew they were all right. I entered the shadow. Instant ice, the wind stronger now, like a wall itself, a torrent. Or a surgeon's knife.

Somewhere here is the Valley of Hope, a place in which to pray for a vision of one's favourite god. Is that what I hope for? How easy to believe if everything is revealed! And how much more dynamic the power of faith, when one trusts and *knows*, but is not yet granted sight. To have hope is to strive without expectation, I realised. To accept, to live – to rejoice in that living. And be ready for whatever comes.

Piles of stones, another sacred spot. I look around. High on the right, the crystal dome, its body still hidden by the guardian walls. I am numb with tiredness and cold.

A pebble-strewn valley. Gushing streams, clear, insistent; like the wind. No sign of a bridge or path. No more chortens. I pause. What time is it? All is shade. Or is it twilight?

Light blue ahead, luminous even without the sun. It must be the effect of altitude. I know that blue. It draws closer and becomes arms that are waving and a head with an Aussie digger's hat.

'This way,' I hear him shout and try to follow where he points. '…place to cross…' The wind steals his words and they are gone. Like the water, the air, the day.

He takes my pack and I follow. 'How much longer?'

'A while yet. I've left my pack farther on. It'll be dark in an hour. We need to move.'

'How's Luke?'

'Struggling. But he's plodding on.'

'And the others?' I never knew how much energy and breath one needs to speak.

'Ahead. None of them waited.' He seemed disappointed. 'But it's not the weather for hanging around in. There's Jacques. And Norbu.' Lizard-like figures against the rock.

We had to step on stones to cross the stream. On the far side my knees buckled. 'Whatever happens, keep between Norbu and me,' said Justin. 'You're off the path, but it's not far. I'll come back when I've got the packs to the gompa.' He walked on. I tried to follow, but my legs would not move.

Norbu was close. 'Nearly there,' he said cheerfully. Tears welled.

Jacques stood behind, struggling for air. His pack was the biggest of all and he was carrying a tube made of Coke cans, with sticks of incense about a metre long to offer at the next monastery. A camera too. We walked together. Somehow there was strength in knowing he was also in strife. Norbu raced about looking for suitable rocks at the next crossing. I stumbled. Jacques stumbled. Norbu laughed. At last, a chorten. The path! How different that felt. And farther on, my pack, which Justin must have left to come back for.

'Here, I carry for you,' said Norbu, as Jacques collapsed onto a rock and started rolling a cigarette. 'It's no problem.' His own gear was in a gunny bag tied to his back. He lashed it on the pack and fastened the buckle around his waist. 'Excellent.' He grinned broadly. 'Easy like this.' He clicked and unclicked several times, then patted the bundle as if it were a baby.

'Why don't you buy one?' But I knew the answer.

He said he earned little as a guide and the work was seasonal. Even his brother, Dorje, only received about thirty dollars a month. 'Too little, heh?' But I could sense no resentment.

Jacques was silent. In the dwindling light his face looked haggard; then he started to cough. But he was smiling as he stood up. 'So much beauty,' he said, inhaling deeply. 'It's insane to rush.'

We climbed a long slow rise and at the top, there it was in its ice majesty, the stern north face of Kailash. In front was a gap in the surrounding mountains; and I could see how the pyramid at the top continued down, over a shoulder, in almost exact symmetry, scarred by horizontal lines. Norbu pointed to three lesser peaks nearby.

'Avalokiteshvasa, Vajrapani and Manjusri. The bodhisattvas who fight against darkness, decay and ignorance.'

I looked up. Justin was heading towards us. I burst into tears.

The monastery was a humble building halfway up the slope. We took the path to the guest shack below. I could no longer do anything except sit on the edge of the wall-to-wall platform that was to serve as a communal bed for Jacques, Norbu, Ruth, Justin and myself. Walls, a ceiling and a dusty concrete floor plus a rough quilt each. No window, no light, apart from the fluorescent white of the mountain in the last glimmer of dusk, so close, so far.

Justin went up to the gompa with Jacques and came back with stories of the cave that was the inner sanctum, pitch dark but for candles, too low for standing. 'We could only bow,' he said. 'Or prostrate or kneel.' There Jacques ritually opened the Coke-can tube and lit one of his great incense sticks, leaving the others for the two monks.

'I'm worried about tomorrow,' Luke whispered miserably.

'I know,' said Justin. 'We've taken nearly nine hours. People normally take six. We need to be off by seven at the latest. It'll be harder than today.'

Suddenly it was pitch dark. He and Peter went down to the river to get water and came back with ice. It took ages for Jacques to boil it on his stove, while Ruth sat in her thick down bag, mixing oats, dried fruit, nuts and powder milk into a muesli. She gave me some walnut cake and was convulsed with coughing. 'Change your socks,' she said between spasms. 'The sweat becomes ice. You'll get sick.'

'The trick's to spread them under your sleeping bag,' added Jacques in an authoritative way. 'They'll be warm in the morning.'

We had our tea and noodles in candle light to the chorus of coughing – even from Norbu. He had a toothache too, but insisted he was going to carry my pack the next day. I felt ashamed but knew it was the only way. Then, gathering what was left of my strength, I went outside. Squeezing out the toothpaste took for ever, followed by an eternity of standing, staring up, hypnotised, into the bejewelled firmament of the sky.

*

It was dark when Justin's alarm jolted us back into the freezer that was our room. I lay beneath my pile of clothes, quilt and sleeping bag, trying to will my fingers and toes into activity. *If they won't obey me, how will my legs?* Anxiety gnawed. I would need at least eleven hours to get to the next gompa. Assuming, that is, I made it to the high pass – the Dolma La, or Pass of Compassion!

Justin was up, preparing breakfast with the water Jacques had boiled for us in a thermos before going to sleep. Norbu stirred and coughed, but stayed in bed. Ruth stirred, coughed and got up. Was she coming early with us too? Justin woke Luke next door and by the time we were ready it was seven thirty, the ground lethal with ice.

Dawn light glimmered over mountains to our left, reflected on the sheer north face as we made our way precariously down the slope to the bridge across the river. Then the climbing began. I felt guilty about being unburdened and offered to take Luke's camera bag. It was shockingly heavy. 'I don't think I can do it,' I said to Justin, gasping for breath and beginning to panic. 'Shall I go back?'

'Keep going or you'll freeze.' He took the camera and left me to plod on at my snail's pace. One foot, then the next. Then the one after. He appeared again after an eternity and I looked back down with a sense of achievement. Still no sign of activity by the guest house, below us now, on the opposite slope. 'It's not fast enough,' he said, trying to push me upwards.

'I can't do it any other way. Please leave me alone. I'll get there somehow.'

And he walked off. Was he piqued? On again. One foot. Then another.

They were waiting for me at the top of a shoulder with my friends, the chortens. A narrow smooth stone, about the length of my foot, was standing upright on a boulder, bathed in the rose-glow of dawn. Such simple eloquence. *Here a human being has been, for how else could the stone have found its verticality?* The glow intensified and for a few moments I was breathing colour as well as air – saffron, pink, gold. But the sun was still far beneath the mountain walls and the wind knifed as I stood still.

Ruth was spreadeagled on her pack, coughing. She looked dangerously pale but said she was okay. Luke was sitting on a rock, breathing in spasms, his face grey. He raised his bottle mumbling, 'Drink water, Mum,' then scrambled to his feet and left. Ruth followed. Only Justin appeared to be thriving. He said he could go faster at this altitude and preferred to walk ahead and test himself, then come back from time to time without his pack. 'We're doing all right,' he said, more gently now. 'That's the first steep section done. There are two more with long stretches in between.'

It was only after he had left that I realised my food was in his bag and all I had in my coat pockets was a water bottle and some tissue paper.

The shoulder extended into a valley. My legs picked up on the flatter ground; but so did the wind which seemed bent on driving me back.

'Cluck-cluck, cluck-cluck, cluck-cluck.' A man and a boy, from behind – sheepskin cloaks and boots, woolly hats, shoulder pouches, sticks. They skipped from rock to rock, glancing briefly at me, and within minutes had disappeared. I paused, drank and went on.

And now the second of the slopes was looming, as steep as the first. High above, I saw the blue of Justin, looking back and waving. I paused again. From below, Amy's head and grey lips appeared. She threw herself on a rock and I joined her on another. 'I need something to eat,' she said, opening her bag.

She had started over an hour after us and caught up already. As a teacher of physical education, she was fit despite the condition of her stomach. I realised I was hungry too and asked to 'borrow' some of her food. 'You're not carrying any?' she said in amazement and tossed over a packet of biscuits. The water was half-frozen in my bottle and I could only squeeze out a few drops. Amy drank from hers and hurried on.

Higher up, the hillside was bright with the colours of discarded clothes in full view of Kailash. It is a place of memorial, where people offer relics of the dead and pray for their well-being. Here too the pilgrim renounces his ego, along with its past attachments. I had read of a rock on which to lie down for this purpose. I looked and saw the man and boy, prostrating full-length. There is also an opening between two boulders, through which the good are said to pass freely, but the sinful cannot! I had no wish to add to my difficulties and sat on the smooth surface after the pilgrims had left, pondering what to put to death.

Self-image, desires, prejudices, reactions and the general stuff and clutter of the soul – it was some backpack! In this powerful ice-crisp atmosphere it seemed possible; but I knew that one such act is not enough. Real change comes from efforts repeated so often they alter one's habits and create new faculties of sensitivity.

At the top of the slope is the Valley of Death – a desolate stretch of rocks and boulders bordered by colossal walls. I added a stone to a chorten at its entrance and entered into the sunless deadly cold. Through army quilted denims it pierced, through tights and trousers, T-shirt and shirt, sloppy joe, jumper, fleece-lined waistcoat, anorak, silk and woollen scarves, woolly hat and hood. Breathing in small gasps, I dragged my feet on, focusing on toes where all I could feel was numbness. And the unrelenting wind, lashing my face like a whip.

Silence. Huge. Dark thoughts stirred. Self-pity and blame. *'He should have waited. Selfish.'* A demon's whisper. *'Look at what you've left behind. Comforts, light-filled rooms, yellow wattles.'* A niggling leer. *'You won't survive.'* Tears pricked me. Grit in the eyes.

I pulled the ski glove off one hand, shuffled inside a pocket for a gauze mask and hooked the loops over my ears, left then right. It took a full few minutes and left me exhausted. I had no breath. Panic. *'I'll drink some water.'* The voice was hoarse. Was it mine? Struggling with the glove, then the bottle top. No water. Ice. The cap would not fit back on. Blackness flooding. Forsaken. Am I dying? *'Don't sit down. You won't get up.'*

A garden. The garden at the kindergarten. It is in the sun all day. Early in the morning before class, the light is soft, bathing every leaf and petal. Yellow daisies, red begonias, blue forget-me-nots… And the pink and mauve cosmos.

From a tiny seed a child has put in – a shoot, a stem and now a bush. Lush green leaves, spreading at the top as it grows taller. The sun calls, the rain soothes; then sun again. Jade buds appear at the tips of fragile stems. A petal unfurls;

and another. Tissue-thin, in the *sun*, quivering. 'The flowers have come! The flowers have come!' A girl's voice, dancing. And suddenly it is mine and I am in a dark room, peeping through a crack in the shutters. The light!

The image lives on. I hold it, *build* it. Yellow streaming, mauve and pink. I pour in my longing. And it is here; I am flooded with sunshine. In place of ice, gold. Instead of air, light. I am light. I am nothing, nothing without it. The Sun. *Christ.*

Sounds from behind. I do not turn. There is no energy. The steps draw close. 'Hi.' San's voice, singsong. Colours rippling. 'Are you okay?' His smile is real. He's puffing, but his legs are strong, long. Like his hair, in a horse tail down his back.

'My water's frozen.' I show him the bottle. He rattles it, then swings his pack down and I marvel how easily he does it. He pours in some of his water and shakes to melt the ice. I still cannot close it, but I drink. And put it in my pocket.

'Where are Luke and Justin?' he asks.

'Ahead. Please ask them to wait. I have no food.'

He hands me a block of 761, rock-hard high-energy biscuit that looks like soap. Then he leaves. I bite. And the tears flow, unstoppable. I cry out, '*Oh, where's the sun?*' But it is really to announce that I am here again, back in life. For I know the answer; I know I'm all right. Only numb.

The sun was above the cliff in front. I could see the sharp diagonal 'wall' where the shadow ended and the light beckoned, the sky a *royal* blue. Huge boulders basked in the glory, but the wind still tore. A structure of stones and there – *in the sun* – was Luke, munching raisins, his food bag open on his lap. San was clicking on his waist buckle. He gave me a bottle half-filled with water and packed my ice block away. Then Cara appeared, dishevelled and intense; and they left together with a brief 'hi' and 'bye'.

It was a beautiful spot. Gratitude filled me at seeing Luke. I sank onto the rock next to him. It was *warm*. He handed me a fruit roll-up. 'Are you okay?' I asked.

'Struggling. I still can't breathe. Take some of my food.' He stood up.

'Don't go yet. It's so sunny.'

'I'd better, Mum. I'll get Dad to come back.'

Something opened then. My head was as woolly as ever but suddenly I could *think*. For the first time I glimpsed what it means to think *outside* the brain. The process was *above* my head, quite distinctly – crisp, clear and not confused with emotions. I was aware of everything in a direct and detailed way.

The long valley ended and the path swung to the right. In front was the third of the steep ascents, the hardest and highest. There was no other way, except back.

After ten steps my heart is thumping so hard I am afraid it will explode. *You won't make it like this. Take one step. Just one. And see how it feels.* It is okay. I try another. But the limit is three. Beyond that the great drumbeat starts up again. *One. Two. Three.* Incredibly slowly, but steady. *Stop. Two. Three.* The tempo comfortable enough that each beat is a breath. *One. Two. Three – Stop. Once. More.* It has a power. Like a mantra. Or a slow-motion, ritualistic dance. And when, at moments, the slope eases, I can expand to *Four* – or *Five*!

What is more, I have energy to look around. To enjoy. I begin to bathe in it. The air, the sun-warmth, the intense red and brown of the rocks, the white mountain, the immensity of blue. And the light. I feel high, but in a controlled way, brimming with gratitude and spirit.

For the spirit world is near. Everywhere. I cannot see it but I am in it as we all are. And it comes to me that the gods worshipped on Kailash by different religions are but aspects of an all-pervading Universal Being, which expresses itself in ways appropriate to our cultures and consciousness. The *rightness* of it all!

'I can't breathe.' He was sunk low on a rock. 'I won't make it, Mum. I have to stop every few steps.' His tone and the greyness of his face alarmed me.

'It's the same with me,' I replied. 'You *are* breathing. It's just that it feels different at this height. Everyone finds it difficult.'

'But I'm *nineteen*!' He drank from his bottle. 'Everybody else is older and they can do it. Dad's right ahead. What's wrong with me?' His lips were bluish. He was shivering, arms limp by his side.

'Luke, it's not a competition, do you hear me?' I was beginning to panic. 'If you're tired, slow down and rest. Often. I'll show you my way,' I explained and we crawled on, like two giant snails. After a while he grew calmer, though his colour still worried me. But when he got out his camera and took a photograph I could see life and interest flowing again.

'You look like two elderly aliens out for a walk,' Justin cackled above us. He appeared drawn but elated, and we sat together and shared some food. 'I'm sorry for not coming back earlier,' he went on. 'But it's only been two hours, you know. I guess I needed to show myself I could keep ahead of Amy. Anyway, do you want a push? It's out of this world up there.'

I declined as before, preferring my own pace, but I felt refreshed. So did Luke. As the two of them went ahead, I reverted to my outlandish rhythm, mulling over Buddha's saying: 'You should thus train yourself: though I am ill in body, my mind shall not be ill.'

Then the tourist group appeared with Peter in front, worn and short of breath but cheerful as always. He said there were twelve of them, the oldest sixty-five years old. They had driven from Kathmandu in Landcruisers together with a truck for baggage. Porters and yaks were carrying their gear.

A white-haired man with ski sticks stopped, stuck out his chest and grinned. Two younger ones with day bags panted behind. Three Tibetans loaded with boxes, canvas and poles were chatting as they sauntered up the path. Then came the drivers and the yaks – horns like pointed handlebars, heads low, lumbering over the rocks, and on their backs garish piles of packs and quilts and cooking pots. Soon they were among us – thick fluffy necks, grunts, wary eyes, body warmth and the tang of sun on leather and breath.

'Oh, it's you.' It was the German lady from the day before, her backside sticking out behind the beast's rump, hanging on for dear life. She looked me up and down with an expression of pain mixed with disbelief. 'How did you get here?'

'I walked.'

'Oh my God. Poor woman!' The yak bumped against a boulder and she cried out as it lurched forward. Behind her came a man on another animal. The path was a series of rocks and the sudden heaves were too much. He let go of the reins and fell. The driver rushed up to help but he refused to get on again.

It takes a further hour but the moment comes. I am on the pass, the sky so near one can almost touch the angels.

In the centre is a giant boulder, festooned with chortens, bones, horns and fabric. From a tall pole, lines of prayer flags crackle fiercely like flames. It is a festival of all-seeing eyes, swastikas, mani stones, scattered grain, coins stuck on with butter, paper money (even dollars) and colour, colour, colour. A few pilgrims are fingering rosaries, whirling prayer wheels, chanting; here and there, a foreigner looking dazed, face turned up in awe towards the Ice Pagoda, soaring into the blue. Above our heads, an eagle, floating on air.

> I climb the mountain,
> In search of miracles.
> There on the top,
> A bird.

Jacques and Norbu were still behind and it was after two. Peter and Justin decided to wait for them, while Luke and I went ahead. It could take a further six hours to reach the gompa.

The descent at first was almost vertical down grey crumbly rock and slate which slid away in puffs of dust. Luke was running, while I clung to the side in terror. 'I can breathe,' I heard him shout. 'Breathe!' Toes, ankles, calves, knees, it was as taxing as going up, but my breathing was easy too and my pace faster.

At the bottom of the first slope was an expanse of ice, the Lake of Mercy. Another legend; I had done my reading. Shiva had a wife named Sati. One day, her father offended them by not inviting him to a party. In protest Shiva materialised a thousand-headed monster which brought havoc to all and sundry, while Sati exploded in flames. Appalled by his wife's death, Shiva went to Kailash to mourn. Sati reincarnated as Parvati and came to bathe in this lake to lure him out of his solitary meditation.

'It's lucky we're not Hindu,' was Luke's response. 'No doubt we'd have to break the ice and bathe in it.' Then he ran on.

Monotony of brown now, the path, the rock, the unrelenting wind. I was alone again, content but indescribably tired. It was a different sort of tiredness. On the section before the pass, my nourishment had been of the spirit. Now as I descended, I felt the body's needs grow stronger and I longed to eat and sleep and be warm.

Justin and Peter caught up on a shoulder overlooking the valley on the eastern side. They said Norbu had reached the pass at three, left his load there and gone back to help Jacques who was struggling farther down. Justin had given the tent and some food, since they would almost certainly have to camp out for the night. They also had my sleeping bag in the extra pack Norbu was carrying.

I begged again to be left to my own pace. Justin was anxious about the time I was taking. 'We've only got two flimsy sleeping bags between the three of us,' he said. 'If we don't make it to the gompa...' He left his sentence unfinished, as we started the painful scramble down the escarpment.

Strangely I was not worried; perhaps I had no energy to be. But perhaps too something of the exercises we had been doing these months was having an effect; for we were now at the sixth, during which all the previous five – mental focus, strengthened will, equanimity, positivity and open-mindedness – are brought together in a daily rhythm. All I knew was that I must go to my limits. Beyond that, it was in the hands of powers greater than me.

The valley went on. And on. At first there was the relief of walking on flat ground and the joyful company of its river. But with each step it seemed to grow longer, while the wind was turning into a gale that blotted out all other sensation. From time to time Justin would re-emerge into my world, encouraging, urging me on. 'Peter's on the other side of the river,' he said on one occasion. 'I don't understand it. Surely the gompa's on this side? The wind's so strong, I can't call to him.'

Another eternity. Then tents. A group of foreigners. 'Where's the gompa?' I try to ask. But only my mind hears it. My throat is raw flesh, muffled beneath bandages. They look at me strangely. Do I look mad, with these layers of padding like elephant skin? 'Gompa?' It is spoken.

A woman takes out a map; but we cannot locate it. A man looks on, then another, as the wind rages to tear it to shreds. The light is fading; there is no time to waste. 'Go straight on,' says one of them with authority. 'It's about an hour's walk.'

Farther on, another city of tents. Could it be *here*? 'Hello,' a man with a charming smile. 'Where do you come from?'

I laugh. The absurdity of it. 'The Dolma Pass. Where else?'

'Oh, I mean, what part of the world?' I tell him and he goes on chatting. Have I been back recently? He's heard it's an interesting country. How did I find it?

'Please. The monastery?'

'Ahead, I presume. I've heard it's about two hours. You can't miss it.'

An electric blue dot in the distance, growing bigger. Gladness rushes through me. 'We must hurry,' says Justin. 'It'll be dark in forty minutes. And freezing.'

We walk on, the sun sinking into the V of two mountains. There is no sign of Peter. The path becomes threadbare, derelict. Something is missing – no chortens. We scale a crumbly rockface. Sheep tracks. The sun has gone and for a few moments I pause – the rose glow, luminous, tangible, filling all things with promise. Is this the Valley of Rebirth?

The sheep trail descends and in front is another river, flowing into the main one from the left, across our path. Luke and Justin are trying out stepping stones. But the current is too fast, the channels too deep. We could wade no doubt, but at what cost? The first stars are with us. There is no time for mistakes. We rush up and down, devoured by the urgency.

The last glimmer of colour. I stand still, fully aware that it is my slowness that has brought this about. Pale darkness over the land. Ice grips; but the wind is suddenly quiet and in the emptiness the water's flow becomes the ticking of a clock. 'Maybe Peter knew something we don't.' Luke's voice, remarkably clear. 'Dad, we should cross the other river.'

It is in several streams, with islands of gravel between. Spread out, its force is weakened. We tread on stones, and at only one place have to jump. Luke is alongside me, Justin waiting to grab us. 'Together, Mum. One. Two. Three…'

It is pitch dark. We have one torch. Thank God for Gyanseng. We lie on our backs, gulping the stars. The radiance! As if the whole firmament is light. It is hard to pick out the constellations, the other stars so bright. We walk on towards the west in a new valley, Justin in the lead, still not knowing if it is the right direction.

Luke sinks to the ground. 'I've got to stop.' The rest follows in quick succession. Justin's cry, 'May our angels guide us!' Then the sound of a scuffle and he is sitting at my feet. He tells me later he somehow pivoted round, off balance, ending up facing the wall of mountains across the river. He exclaims again and in the instant I see it too. 'Look!' From the zenith of the heavens a star flying across the sky, on and on, until it falls behind the horizon…

Within a minute he has found it. Five stones, the top one as round as a golf ball and red in the torch beam. Then the footprints. We hug one another, the light from Justin's hand making a crazy dance as it illumines more and more of the little piles of stones.

We were there within an hour. First we saw a light, moving then flashing. We signalled back. Twenty minutes and we heard voices. Then the room, bare-board beds, candles, smiles, hugs, thumps on the back, quilts, tears, steaming mugs of tea, noodle soup – and thin slices of carrot thrown in by someone to honour the occasion. It was ten o'clock. We had been going for fourteen and a half hours.

But it was not yet the end.

I heard their voices first, then the scraping of shoes on concrete. It was well after midnight and all was quiet except for the regular breathing of sleep. More voices, a light flashing outside, a gentle knock and in walked Jacques and Norbu, bear-like figures, exhausted but grinning in the barrage of torches as if their mouths would split.

The third day. We awoke to a glorious morning – fresh, crisp and scintillating. A delicate chirping punctuated the stillness. There were no trees and I could not find its source. Below was the river, much too fast and deep for us to have been able to cross in the dark; and behind us, the slope to the simple gompa and the escarpment, rearing up into the cloudless blue. Beyond again, hidden now, would be the south face of Kailash, with its famous cleft which some see as a swastika, others a cross – and which seemed to me, when we saw it earlier, like a series of vertebrae on a spine.

Legend attributes it to a contest between Milarepa, one of Tibet's most loved poet-saints, and a priest of the Bon faith. It was agreed that whoever reached the summit first on an appointed day would become its lord. The Bon priest set off in the dark with his green cloak and magical drum, while the Buddhist slept on until dawn. Unruffled, he donned his coat, snapped his fingers and was at the top as the first ray of the sun touched it. Seeing him already there in meditation when he arrived, his rival threw himself into a fit and fell down the mountain, his drum clattering behind, scarring the rock.

Another of Milarepa's deeds is associated with the gompa but that too was hidden from our sight as it was closed for winter. Within it is a cave, the roof of which he is said to have raised with his bare arms. He lived there many years, eating only nettles, which made his skin go green. His teachings are based on renunciation and contemplation and he is normally depicted with a hand cupped to his ear, listening for the music of the heavenly spheres. There is a story that his only possession was a clay pot, and that when one day he broke it, he composed a song to celebrate the joy of self-denial.

The door to the caretaker's room was open and I went in to ask for hot water. A man was fanning the fire beneath a kettle, his wife (so young to be a mother) nursing a baby, wrapped in dirty rags and lambskin. I asked how old it was and he counted sixteen days on his fingers. I touched its red cheek. The water boiled and he filled my thermos.

'Not even a god can change into defeat the victory of a person who has conquered himself,' said the Buddha.

I immersed myself in its meaning, exploring thoughts and images related to it. Every time we succeed in overcoming egoism, it is as if we have triumphed over a demon. But what is the force that achieves this? I tried to build it in imagination, as richly and vividly as I could. Then it was time to let it go, easier here than ever before. Details erased, one by one, until nothing remained and I held for as long as possible the 'space' of uncluttered consciousness.

Sometimes, nothing happens in such moments; at others an image may come, a thought, a light out of the darkness, directly or indirectly connected with the saying. But as I return slowly to daily life, it is always with a new vigour. On that particular morning, the image of Victory seemed to give out a feeling of something new arising, and when it had gone, a clear picture arose against the dark background: a rose, dawn-pink, radiating light.

Justin came back from an early-morning jaunt, happy as a lark, with tales of magical frozen waterfalls. I set out as the rest of the group emerged, stretching and blinking in the glare. Compared to the day before, today's walk was simple – up a little, down a little, as the river sank into a canyon on the left, plunging helter-skelter towards the plain.

A flat boulder, a chorten and the valley fanned out into a vista of brown and mauve, blurring in the distant white of Gurla Mandhata and the ultramarine of the lakes. Darchen was still two hours away and one by one the others overtook me, but it no longer mattered. In the immense space I could feel myself expanding. *My body is here, but 'I' go way beyond. I am in the air, the light, the mountains. I am in Justin, Norbu, Luke, Peter, Tutu. And they in me.*

I put all my will into being aware, for I knew the experience would become no more than a memory, until such time as I could find it anew in the 'ordinary' world. And though the Ice Mountain was hidden, I built a small chorten, of stones and gratitude.

I was home. We all were. Even Jacques. And to my relief Tutu and LT seemed as jubilant as the rest of us. They and Quzha had prepared a hot meal and in the hubbub of people loading up the truck, Justin and I wrote out the haikus we had composed as we walked the kora – Justin's for LT, mine for Tutu:

> I thought I came here
> To do the kora. But no!
> I did my washing.

> Sitting in my room,
> Contemplating their footsteps;
> There it is – Kailash.

4

Sacred Lake Manasarova. A day of rest! Thu and I were up early enough to have a discreet 'shower' in the piping hot, rust-red spring near the settlement where we were staying. How good just to be, to think, to write, to move one's limbs without having to drive them! And, though it was out of sight behind gnarled rock, how different is a lake from a mountain!

During the drive from Kailash, I had been in the front with Cara. Like others we had met, she was at a fork in the road. Coming up to thirty and having lived and worked in various parts of the world, what now? Her roots were in Italy, but she had made a break with the Christianity that was the backbone of her education. Nor had she found a direction in the East. Indeed she had been disturbed by the male dominance and superstition she had seen in many places. We had spoken little until then, but I recognised in her the kind of inner homelessness I had known myself, a feeling of estrangement from one's own culture. And in the dust and space and afternoon sun, our conversation turned to East and West – and Christ.

She described Japan which she knew well and liked: the pagodas with their roofs like birds' wings, the exquisite

Shinto shrines to nature, the meditation gardens of rock and raked sand, the solitary 'gateways' leading nowhere. 'There's such peace,' she said. 'And a sense of union with what's around.'

She also spoke about the Catholic rituals of her childhood, and her memories of cathedrals and chapels, of stone, incense, candles, coloured glass and the chanting of prayers. For her now such scenes had become dark and suffocating, cut off from the environment. 'It's as if through Christianity our relationship with nature has disappeared,' she said.

Yet it was not always so. In pre-Christian Europe, as in the East, places of worship were often in the open. And in the first centuries AD, there was an awareness of Christ's connection both with nature and the entire cosmos. In Celtic Ireland he was hailed as the Lord of the Elements; and in many of the sects destroyed by the Roman church, spoken of as having come down from the stars and sun. Then, as the emphasis grew on the personal relationship of each soul to the Christ, the other aspects were cast out as heresy and paganism.

'It's like two extremes,' I said. 'In old China, being "spaced out" into nature and the Tao; in Europe, so absorbed in the inner life of the soul – and one can trace the gradual movement from one to the other through history.'

There was a loud banging on the roof and Quzha stopped the truck. Jacques jumped out and wandered off by himself. No one knew why. We waited. Sand and gravel, and the deep blue of sky and the water ahead. 'What previously was outside, has entered in,' I added.

'And you connect this with Christ?'

'Yes. Before, people found divinity by looking outward and upward. Now we have to look within as well. I see Christ as the universal "I" of humanity, which has gradually come down to earth. It belongs to no race or part of the world – nor, exclusively, to any religion. I believe too that many in the ancient world knew that this was happening.'

Jacques returned and we piled back in. We were quiet a long time, then Cara said, 'If that's the case, what's gone wrong? How can so much destruction have come out of it?'

'I guess, as we come into ourselves fully, we stir up what lurks inside as part of our nature. We can't deal with it overnight; but far more people are able now than before to take responsibility for their own "stuff" without projecting it outwards. And as we grow, I think we'll find again the kinship of Christianity with the external world. Even the Tao!'

'My God,' said Cara suddenly. 'I mean, what's in a name? Would it be Christianity recognising the Tao – or Taoism recognising the Christ?'

Quzha drove down to the lake. In the late light it had a fairytale quality, mauve-blue against the distant snow and orange-red cliffs. Behind us loomed a bulbous hill, topped with stupas and a rainbow arch of swaying flags – the Chiu Gompa, dedicated to Padmasambhava, the holy man from what is now Pakistan who came to Tibet in the eighth century to rid it of demons and spent his last seven years in a cave here.

Across the valley behind the gompa was a cluster of households, surrounded by walls. We entered one, into a spacious yard, bordered by a single-storey house and a number of outbuildings in which two small rooms were made available with enough space in each for five bodies lying close together. Jacques, Norbu and Quzha were put up with the family. We had no beds but everything was clean. Cloth patterned with flowers and peacocks lined our ceiling and thick stone walls; and the host, a handsome man with flashing teeth, spread out carpets on the gravel floor. There was scarcely any light through the single window, but with candles, quilts and sleeping bags it became quickly cosy – if not exactly warm.

In the evening we were invited into the family's room. Warmth glowed from a stove with a bronze-coloured flue, on which a large pot and kettle were steaming. For two hours each night there was even electricity from the gompa's generator and a naked bulb illuminated the shiny earth floor, the carpets on the walls, the woven blankets and rugs. Cushions and wide benches lined the sides serving as beds as well as seats. There were books, framed pictures of saints and a sketch of the Dalai Lama. The teacups were of red lacquer with ornate silver lids.

A little girl in an anorak and apron toddled back and forth between the man and his wife. Inside a basket was a gurgling baby, cushioned in fleece. The host's three beaming brothers crowded in, one still a child, also his old father, mouthing mantras unceasingly to the rhythm of a prayer wheel. The boy fed the fire with animal droppings, while our hostess pinched dough from a coil around her wrist and flung the pellets into a meat stock. Norbu told us their livelihood came from sheep, that the old man claimed to be able to do the Kailash kora in eight hours and that his wife had been round over two hundred times!

'If a hundred and eight guarantees a place in nirvana,' quizzed LT, 'why does she do more?' There was a discussion in Tibetan and laughter.

'She enjoys it,' said Norbu at last.

Out of hospitality, the family removed their pots to let us cook first and it was nearly midnight by the time we had finished. I was coughing again. So was Cara. And Ruth exploded like a steam engine through the night.

Rugged up in everything I had, but still cold, I was away before sunrise. As I climbed the crag towards the gompa, the vista over sky and lake growing with each step, the sun's power began to pulse into the atmosphere, illumining the walls of whitewashed stone with their stripes of earth-red along the tops and black around the windows. White, black and red, colours that appear in so many fairy tales and legends of the world. Red for the blood, and the heart at its centre; black for the unfathomable will, in human beings and nature; white for the light that is our thinking.

A door was open and I ventured into a room with prayer barrels, leading to steps, winding alleys, more steps – and so to the stupas of piled stones at the top, the fragments of mani slabs, the heaps of yak horns and the fraying flags. There was no sign of the two monks who lived there. On a flat roof below stood four tridents – three-pronged staffs of Shiva and Poseidon, Greek god of the ocean, and the same symbol of trinity in this monastery of Tibet. Away in the distance, Mt Kailash.

I thought of the Dalai Lama's vision of Tibet as a sanctuary. The earth belongs to no one. From some parts we reap the fruits of agriculture, on some we have our industry and homes. But there are other places, such as national parks and forests, whose offering lies in not being exploited. And if the people here are willing to enshrine their high wilderness as a protected area – and are allowed to do so – it will be a service for all mankind...

The sun rose as liquid fire splintering into a thousand flames on the lake below. Apparently Beethoven could experience the sunrise as music. I am far from that, but I have learnt at least to hear the silence.

I walked down to the rhythmical splash and creak of tiny waves and ice crystals on the water's edge; then fast along the beach of pebbles to keep warm, pausing at intervals to take in what was around. The two activities were separate. 'When eating, I eat; when sleeping, I sleep' is an archetypal morsel of Zen pithiness. Walking was enough in itself. Likewise, standing and taking in.

I came to caves in the cliff, then a sad-looking woman with a cluster of children. A man approached smiling but his greeting seemed to have barbs. I wondered if he had been drinking for he leered a bit, his eyes shifty. Judging by the mess around the cave they had been there for a while. 'Where did you learn English?' I asked.

'In India. Chinese make trouble. We go. Then come back.'

'And is it easier now?'

'You think so, perhaps. You foreigner, not see what change. No food, we poor. You have Dalai Lama picture for my family?'

I walked on, hard, absorbed in the rhythm of legs moving, one after the other. How *do* they move? In these high places, where one breathes light as well as air and seems to need less physical nourishment, the distinction becomes clearer between the body and the will which empowers it. And words formed themselves, tuning in to my footsteps:

> Yes, I've heard about the brain,
> About nerves and electricity,
> But tell me, where does it come from,
> This simple power of legs moving?
> You say the brain does all this,
> That static contoured organ behind bone.
> Then tell me this...
> Who – or what – is using this brain?

I stopped, the sun hot now, a gentle but freezing breeze soughing across the crystal water. Were this in the West, there would perhaps be sailboats and outboard motors. And if it were the China we had been travelling through, it would be packed with people and rubbish. Here in Tibet it is a place of holiness, and no matter where I listened or looked there was nothing to disturb it but the clutter of my own mind.

> I've learnt about muscles, too –
> Blood sugar, calories, adrenalin.
> It all makes sense,
> But for one little fact:
> This power that I walk in
> Comes not only from inside,
> It's all around and flowing through.
> And somehow, by some magic I don't understand,
> I tap it,
> Each day, each footstep,
> Each smallest contraction of a muscle fibre.

The sun was still warm in the yard when I got back. Beneath strings of drying clothes the little girl was stumbling forwards, hands up high for balance, into Thu's arms. Against the west wall were people reading, writing, chatting – Quzha holding the baby, singing to it with Norbu. Its mother was next to them, rugged up with a scarf around her head like a balaclava, her skirt as warm as a sleeping bag. The sun moved. Shadow fell. It was suddenly cold.

We left in freezing darkness. Back to the bumps and our travelling companion, the dust. We knuckled down in silence under a mound of bags, the tang of petrol in the air. Dawn came and there were moments of comparative warmth; but our road was headed east now and only those up front were in touch with the sun. East towards Mt Everest.

There had been a time before our journey began, when I was filled with the idea of climbing it. I had met an Australian who had been to the top twice and was comforted to see that he was not a hunk of muscle but tall and wiry like myself. 'I happen to have a constitution that adapts well to altitude,' he said with humility, his face long and with the same high cheekbones we later saw in Tibetans. 'It's a question of how readily one's blood absorbs oxygen.' Something else he said affected me. 'I've seen what happens when a person loses his will. It's like losing one's humanity. It's the will that keeps one going when the body's beyond its limits.'

I contacted someone who was to lead an expedition soon after. It was then I heard how much it costs. Apart from all the equipment, human support and time devoted to training, there is a fee of around eighty thousand dollars for each group; and a waiting list of several years. On the Nepal side, at least. The way up and down is only deserted during the seasons when climbing is impossible, and is disgracefully polluted with the trash left by climbers.

The idea waned; but the image of the mountain still glowed. It may not have the legends and powers associated with Mt Kailash, I thought now, but its height is a symbol of holiness. The struggle to lift oneself upwards.

The truck stopped. Bare walls, earth road, squat mud houses, no sign of vegetation. Voices, then a Western man with a Chinese army jacket, striped woolly hat and a week's growth, appeared at the back. 'Any chance of a lift?'

'Have you spoken to the driver?'

'He said to ask you.'

'Then jump in.'

He looked dishevelled and extremely grateful. He had been hitching and walking in the area for a number of weeks, and been stuck at the village for three days. 'This is only the second truck that's been through,' he said. 'I was beginning to think I might be here for ever.' His name was Ian and he came from England. He had also trekked to the advanced base camp at Mt Everest. 'You have to go there,' he said simply. 'It's incredible.'

It would take four days of hard driving to reach Rongbuk Monastery, the last settlement on the trail there. On the first day I launched into the voluminous *Modern Times*, lent by LT. It begins with a reference to the culture-shaking impact of Einstein's theory of relativity which, as the author sees it, has spread from physics where it belongs into the domain of human values where it has become destructive. The old pillars of moral truth, such as the Bible, have toppled in the slurry of opinion and relative perspective and there is no longer an agreed standard of appropriate behaviour or belief.

On the second, I succumbed again to giardia. Ian had it too; and Jacques was headed for it. His way of dealing with it seemed to be to burn it out with contempt, mine to starve it, while Ian accepted it as a likely companion for the rest of his time in Tibet. Back at Saga that night – in low-slung buildings by a yard that seemed to serve as a communal toilet and garbage tip – I climbed onto my grubby bed, fully clothed and piled up with blankets, shivering.

The others went out and I lay in the darkness, listening to the sounds of trucks and people coming into the yard. When I got up later, it was flickering with tiny fires, cloaked bodies silhouetted against the flames amidst smells of dung smoke, toasting tsampa, yak cheese and urine. The group came back with stories of the best meal in centuries. I dozed again, to be woken at intervals by Ruth's coughing. It seemed each time it would never stop, the convulsive spasms racking her chest and windpipe like a vulture tearing at flesh.

On the third day came the turn-off to the rough road that winds south-east towards Tingri. I was feeling better and plunged again into *Modern Times*, which was leading me through the First World War to the Russian Revolution, the Depression, the rise of America and the Second World War.

I enjoyed the wide panorama it gave but wondered why the central story of our times, the evolution of consciousness, is so little touched upon by historical writers. As with our daily news, so with history, what clamours for attention is the stuff of war, scandal, economics and politics, while what is slowly maturing in human souls behind these outer symptoms – the struggle for a new morality, the search for meaning and global understanding – is largely ignored.

We reached Tingri after nightfall, our accommodation as basic as ever, but with cheerful wallpaper and a cosy kitchen of steaming pots and dung stoves. Jacques came to life in its rustic warmth, and Luke and Ian elected to eat there too with Quzha and Norbu. But the only food was yak meat and those of us who needed vegetables put aside racial prejudice and headed for the Chinese place across the street.

When we rejoined them in their twilight den, they were drinking chang, the local firewater made from barley. A small girl was hiding her face in her mother's skirt, while Quzha and Norbu spoke the throaty sounds of their language with the locals. Then Norbu began to sing, slowly at first and quite softly, but gradually gaining in strength and intensity until the veins on his neck swelled and seemed about to burst and his eyes were focused far away in a place where I could not follow.

It was at Tingri we had our first glimpse – from the two-storey tower, open to the air, which was the pit toilet – of Mt Everest. It was there too that Ruth left us, to go straight to the border without the detour to Rongbuk; Ian as well. It was as if he had been with us the whole journey. With his good nature and familiarity with rough travelling he had merged easily. In her own way Ruth had blended too. The hunger and squash, coughing in the night, the trek up the Valley of Death, a touch, sunrise on ice – such things are the stuff of companionship.

At noon we had our second glimpse of the mountain, from a bristling community of chortens on the last pass before the Himalayas. Behind us to the north, was ridge upon ridge of chiselled mauve-brown rock, its history of upheaval revealed in the chaos of its striations; ahead, across valleys and foothills of burnt sienna and dusky olive, the long line of white, its pyramids and jagged angles like an almighty ice dragon against the blue. 'Qomolangma,' said Norbu. 'Everest. Mother Goddess of the Universe.'

Simply to sit and gaze was a feast.

We descended into the dry valley, winding through villages of mud and stone, replenished by streams of melting snow. In one there was a guest house and while the others clambered out to see if we could get some lunch, I stayed to watch our gear. Faces appeared, children first – smiles, stained teeth, bright eyes and runny noses; then adults, the women with baskets on their backs. The more adventurous climbed higher, hands held out for gifts, peering into the alien world of the truck and exclaiming, 'Inji! Yagadoo!' Foreigner! Good!

An older boy swung a leg over the tailgate and I waved him away with a 'No'. Another pushed forward. It was like a tide rising and all I had, to hold it back, was the strangeness of my presence and the authority of my voice. I realised that it was with a similar 'psychology of superiority' that the British had grabbed much of India and built their empire.

The poverty was worse than we had seen elsewhere, the children's faces ingrained with mud, their hair matted and stiff, grit in their eyes, though at least they had shoes and there was padding in their clothes. Two small ones were focused on something on a flat rock the height of their waists, totally still, pink buttocks showing through the slit in their pants.

'Guess what's on the menu,' says Amy cheerily, bringing me a bowl of instant noodles and potatoes. San starts juggling and eyes turn with wonder as he varies his rhythm, crossing his arms under his knees and behind his back. Luke stretches out on the ground with his camera to catch a child's game, while little bodies climb up Jacques's legs to reach for sweets. The top part of Peter emerges on the roofless latrine tower next to the truck, waving a roll of pink paper and grinning. The crowd grows, as do the number of outstretched hands, as we rumble off into the wilderness. What thoughts and feelings must these transient foreigners provoke in the people who live here? Interest, bewilderment, resentment? Hope?

Jacques threw some sweet wrappers out of the back and Cara erupted. 'You make out you're the only one who has any love for Tibet, and here you are littering the place like the Chinese do.'

'Mind your own business. What's a piece of paper in this wilderness? We create far more pollution by driving in this truck.'

We were tired. The tension had been building for several days. It was there between Thu and me too, as anxiety began to grip about the coming trek to the advanced base camp; and it was out of sensitivity to this, perhaps, that there was a unanimous vote that Luke, Thu and I take the only three-bed room at the monastery of Rongbuk when we got there at twilight – the others sharing a dormitory. The valley was in shade, the air biting cold. At its far end, still bright with sun, the pinnacle of Everest streaming cloud like a volcano.

The first priority was food. A monk appeared, dressed in climbing boots, army fatigues and an orange jacket, and offered to cook us a meal. When the cheering died down, he described the ingredients. The novelty was eggs. We could have two each to supplement the noodles and potatoes. He was no stranger to business and his price was not cheap. A number of us followed him into his snug soot-black kitchen, cluttered with boxes, makeshift cupboards and cooking utensils. He also let us know he had a Walkman for sale and Norbu showed interest; but it was beyond what he could afford.

Our room was a deep-freeze. We lit candles and the few twigs Norbu had brought us earlier. Whether the temperature rose I doubt, but the flicker and crackle of the flames gave some inner warmth as we sorted out what we would carry the next day. The plan was to drive on to the base camp and trek from there. It would be hard going, there and back in a day, but everyone seemed keen, even Cara who had sprained her ankle jumping out of the truck after her argument with Jacques.

Luke was worried about his breathing; advanced camp was at five and a half thousand metres, almost the same as the high pass on the kora where he had had trouble. Thu was uneasy as well, haunted by memories of her earlier ordeal. 'I don't want help that's grudging,' she said at one stage. 'I'd prefer you go on ahead and prove whatever you need to prove.'

But I no longer needed to vie with anyone, even myself. 'We can all get there,' I said. 'It's just that you get into a doze when you're high up, Thu, and it scares me.'

Besides, though I had not said it, I did not know whether I was up to it myself.

For once, our delay in leaving was not because of the foreigners but Quzha who fell asleep again after being woken. Ice crystals glinted like stars in our headlights, the mountain a transparent yellow against a pre-dawn sky of white and indigo and pink. San started to hum and it spread from one half-buried body to another like a mist rolling over the land, a medley of tones and rhythms splashing together as the light grew. Only Jacques was not there; he had decided to go his own way for the day.

Quzha took it slowly and we reached the base camp of rock and river-smooth pebbles without mishap. There, to our discomfort, Norbu told us they would stay in the truck and wait for us. 'No problem,' he replied as we pressed them to go back. 'We can sleep here as easily as there.' We promised to return by seven. We had nine and a half hours.

The path rose gently, accompanied at intervals by a friendly chorten, on one side a chaotic ridge of gravel and pebbles intermingled with ice. Luke was exultant: 'I can *breathe*,' he shouted. 'I'd like to go on ahead.' Thu was in good spirits too. Little by little, as we climbed and came into the sun, the ridge of scree revealed itself as a glacier, the slow systematic master sculptor of the whole valley, reaching massively from far away Everest to the base camp.

We came to a ravine, carved out by ice and melting snow rushing to the hidden river beneath the glacier, only Cara behind us, struggling with her ankle. We filled our bottles with water, our souls with the music – of limpid pools, crashing spray and the gurgling of vortices. Bare rock beyond, the path indistinct; the glacier now a wall of crystalline pinnacles and behind it, pure white peaks against the sky. Within the vast silence, a crash of rock or ice. The creaking joints of a giant.

We lost our way among the sharp rocks and when we found it Thu needed to rest; ahead, insect figures inching upwards. A few minutes later and she was slowing again as the gradient began to bite. Four hours had gone by. I realised I was going to have to make a decision. 'You go on,' she said breathlessly before I had spoken. 'I'll rest, then turn back.' I hesitated, unable to decide.

'Go on,' she repeated. 'You *must*.'

Is gravity less strong at altitude or does one come closer to its opposite, to the same universal sun-seeking force which draws the sap upwards and makes plants grow tall? The higher I went and the more I exerted myself, the lighter my body seemed to become and the clearer the thought: It is not food alone that feeds us, but the ocean of spirit-will in which we live. Is that what the old sages referred to as the Tao?

The slope was a trickster, as so many are. I reached the top, but it was no more than a shoulder – or a hip. It continued, steeper. I met up with Tutu and LT. They were going slowly, pausing frequently, but still determined. The path disappeared among boulders. At some places I had to clamber up and down; at others leap from one to another, aware of the risk but trusting the flow. Surfing must be like this – being *there*, on the roller's crest, ever on the verge of being pulverised into chaos. Is this how an eagle soars?

The feet seemed to know where to go and I kept watch from above, only occasionally having to intervene and make a decision. It was not a trance; I knew precisely what I was doing but only as it happened. Yet I was tuned in at the same time to what was around – the mountains, the valley, the air, the snow.

The path again, climbing sharply; and then in the way of mountains, suddenly I was there. The ground was level, a wide shoulder, beyond which was the huge north face of Everest, its peak, still trailing clouds in the cloudless sky, so near yet over three kilometres higher. It was too much to grasp, for we were high already.

Advanced camp was in an empty bowl on the left and on the right, below now, that jewel-like river of ice pyramids with their jagged tips gleaming in translucent blues and greens. Glare was everywhere and a torrent of wind powering in from Everest.

I walked along the ridge to its far end, where the ground falls away into a vast white domain in which the roots of the mountain are embedded. I had the feeling of looking into something that is normally hidden. Like the floor of an ocean.

'Dad! Far out! How's Mum?' His voice was strong.

'She won't reach the top, I'm afraid. She's okay, though.' My words were swallowed even as I spoke, by the wind and the silence behind it. Better not to speak but to hug, to be grateful. Peter was there too, Amy and San, bathing in the landscape.

Ah, how much easier to be a bird or an angel! Yet what a work of art one's body is and what a companion on the way. How much I long to go higher – and what a wonderful teaching not to be able to!

I realised why the image of Everest had lived so strongly in me. In ordinary life it is hard to disentangle ourselves from the environment, for it feeds and supports us. Up here, nature's bounty is taken away. One is alone, battling to keep body warmth and moisture, and even the air itself, from being sucked away. Everything conspires to draw one out – the whiteness and glare, altitude and wind, the absorbing blue of the sky. And in the effort to hold oneself together is revealed the activity of the spirit.

Apart from my companions, I could see nothing that had life. And yet I was nourished. It was something as objective as the effect of warm soup in a cold hungry body. The colour is sustenance, so is the light, the silence, the space. The beauty. Though tired physically, I was replenished, and this in turn brought strength. It is not a substitute for food but something in addition, which we need just as tangibly – and of which we are so often deprived.

Tutu appeared, worn out, but jubilant. 'LT turned back,' she said, gasping for breath. 'I told him... we were nearly there... but he wouldn't... listen.'

We had less than four hours in which to get back. As we reached the ridge's end, a current flashed through my spine, and I rushed forward. Luke ran too. 'Mum, you made it! *How?*'

'I don't... know.' Her words came slowly, smothered by breath and smiles and the wish to take in the magic of where we were, as she sank onto a rock. 'I was sitting, gasping...' Then LT had appeared, saying that there was still a long way and it would be better to go back. 'I felt so sad. I stood up to follow... but my legs wouldn't move. I thought I was paralysed. Then I turned to the slope... and they walked. I can't explain. They were being moved.'

★

The eighteenth day since leaving Lhasa. There was no hurry. It only remained to get back to Tingri by evening, allowing a final day for reaching the border at Zhangmu.

Though for Thu and me the journey had a long way to go beyond the Himalayas, leaving Tibet would be an ending; for the crossing into Nepal means not only moving from the north side to the south of this great divide, but a transition to a different climate, geography and culture. On one side, the huge sphere of Chinese influence; on the other, that of India.

Something was tugging at my mind. A century ago people seemed to exult in the gulf between East and West. Fifty years later, Jung was writing of the East as the intuitive, feminine, unconscious mind and the West as its rational, masculine counterpart. He saw them as two parts of a whole, as in the human psyche. With the advent of

Africa, Asia, South America and the Pacific into world affairs, there came the idea of North–South polarity and the diffident categorisation into First, Second and Third Worlds, based on material well-being. So, my question: beyond the disparities of politics and wealth, of tradition and outer appearance, is there still a difference in essence between East and West?

Or is it more accurate today to think of humanity in terms of individuals, each one brought up in a given climate and culture, yet each of us as different as a different world, though we share the same basic needs and feelings and body structure?

Our last day in Tibet. I was up with the light and as I walked out of the village of Tingri for a last look at Mt Everest, I saw Jacques coming towards me. 'Here I breathe,' he said, emphasising each word. 'In France the mountains have been tamed and so have we. We're obsessed with hygiene and regulations. Here, despite the Chinese, the sacredness remains.'

'And where do you belong?'

'That's what I don't know. Yet perhaps I do. I know I could never really be a Tibetan. But the West is not my home either. Like the nomads, I'm homeless.'

We gathered by the truck as a group for the last time to thank Quzha and Norbu and say goodbye to those who were leaving us. To Quzha we gave the two tents we had used once; to Norbu, the Walkman we had secretly bought from the monk at Rongbuk. They were happy – the former with the habitual calmness which had been a backbone of the whole journey, the latter like a child with a toy.

It was a raw day, not only cold but damp. As we pulled away in the truck we looked back, huddled beneath quilts (Norbu already glued to his headset) until we could see no more the waving arms of Cara, Tutu and Jacques, who were planning to hitch back to Lhasa and stay longer in Tibet.

It started to sleet. On the mountains it was snowing. Until now, we had had the sun each day. For the first time it had the inward feeling of winter.

Then the last lap began, as we snaked down the dirt road, into a different world of gorges, streams, waterfalls and trees – the southern slopes on which the winds from the Indian Ocean offload their water before driving on, arid, across the high plains. 'Thank God we have Quzha for a driver,' said LT, as we looked over the sheer drop to the river far beneath.

In Zhangmu we zigzagged yet farther down, past a flurry of new constructions, shops overflowing with produce, trucks, garbage, telegraph poles, stalls, people in Chinese clothes and the brighter fabrics that come up the valley from Nepal. The main street was paved and rivulets along its edges mirrored the crashing of waters in the ravine, as the rain fell.

At the Chinese hotel in which foreigners were obliged to stay, it took all of twenty minutes to locate a staff member, who disdainfully led us to our rooms. Despite our protests, Quzha and Norbu insisted on sleeping in the truck. The sheets were clean, the toilets foul and there seemed to be no water. Our window had a vista of valley and peaks and billowing cloud, but on the flat roof below were piles of rotting garbage and plastic.

For a few moments, the old 'China syndrome' threatened to swamp me, but I managed to stand aside and it subsided. Slowly, slowly I was learning – it had taken all these years – to be a master in my own home. Emotions can be like ivy that runs over everything; or they can be a garden, where there is a balance between the wild and the tame, and the presence of the gardener is clear.

What lingered on was a touch of the sadness that comes with descending from high country; and the subtle anxiety of drawing close to yet another border.

Postscript

Weeks later, in the comparative comfort of Kathmandu, as the wealth of impressions and emotions from the long journey began to fade and it became possible for us to look back with more objectivity, Justin recorded our shared thoughts in his journal.

★

Long ago, human beings could commune, in dreamy but vivid pictures, with the spirit in all creation. With the coming of the intellect – in a few at first, then everyone – there dawned the differentiation between self and environment, self and other, which is intrinsic to our emancipation from nature. To the East, the world is indebted for the preserving of the old spiritual wisdom; to the West, for the pioneering of the rational mind that frees us from tradition and helps us face reality on our own.

Now the world's cultures flow into one another. East receives from West; West from East. And a third level of consciousness begins to grow, without constraint of race or language – though certainly it is held back through cultural, economic or political tyranny. The devotion of the East and the self-dependence of the West are brought into a dynamic unity, at the centre of which is a newborn delicate sense of the divine in oneself and others and all things, through dream no longer, but the awakeness of the day.

From this arises the possibility of a morality based not on duty but freedom. By means of it we seem to have to create almost everything anew (even how to relate to our children and those who are crippled or dying), in place of the instincts and social conditioning whose time has passed.

Thank God for nature's resilience – and its limits. Thank God for the old cultures that have somehow held on, so that others can gain the essence they have been carrying. Thank God, too, for what we learn from the destruction we have wrought, ghastly as it is, for it takes us to the brink of our existence, the uncertainty of our future – and obliges us to face ourselves.

That, too, is the new consciousness – knowing one's weakness and capacity for evil, but knowing too that within, however deeply buried, there lie the seeds of renewal. Worldwide this initiation is taking place, in ways that are unique to each person.

Through our realising this there comes into being a growing world community, of people who may not meet in this life but can know they are united.